IMPORTING

IMPORTING
A practical guide to an exciting and rewarding business

Anne Curran
Glen Mullett

Self-Counsel Press
(*a division of*)
International Self-Counsel Press Ltd.
Canada   U.S.A.

Copyright © 1979, 1995 by International Self-Counsel Press Ltd.

All rights reserved.

No part of this book may be reproduced or transmitted in any form by any means — graphic, electronic, or mechanical — without permission in writing from the publisher, except by a reviewer who may quote brief passages in a review. Any request for photocopying, recording, taping, or information storage and retrieval systems of any part of this book shall be directed in writing to the Canadian Copyright Licensing Agency, Toronto, Ontario.

Printed in Canada

First edition: February, 1979
Second edition: September, 1981
Third edition: May, 1993
Fourth edition: April, 1994
Fifth edition: November, 1995

Canadian Cataloguing in Publication Data
   Curran, Anne.
   Importing

   (Self-counsel business series)
   Includes bibliographical references.
   First-2nd eds. by Ernest Y. Maitland
   ISBN 1-55180-041-1

   1. Foreign trade regulation — Canada. 2. Tariff — Law and legislation — Canada.
3. Customs administration — Canada. I. Mullett, Glen. II. Title. III. Series.
KE1955.M34 1995   382'.5'0971   C95-911016-X
KF1993.A75M34 1995

Cover photography by Larry M. Lahoski

Self-Counsel Press
(*a division of*)
International Self-Counsel Press Ltd.

Head and Editorial Office	U.S. Address
1481 Charlotte Road	1704 N. State Street
North Vancouver, British Columbia V7J 1H1	Bellingham, Washington 98225

CONTENTS

INTRODUCTION   1

1 GETTING STARTED   3
- a. Choosing a product   4
- b. Finding a supplier   5
- c. Estimating the cost of your product   9
- d. Researching the sales potential of your product   10
- e. Deciding how to market your product   12
- f. Setting up your business   13
- g. Placing your first order — to use a broker or not?   13
- h. Planning for your business   14
- Recommended reading   15

2 PAYING FOR YOUR GOODS   18
- a. Establish your base   18
- b. Common shipping terms   19
- c. Documents used in importing   20
  1. Transport documents   20
  2. Commercial documents   22
  3. Insurance documents   22
  4. Financial documents   23
- d. Payment alternatives   23
  1. Open account   23
  2. Documentary collections   23
  3. Documentary credits (letters of credit)   25
  4. Payment in advance   26
- e. Reimbursement methods   26
- f. Managing the risk of foreign exchange   28
  1. Forward rate contract   28
  2. Foreign exchange options from your bank   29
  3. Foreign exchange options and futures on the stock market   29
  4. Foreign currency account   29
  5. Back-to-back financing   29
  6. Leads and lags   29
- Recommended reading   29

3	**CANADA CUSTOMS AND *CUSTOMS 2000***	30
	a. The changing landscape	30
	b. Overview of Canada Customs	31
	c. Acts administered by Canada Customs	33
	d. Electronic Data Interchange (EDI) Systems	33
	e. Voluntary compliance and enforcement	34
	f. Procedures today and tomorrow	34
	g. Responding to business	35
	Recommended reading	35
4	**THE HARMONIZED SYSTEM TARIFF**	36
	a. The Tariff's seven schedules	36
	1. Schedule I	36
	2. Schedule II	36
	3. Schedule III	36
	4. Schedule IV	37
	5. Schedule V	37
	6. Schedule VI	37
	7. Schedule VII	37
	b. The tariff format	38
	c. Punctuation and wording	46
	1. Commas	46
	2. Semicolons	46
	3. Colons	46
	4. "And," "or," and some unusual terms	46
	d. The General Interpretive Rules	47
	1. International rules	47
	2. Canadian rules	49
	e. Essential character	49
	f. Tariff classification and other rulings	49
	g. Parts and accessories	50
	h. Notes	51
	1. Legal notes	51
	2. Explanatory notes	51
	i. Schedule II codes	51
	j. Classification worksheet	51
	Recommended reading	52
5	**THE NORTH AMERICAN FREE TRADE AGREEMENT**	54
	a. Tariff elimination under NAFTA	54
	b. NAFTA's tariff treatments	55
	1. The United States Tariff	55

	2.	The Mexico Tariff	56
	3.	The Mexico–United States Tariff	56
c.	Marking rules under NAFTA		56
d.	HS classification and the definitions of terms		57
e.	The Rules of Origin		57
	1.	Article 401(a)	57
	2.	Article 401(b)	58
	3.	Article 401(c)	59
	4.	Article 401(d)	59
f.	The De Minimis rule		60
g.	The NAFTA Certificate of Origin		60
Recommended reading			61

6 VALUATION: DETERMINING VALUE FOR DUTY — 65

- a. What is valuation? — 65
  1. Point of direct shipment — 65
- b. Methods of determining value for duty — 66
- c. Applying the transaction value method — 68
  1. Have the goods been "sold for export" to Canada? — 69
  2. Are the purchaser and vendor related? — 69
  3. If the answer to the second question is "yes, they are related," has the price of the goods been influenced by the relationship? — 69
- d. Applying the other five valuation methods — 70
  1. Transaction value of identical goods — 70
  2. Transaction value of similar goods — 70
  3. Deductive value method — 70
  4. Computed value method — 70
  5. Residual method — 71
- e. Some commonly asked questions about valuation — 71
- f. The customs valuation questionnaire — 72

Recommended reading — 73

7 CALCULATING THE GST AND OTHER TAXES — 74

- a. The GST — 74
- b. Excise taxes and duties — 75
- c. The excise act — 75

Recommended reading — 75

8 THE SPECIAL IMPORT MEASURES ACT AND OTHER NON-TARIFF BARRIERS — 77

- a. The Special Import Measures Act (SIMA) — 77
  1. The six steps of the complaint process under SIMA — 78
  2. SIMA's other functions — 80

	b.	Other non-tariff barriers	81
	Recommended reading		82
9	**IMPORT DOCUMENTS FOR YOUR GOODS**		**87**
	a.	The importing process	87
		1. The commercial invoice	87
		2. Request for Business Number	88
		3. The Cargo Control Document	88
		4. The Canada Customs invoice	96
		5. Other forms	97
		6. Canada Customs Coding form (B-3)	100
		7. An Adjustment Request	100
		8. Application for Duty Remission	100
		9. The Drawback Claim	100
	b.	Returning products to an American supplier	103
		1. Declaration for Free Entry of Returned American Products	103
		2. Commercial or pro forma invoice	103
		3. Certificate of Destruction/Exportation	103
	Recommended reading		104
10	**DETERMINING THE LANDED COST OF YOUR GOODS**		**107**
	a.	What do landed costs include?	107
	b.	Purchase price	107
	c.	Finder's fee and foreign commission fee	108
	d.	Packing and shipping charges	108
	e.	Duty and taxes	109
	f.	Bank charges	109
	g.	Customs broker's fees	110
	h.	Calculating your landed costs	110
	Recommended reading		110
11	**RELEASE AND ACCOUNTING TO CUSTOMS**		**113**
	a.	How it's done by a customs broker	113
	b.	Importers doing their own processing	114
	c.	The B-3 entry form	114
	d.	Other entry forms	119
		1. E-29-B form for temporary imports	119
		2. Another kind of temporary import	119
		3. Warehouse and ex warehouse entries	121
	e.	When your entry is incorrect	122
	f.	Goods imported by mail	122
	g.	Goods imported by courier	123
	Recommended reading		123

12 DUTY RELIEF — 126
  a. If your goods are faulty — and other problems — 126
    1. Refunds on damaged or deteriorated goods — 127
    2. Refunds on shortshipped, lost, and pilfered goods — 127
    3. Refunds on defective or inferior goods — 127
    4. Refunds when clerical errors are made — 129
    5. Refunds on parts and equipment replaced — 129
    6. Refunds on duties overpaid as a result of an error or change in tariff classification — 129
    7. Refunds as a result of errors in valuation — 129
    8. Refunds when goods are diverted for a special use after importation — 129
  b. Machinery Remission program — 130
  c. Customs Drawback program — 133
    1. Imported goods that are later exported — 133
    2. Imported goods or materials used in or incorporated into goods manufactured or produced in Canada and then exported — 133
    3. Imported goods or materials used or consumed in the manufacture of Canadian-made exports — 137
    4. When the same quantity of domestic or imported materials is used in the manufacture of goods for export — 137
    5. Goods deemed exported — 137
    6. Imported goods or materials used in the manufacture of goods for domestic consumption — 137
  d. Deadlines, deadlines, deadlines — 138
  Recommended reading — 138

13 INVESTIGATIONS AND ENFORCEMENT — 140
  a. Self-assessment — 140
  b. Seizures and forfeitures — 142
  c. Responsibilities and powers of Customs officers — 142
  d. Customs' inspection of imported goods — 142
  e. The adjudication process — 143
    1. Civil penalties — 143
    2. Criminal penalties — 144
  f. Correcting errors in your entries — 146
  Recommended reading — 146

14 BUYING A CAR FROM THE UNITED STATES — 147
  a. The Automotive Products Trade Agreement or Auto Pact — 147
  b. Reduction of duty rate under NAFTA — 148
  c. Requirements for imported vehicles — 148
  d. The inspection and approval process — 150
    1. Border entry — 150

2. Vehicle modification		153
3. Inspection and certification		153
4. Licensing		153
e. Calculating duty and taxes		153
f. Caveat emptor		154
Recommended reading		155

APPENDIXES

1. Trade administration services and Customs Border Services offices		157
2. "D" series Memoranda		158
3. Other acts and regulations administered by Canada Customs		163
4. Customs Valuation Questionnaire		165
5. Industry organizations and government ministries		167
a. Federal government agencies		167
b. Provincial government agencies		168
c. Industry and related business organizations		168
6. Customs office codes		169
7. List of countries, currency, and codes (including U.S. States)		173
8. U.S. foreign trade zones		175
9. U.S. port of exit codes		178
10. Units of measure		184

GLOSSARY 185

SELECTED BIBLIOGRAPHY 192

SAMPLES

#1	Supplier contract	6
#2	Costing out Zimbabwean baskets	11
#3	Letter of credit	27
#4	HS Tariff — table of contents	39
#5	NAFTA Certificate of Origin (form B-232E)	63
#6	Calculation of duty	68
#7	Customs brokerage invoice	76
#8	SIMA Index	79
#9	Typical commercial invoice	90
#10	Request for a business number (form RC1-E)	91
#11	Request to convert to the business number (form RC6-E)	95
#12	Customs Cargo Control Document (form A-8A)	96
#13	Customs Cargo Control Abstract (form A-10)	98

#14	Canada Customs invoice	99
#15	Application for Permit (form Ext-1466)	101
#16	Permit (form Ext-1054)	102
#17	Declaration for Free Entry of Returned American Products (form 3311)	105
#18	Certificate of Destruction/Exportation (form E-15)	106
#19	Bar code	113
#20	Canada Customs coding form (form B-3)	116
#21	Page from Customs Regulations on temporary imports	120
#22	Customs Postal Import form (form E-14)	124
#23	Requesting Refunded Duties and Taxes (form B-2G)	125
#24	Adjustment request (form B-2)	128
#25	Application for Duty Remission under the Machinery Program (form K-122)	131
#26	Drawback Claims (form K-32)	134
#27	Certificate of Importation, Sale or Transfer (form K-32-A)	135
#28	Drawback Certificate of Sale or Exportation (form K-32-B)	136
#29	Vehicle Import form 1 (form 13-0132)	152

WORKSHEETS

#1	Questionnaire for the novice importer	16
#2	Classification worksheet for the HS Tariff	53
#3	The NAFTA worksheet	62
#4	Calculating your landed costs	111

FIGURES

#1	Payment terms and risk	24
#2	Revenue Canada, Customs, Excise and Taxation program branches	32
#3	Establishing the point of direct shipment	67
#4	The complaint process — Special Import Measures Act	83
#5	Marking requirements (as specified in the Customs regulations, D11-3-1)	84
#6	The typical importing process	89
#7	Time limitations for refunds and drawbacks	139
#8	Commercial seizures	141
#9	The enforcement process	145
#10	Ports designated to handle motor vehicle importations	151

NOTICE TO READERS

Laws are constantly changing. Every effort is made to keep this publication as current as possible. However, the author, the publisher, and the vendor make no representation or warranties regarding the outcome or the use to which the information in this book is put and are not assuming any liability for any claims, losses, or damages arising out of the use of this book.

The reader should not rely on the author or publisher of this book for any professional advice. Please be sure you have the most recent edition.

Note: The fees quoted in this book are correct at the date of publication. However, fees are subject to change without notice. For current fees, check with the appropriate government office nearest you.

INTRODUCTION

Welcome to the fifth edition of *Importing*. When we published our last edition in April, 1994 (the second for these authors), the North American Free Trade Agreement (NAFTA) had just gone into effect, creating the largest free trade zone in the world.

As a result, we completely reworked chapter 5, previously devoted to the Free Trade Agreement (FTA), and made changes to several other chapters dealing with subject matter affected by NAFTA. No new agreements or major shifts in federal government policy have since occurred, but this latest edition still contains many changes, prompted by Canada Customs' continued streamlining of many customs procedures.

The need to streamline became apparent back in the 1980s when Canada adopted first the transaction value system of valuation and then the Harmonized System Tariff (HS Tariff) in order to conform with other members of GATT (General Agreement for Trade and Tariffs), including the United States, our major trading partner. This signalled a basic shift away from the protectionist stance we'd maintained in our previous trading activities toward a policy of actively fostering international trade. The result, not surprisingly, was that our trading activities began to grow. Canada Customs foresaw the impact this would have on its structure and procedures and developed a plan that would allow it to keep pace. Fuelling this decision was the pervasive interest and growth in electronic technology worldwide — technology that could be adapted for use in customs-related activities.

Since then Canada Customs has made many changes, and continues to make new ones as one innovation leads to another. This edition is an attempt to keep you up-to-date on basic importing procedures. Future editions will continue to incorporate changes made by Canada Customs.

As you may have already noted, this book is divided into 14 chapters. Chapters 1 and 2 are written with the person new to both business and importing in mind. They deal with the real basics: choosing a suitable product or products, identifying a supplier, deciding whether or not to use a customs broker, and paying for your goods. Chapter 3 is likewise an introduction, this time to Canada Customs and the changes now being made to Customs' procedures as a result of computerization.

Chapters 4 through 14, the bulk of the text, provide a more detailed explanation of the technical side of importing, covering topics such as the HS Tariff, NAFTA, the transaction value method of determining value for duty, the Special Import Measures Act, accounting to Customs, duty relief, investigation and enforcement procedures, and a final chapter on how to import a vehicle from the United States.

Each chapter starts with a summary that identifies the information covered and ends with a recommended reading list for anyone interested in taking their research further. We've provided real-life examples of much of the theoretical material being discussed and included samples of forms commonly used in related procedures as well as worksheets to help you plan. At the back of the book is a glossary, along with a list of general references and organizations, and appendixes pertinent to subjects covered in specific chapters.

Those of you who have never been involved in importing or small business will want to begin with chapter 1. But if you've already started your business or are taking a course on the subject, you may decide to skim the first few chapters and begin reading carefully at chapter 4.

Remember, this book is an introduction to the subject of importing and by no means covers all aspects of the industry in detail — the Customs' regulations that govern it encompass several volumes in themselves. We suggest that once you're comfortable with the material covered here, you acquire one of the more technical industry texts and keep it on hand as a secondary reference. We name several such volumes in our reading lists.

Please note: Because of the changes Canada Customs has made in recent years, and is continuing to make, the Customs information and forms are time sensitive. If you're reading this more than a year after its last publication date, check with Canada Customs before going ahead with any of the procedures we've described or contact Self-Counsel Press for a copy of the latest edition.

In 1994, Canada Customs changed its formal name from "Revenue Canada, Customs and Excise" to "Revenue Canada, Customs, Excise and Taxation." As you will see when you read this book, one or the other title has been used, depending on the activity, event, or publication being cited and the department's official name at the time.

1
GETTING STARTED

In this chapter you'll read about the basic steps you must take in establishing and developing a small import business. Much of the information provided here is general in nature and is designed for the reader with no experience in either importing or small business.

So you'd like to start importing, would you? You're not alone. Each year, thousands of Canadians trek off to one corner of the globe or another and return with a plan to start importing the artifacts or jewellery they saw on their travels.

The scenario they envision usually runs along these lines: they import their product in number (since it sells for practically nothing in the third-world markets they visited), it's an immediate hit on the North American market and they make huge profits, they then use their money to go travelling again in search of new products to handle. A few years later, their fortune made, they retire early to one of the countries they've been importing from and live in relative luxury for the rest of their lives.

This description is closer to a fairy tale than an authentic importing business. But that's not to say that importing isn't profitable, or that you can't eventually lead the life of your dreams, if you are prepared to put a lot of planning and hard work into it first.

Almost half a million importers have registered with Canada Customs since it initiated its Importer Number program (now being replaced by the Business Number program) in the late 1980s. In 1994 alone, $202.5 million worth of goods were imported from around the world, up more than $50 million from 1992, and more than $90 million from 1986.

Traditionally, exporting, not importing, has received the most attention from Canada's provincial and federal governments in the form of programs and funds to assist in the promotion of Canadian goods abroad. The reason is not difficult to understand — exports stimulate economic development. Also, imports often compete successfully against Canadian goods produced at higher cost, prompting Canadian manufacturers to protest that our own industries are being undermined by foreign presence in the marketplace.

As you will read later, the Canadian government maintains tariffs and other controls on many imported products as a means of both protecting our own industries and collecting revenue. Yet the imports continue to flow in — and will doubtless increase as our world reorganizes itself over the next decade into international trading blocs like the already-formed European Union (EU) and NAFTA, implemented January 1, 1994.

As the face of international trade continues to change and reform, so does the internal organization of Canada Customs. In 1989, senior managers in the department initiated "Customs 2000," a ten-year plan to streamline many procedures through computerization and other innovations. Their purpose was to make their operation more efficient by speeding up and simplifying the importing process — and now six years into the program, they've gone some distance toward realizing their goal.

You will read more about NAFTA and Customs 2000 in later chapters. For now, suffice it to say that the importing sector is undergoing many changes — changes that you as an importer will have to keep track of as you develop your own business over the next few years. Unchanged, however, are the basic steps you must take to get into the business in the first place. Let's have a look at those steps now, bearing in mind that we'll be dealing with much of the technical subject matter in more depth in later chapters.

a. CHOOSING A PRODUCT

You can always start an importing business without having a specific product in mind — many people do, fired more by the notion of being able to travel than by the market potential of one imported item or another. If this is your plan, you should have a generous cash reserve set aside for this purpose — or be prepared to run out of money. A more sound approach is to know what you want to handle and even to have a few examples on hand to show potential buyers. Or you might draw up a list of a few products you're interested in and compare the merits of each before making a final choice.

Once you have a product in mind, consider its source. Where is it from? Who makes it? If it's handmade by a small group of artisans, as so many artifacts from the third world are, how many can they realistically produce for you within a specified period of time? Are they well organized to do business "western style"? North American consumers have high standards and expect imported goods to be of a consistent high quality. But quality controls are hard to maintain, especially when the supplier is a basketmaker who lives in the Zimbabwe bush and relies on his neighbors to supplement his export supply. How do you get in touch with this person when you need to re-order? And does he have an efficient and reliable means of shipping your goods? He might turn out to be an excellent source for you — but it's still important to ask these questions.

You should also give some thought to the political and economic conditions of your supplier's country, especially if it is in the third world. Obviously a nation embroiled in a civil war, as Ethiopia was for so many years, is not a reliable place in which to do business.

Consider as well what your product is made of. A shipment of wooden drums with stretched cowhide drumheads will pose no serious problems to Canada Customs officials. But ivory jewellery or elephant-hair bracelets certainly will. The elephant is listed in the Convention on International Trade in Endangered Species (CITES) and, as a signatory to this agreement, Canada bans importation of any products made from elephant parts.

The convention also bans several other kinds of plants and animals. If you enter Canada with a plant or animal on the CITES list and do not have the proper documentation, it will be confiscated. Some species protected under CITES are —

(a) Otters

(b) Wolves

(c) Elephants

(d) Rhinos

(e) Marine turtles

(f) Bird-wing butterflies

(g) Cacti

(h) Orchids

If you're thinking of importing a wooden product — handmade carved goods, for example — you might also think about consumer resistance to buying something made at the expense of the world's dwindling forests. This is a major environmental issue among North Americans today and might well influence the end sale of your product unless it's carved from a particularly plentiful and easily replaced wood.

b. FINDING A SUPPLIER

Finding a supplier is one of the most difficult and important steps in organizing your business. If you are fortunate enough to have friends or relatives who live in the country where the goods are produced, you might ask them to help out. In this capacity, they can search out reliable manufacturers, bargain for a fair price, and ensure that the goods are properly packed and shipped. This sort of arrangement eliminates a lot of trouble and confusion. However, it can still result in problems because it's often more difficult, for example, to organize your affairs in a business-like manner when you are dealing with someone who is close to you.

You can otherwise find suppliers by writing to the consulate or embassy of the country you wish to do business in and asking them for some help. Like Canada, most countries are keen to promote their own products and industries, and their embassies usually have lists of manufacturers and suppliers interested in export trade, as well as trade publications you can subscribe to. Make your letter business-like, explaining who you are and requesting suppliers' names and information on trade with Canada. Once your business is operational, consul officials may also be willing to put you in touch with government and industry representatives within their country and to involve you in some of their own promotional activities here in Canada.

After you've found what seems to be a reliable supplier, plan to visit him or her as soon as possible, even if it means spending extra dollars when you're still paying out start-up costs. By meeting your representative in person, you have a chance to check out the operation and ensure that he or she is not just a go-between or wholesaler. As much as possible you want to deal directly with the manufacturer of your goods — agents or wholesalers, though sometimes necessary, also cost you money and force you to push up your prices here in Canada.

You might also consider drawing up a contract for your supplier to sign, in which you clearly specify your requirements. This approach works well if the supplier is a third-world artisan inexperienced in exporting products and unaware, for example, of packing needs for international shipment. We've provided an example of such a contract (see Sample #1), developed by a Vancouver-based import company specializing in goods from Africa, as a result of problems they experienced when they first started importing. While it is not easily enforceable, the contract gives both parties an understanding of what is expected from each.

It's important to remember that the importing process also involves exporting — that is, the exporting of your goods from another country with its own separate rules and regulations. We tend to forget that reality when we focus on our own requirements as provided under Canadian legislation. But your foreign supplier is also subject to limitations and requirements, especially if he or she lives in a country that views export trade as a conduit for much-needed foreign funds. By being aware of that fact, you'll be better able to deal with your supplier and some of the problems he or she is up against.

By the same token, it's worth your while to study the cultural formalities of the country in which you're interested in doing business. What is considered polite in Canada may be thought inappropriate or even insulting to someone from another part of the world. You could eliminate some problems by being aware of cultural differences and willing to abide by the other culture's behavioral code.

SAMPLE #1
SUPPLIER CONTRACT

fever-tree Trading Co.

SUPPLIER CONTRACT WITH FEVER-TREE TRADING CO.

DATE:_____   SUPPLIER:_____

ADDRESS OF SUPPLIER:_____

This is to confirm that I have read and understand and will agree to abide by the following statements.

1. Supplier will obtain goods for price on order form.

2. Supplier will pack and ship goods according to instructions from Fever-Tree Trading

3. Supplier has received 50% of money owing for goods listed on order form in the amount of _____, $CAN_____.

4. Fever-Tree Trading Company will remit the remainder of the total cost of the shipment on receipt of the goods in Vancouver, Canada.

5. Fever-Tree Trading will not pay for extra costs incurred due to failure of the Supplier to comply with the instructions for shipping; (name and telephone numbers must accompany shipment to speed customs clearance in Canada)

6. Fever-Tree Trading will not pay for any goods arriving in Canada that are of inferior quality. It is the responsibility of the Supplier to select goods that are in good condition before shipping. (clean, unbroken, unrepaired, well made)

7. Fever-Tree Trading will not pay for goods broken during shipping if it is clear that the Supplier did not pack the goods with care before shipping. (items unwrapped or unprotected from other items)

I,_____agree to the above conditions.
         (Supplier)

I,_____agree to the above conditions.
       (Fever-Tree Trading)

Date_____

SAMPLE #1 — Continued

fever-tree Trading Co.

INSTRUCTIONS FOR SUPPLIERS

ADDRESS TO:

DOCUMENTS: All forms <u>must</u> be included in the shipment

1. Form "A" Certificate of Origin, Original copy only

2. <u>INVENTORY</u>: MUST include the following:

   (a) a detailed description of <u>each</u> separate item including the material the item is made from (grass, bone, stone, leather etc.)

   (b) unit and total cost of each item

   (c) correct number of each item

   (d) any additional charges listed separately from goods with a clear description of what the charges are for (shipping, handling, packing, taxes, etc.)

   (e) Bank exhange rate for Canadian dollar at time of shipping

3. Invoice

TERMS OF PAYMENT:

1. 50% of total cost of goods to be paid at time of order

2. A signed and witnessed receipt for order and payment and agreement to ship as ordered on order form

3. Remainder of total cost of shipment paid on receipt of goods as ordered

*** Extra costs added because of failure of Supplier to ship according to the above directions will be subtracted from the remainder of amount owing

4. Payment to be made to Supplier by bank draft,

SAMPLE #1 — Continued

FEVER-TREE TRADING CO.

INSTRUCTIONS FOR SUPPLIERS (cont.)

<u>TERMS OF PAYMENT</u> (cont.)

or by cable to Supplier's account

5. Shipping costs can be paid either by the Supplier and included on the inventory

or

by Fever-tree C.O.D. on receipt of the shipment

<u>PACKING OF GOODS</u>:

1. Goods must be shown to be packed with extreme care

2. Items must be packed so there is no movement within the container

3. Each item should be wrapped separately so that it does not touch any other item

4. Packing material is to be clean so items are not marked

5. Containers should be clearly marked if they contain breakable items

6. Containers must be sturdy and packed so they do not fall apart in transit

7. A packing slip listing each item in the container must be included on top of the goods

*** It is important to understand that shippers do not handle goods with care. They use fork lifts and cranes to transfer containers. These containers are often dropped or turned upside down during shipping. Weak cardboard containers often collapse or are torn apart during travel. If you must use a cardboard container, please make sure that there is adequate padding around the items and that there are no empty spaces in the container. It is also necessary to tie the carton with heavy cord in case the cardboard tears.

Thank you very much for considering all the instructions listed above. We have had a long experience with shipping goods to Canada and know that it is necessary to follow each direction carefully to avoid extra expense.

c. ESTIMATING THE COST OF YOUR PRODUCT

The first expense you're likely to consider is the cost of your product from the market stall, craftsperson, or manufacturer you bought it from.

Let's use the Zimbabwean baskets we mentioned earlier as an example and place you in an open-air market not far from Zimbabwe's second largest centre, Bulawayo, when you first spot them. The price to you for a well-made handwoven carrying basket is a mere Z $10 — or about C $2*, for the purpose of this discussion — and several other baskets of varying dimensions are no more expensive. You buy three as marketing samples, make a mental note of the place, and climb back into your car.

Back in Bulawayo, you consult with a local retailer about purchasing the baskets in number and take her name when she expresses an interest in acting as your supplier. Her charge, you agree, will be a straight 10% of the cost of the goods — the next cost you must consider.

Three months later, back in your Kelowna office, you send a letter to your supplier asking her to provide an estimate, in Zimbabwean dollars, for shipping 500 baskets by air (since Zimbabwe is landbound and baskets are light anyway) to Canada. At the same time, you ask her how she wants to be paid. She comes back to you with four figures: the total cost of the goods (including her commission), transportation of the goods from the countryside to the airport, insurance, and transport to Vancouver. The only surprise is the international transport figure — it's more than you anticipated because shipping charges are calculated according to both weight and volume, and baskets are a bulky item to transport. You note down her estimate and the cost of organizing payment by money order, as she has requested. Then you check on the cost of transporting the goods from Vancouver to Kelowna.

Next you make a trip down to Canada Customs, where an officer directs you to the Harmonized Commodity Description and Coding System, or HS Tariff. The tariff lists every conceivable product imported into Canada and the rate of duty you're required to pay on each. After reviewing the tariff's table of contents and finding that basketware is dealt with in chapter 46, you turn to the chapter and locate the category for handwoven baskets, tariff item 4602.10.92. Then, turning to the front again, to Schedule III of the tariff, you find Zimbabwe in the countries listed and discover that three tariff treatments apply to Zimbabwean goods: the Most Favoured Nations or MFN treatment, the British Preferential Treatment or BPT, and the General Preferential Treatment or GPT. Back to your tariff item, you note the duty amounts: 9.5% under the MFN and 5% under the GPT (there's no reference to BPT). Then you make a quick calculation to arrive at a ballpark figure of the amount you'll have to pay Customs, not including the goods and services tax (GST), if you decide to place a small basket order.

You also consider any other requirements your product may have to meet for entry. Called non-tariff barriers because they discourage imports by increasing product cost, these requirements include labelling, as stipulated by the federal Consumer Packaging and Labelling Act, quotas on goods listed in *The Export and Import Permits Act Handbook*, and other duties. None of them applies to baskets, but you make a mental note to check them again when you diversify to Zimbabwean textiles — as you've planned, if all goes well with the baskets.

Now you give some thought to where you're going to store your goods once they've arrived. You live in a one-bedroom

---

* Unless otherwise noted, all dollar figures throughout this book are in Canadian funds.

suite, so home storage is out of the question. But what about renting a garage in your neighborhood or one of those U-lock storage facilities? You even consider renting space in a bonded warehouse (that way you can avoid paying duty on your goods until you take them out), but veto the idea because your shipment is going to be too small. You check the rates for the other alternatives and determine your next cost figure.

Finally, you think about how you're going to distribute your goods. Are you going to drop them off using your own car or do you plan to hire someone to do that for you? In either case, you must allow for these additional transport charges before you can add up all your costs.

This brings you to the important matter of determining your profit... and your next step. Sample #2 shows how all these costs have added up for importing your baskets.

d. RESEARCHING THE SALES POTENTIAL OF YOUR PRODUCT

Now that you have a general idea of how much you must sell your product for, you can check the prices of comparable products already on the market and start talking to prospective customers. By "customers," we mean retailers or service professionals (interior designers, for example) who would be interested in purchasing your goods on a wholesale basis. We are assuming, for the purposes of this discussion, that you intend to operate a wholesale business. But it doesn't really matter what type of business it is — you will have to know your competitors' products and prices.

Many books have already been written on conducting market research, including an excellent Self-Counsel Press publication entitled *Marketing Your Product: A Planning Guide for Small Business* by Donald Cyr and Douglas Gray. We have no intention here of repeating their advice, but would like to make a few suggestions based on our own experience.

The first is this: Identify your market. By developing a profile of who is most likely to purchase your goods — their age, circumstances, purchasing power, and buying habits — you can better identify who to approach with your samples. Spend time defining your product as well. Is it something someone would buy on impulse? Is it a convenience or a luxury item? In what way is it different from competing products? How is it better?

Next, do a little research on similar or related products. A library that specializes in servicing researchers — like some larger public libraries and university facilities — usually has industry periodicals and scholarly journals with information on various industries. Also check with federal and provincial government departments involved in business development, and with relevant trade, professional, and business associations.

Now make a list of who you intend to approach with your samples. Most companies are more than willing to look at new product ideas for their business, particularly when you phone ahead to explain who you are and make an appointment. Take a full range of samples with you and some literature describing your goods and the price range, along with a business card. Then visualize how you intend to present yourself, making a list of some of the questions you plan to ask. Remember, while you are trying to interest the company in your goods, your first priority at this time is to get more information on the market to which you hope to sell.

Needless to say, the more knowledgeable and professional your presentation, the more likely you will be to get what you want. No one knows the market better than other successful entrepreneurs, and most of them will usually tell you what they

SAMPLE #2
COSTING OUT ZIMBABWEAN BASKETS

1. **Per item cost from Zimbabwean supplier:**
Tray with handles	Z $9.33	C $2.36
Basket with handles	10.66	4.71
Fruit basket	2.66	1.18
Trinket basket	2.66	1.18
Wastepaper basket	6.67	2.95

2. **Cost of a small shipment:**
Tray with handles	100 @	C $2.36	$236.00
Basket with handles	100 @	4.71	471.00
Fruit basket	100 @	1.18	118.00
Trinket basket	150 @	1.18	177.00
Wastepaper basket	50 @	2.95	147.50
TOTAL			**C $1 149.50**

   VALUE FOR DUTY *(add following expenses)*   C $1 149.50

3. **Shipping costs:**
   Insurance and freight from Harare, Zimbabwe, to Vancouver
       30 kg. @ Z $15.00 = Z $450.00   C $113.92
   Terminal charges (air freight)   20.00

4. **Duty under the MFN or GPT tariff treatment:***
   GPT rate (5%) applies because supplier provides a
   Certificate of Origin (form A)**   57.48

5. **GST on total of value of goods + duty**
   ($1 149.50 + $57.48) × 7% GST   84.49

6. **Customs broker's fee to complete your entry**
   ($65.00 + 7% GST)   69.55

7. **Shipping to your home in Kelowna from Vancouver*****
   ($130.00 + 7% GST))   139.10

8. **Bank fees for international money orders**
   (payment in two parts)   @ $8.00   16.00

9. **Mailing charges, by special delivery (twice)**   15.36
   TOTAL   **C $1 665.40**

* Depending on your agreement, your customs broker will pay these costs for you and then include them on the invoice to you.

** The Certificate of Origin is discussed in chapter 9; without one, duty would be calculated according to the higher MFN rate.

*** Represents total cash outlay, but not total cost because GST is recoverable.

think, or give you the names of others who might be interested in your goods. Take notes in the course of your conversation (or right afterwards) and keep a log and a contact list.

It's important to note that some of those you visit may want to place an order for your products right away. But before you decide to take them up on it, be sure you can meet the deadlines you agree to. If you're planning to handle a giftware item, for example, and your purchaser is ordering for the Christmas shopping season, the order should be delivered before the end of September. Failing to meet the deadline may result in your losing a customer and your credibility in the marketplace at large — word spreads fast when a supplier is undependable.

With all your information now before you, you can review the costs and profit you estimated at the end of section c. above and give further thought to how you want to market your product. You might also consider taking your research one step further — by importing a limited number of the goods you want to handle and selling them yourself in a short-term retail market, like a weekend craft market or a seasonal theme show.

We're jumping the gun a bit by raising this last possibility since we have yet to discuss the ordering and transport of your goods, but the point is still worth making. Local markets and annual events like the fall home show provide you with an excellent opportunity to test the market without risking too much capital. In such a setting, you can talk to consumers yourself and develop a better understanding of their preferences and buying habits. Markets and shows also give you a chance to get your business off the ground when the economy is depressed and the risks associated with opening a permanent retail outlet are too high. In fact, some importers operate full time as itinerant sellers, appearing at booths in fairs and shows year round.

e. DECIDING HOW TO MARKET YOUR PRODUCT

At some point you will have to decide if you are more interested in retailing or wholesaling. Some businesses operate as both wholesalers and retailers in a conventional retail setting.

Obviously, a strictly wholesale business is easier to establish and less expensive to maintain since you have none of the costs of opening and maintaining a permanent storefront. As a wholesaler, however, you must still show your goods. And while you can carry display cases with you as you visit one retailer or another, you may also want a permanent display area or showroom. This means spending more money again, but because you don't have to be in a high traffic area, it will still cost less than a retail storefront while giving you more flexibility in promoting your goods.

In wholesaling you can also maintain normal business hours, while in retailing the hours are long with most statutory holidays being just another working day. This is an important point to consider if you've never been in retailing before.

As we've already mentioned above, and depending on the nature of your goods, of course, you might consider itinerant selling to begin with at craft fairs or theme shows. In this case your costs are limited to paying for a booth or a table (often on a per linear foot or square foot basis), the cost of transporting you and your goods to the event, and accommodation costs if the event is in another community. Fairs and shows are held at specified times and in many communities across the country, allowing you to wholesale to merchants as you travel to and from the various events.

As you think about the wholesale/retail alternative, remember that if you engage in both wholesaling and retailing, you must retail your goods for the same price that you would expect other retailers to sell them for. In other words, you cannot set up a booth at a craft fair and undercut the retailers to whom you plan to wholesale once the market is over — retailers will simply refuse to buy your products.

Itinerant selling allows you to build up your business gradually at minimum expense. As you grow, you can begin to consider moving full time to a small retail operation, such as a permanent cart or kiosk in a shopping mall, then to a storefront or to a full-time wholesale operation.

f. SETTING UP YOUR BUSINESS

Having identified the goods you plan to import, how much you can make from them, and your target market, you are now in a position to set up your business. As with marketing, many books have already been written on this subject. Our intention here is simply to highlight some aspects of the subject as it relates to importing.

A major question for new importers is, how much money do I need to get started? Obviously this depends on the type of product they are planning to import and how they intend to operate their business: part time or full time, as a wholesale or retail operation, in a fixed location or on an itinerant basis.

Unless you have money set aside for the purpose, you probably must think in terms of starting modestly and building up your business over a period of several years. It's unrealistic to expect to support yourself immediately on the basis of the business alone. Consequently, many new importers hold a second job or depend on their spouse's income to pay the mortgage and the grocery bills.

In addition to the cost of your first shipment, as discussed earlier, you may face some minimal start-up costs such as the following:

(a) Incorporating your business, if you decide against starting as a proprietorship

(b) Purchasing a business licence from the local government authority

(c) Designing and printing letterhead and business cards (preferably with an eye-catching logo)

(d) Developing promotional materials, including photos, for the products you intend to handle

(e) Purchasing and operating a business telephone

(f) Renting and/or purchasing office equipment including a desk, chair, filing cabinet, light, computer, and fax machine

(g) Purchasing general office supplies

(h) Setting up a business account with a financial institution that has international ties

(i) Retaining an accountant to provide assistance and advice in developing accounting systems

The simplest and most economical way to set up is to allocate a room in your home as your office space and use your private telephone line for the few business calls you'll be making during your first months of operation. Then, as your business builds up, you can consider moving into separate business quarters. Depending on the goods you're handling, you might store these, too, at home until you relocate.

g. PLACING YOUR FIRST ORDER — TO USE A BROKER OR NOT?

With the basic structure of your business now in place, you are in a position to make your first order. This includes determining how you are going to have your goods transported, reaching agreement with your supplier on how he or she will be paid, applying for an importer number and GST registration number from the federal government, and deciding whether or not to use a customs broker.

Because of the importance of sound financing in import transactions, we have reserved chapter 2 for a more complete discussion of this subject and suggest that you read it thoroughly. Your financial decisions will depend, of course, on several factors: the size of your order, your experience and relationship with the supplier, the export regulations of the country where your goods are produced, and foreign currency exchange rates.

You can apply for an importer number by visiting your nearest Canada Customs office and completing the relevant form. Depending on which office you're applying through, it may process your application and give you a number right away (there's no charge).

This is also the time to ask yourself whether you want to use a customs broker. A customs broker looks after all the details of processing your shipment through Customs once the shipment has arrived in Canada — and will even apply, on your behalf, for your importer number if you have not already filed for it yourself. A broker ensures that you have proper documentation, that your goods are classified under the proper HS Tariff item and receive the correct tariff treatment, and that the correct rate of exchange is applied. The broker then pays all duty and GST owing (although he or she may require an advance from you for this, depending on credit terms) and will even arrange to have your goods stored or delivered. At the end of it all, you receive an invoice for the duty and GST plus brokerage services. This last fee is an additional cost, but it can be nominal, depending on the size of your shipment and your particular needs.

When you retain a customs broker, you sign a general agency agreement which gives your broker power of attorney to complete all accounting documents, pay all duties and taxes, etc. You may also sign a master carrier authority, authorizing all major transportation companies to turn over any arrival notice of your goods to your broker. That way, you don't have to inform your broker of incoming shipments; he or she will already be advised. And, usually, you also complete a credit report.

Customs brokers are very useful, particularly if your time is limited or if you feel it would be better spent in other business-related activities. In fact, if you are dealing with a good supplier, a good transportation company, and a good broker, you should have to involve yourself only in the actual ordering and receiving of your goods. Whatever you opt to do for your first few shipments, you may well decide to hire someone to handle all your customs and tariff processing in house once your business has begun to grow.

h. PLANNING FOR YOUR BUSINESS

Your business, from start-up to future growth, should be accompanied by planning: keeping orderly records, doing market research for each new product you decide to handle, and having a firm idea of where you want to take your business over the next several years. The easiest way to address these important considerations is to develop a business plan.

There are several books available on this subject today (see Recommended Reading at the end of this chapter), and courses are also offered at local colleges and night schools, and by institutions like the Federal Business Development Bank through its C.A.S.E. counselling and management programs (C.A.S.E. stands for Counselling Assistance for Small Enterprise). The process is not difficult, but it takes time and obliges you to examine every aspect of your operation from office costs to market campaigns and predicted sales. It is a good exercise in itself, particularly if you are new to entrepreneurial activity. The document can be reviewed and adjusted on a regular basis and becomes an invaluable tool both in promoting your business and in giving you direction as it evolves.

Planning also means assessing and taking advantage of business opportunities as they appear, often by belonging to relevant trade and/or business organizations. Groups like the chamber of commerce, Rotary Club, Board of Trade, and the Canadian Importers Association, provide you with an invaluable network of contacts in the business community, giving you a chance to exchange ideas with others involved in the same or related business activities and to keep apprised of upcoming events.

Having encouraged you to "think importing," we suggest that you now complete the following questionnaire in Worksheet #1. As with the information in this chapter, the questionnaire identifies the various steps involved in beginning a small import business and includes some questions you should ask yourself before taking your ideas beyond the planning stage. Complete it now to help you focus your thoughts and ideas.

RECOMMENDED READING

Government of British Columbia. *So You Want to Import.* Vancouver: B.C. Business Information Centre (601 W. Cordova Street), 1992.

Green, Mary and Stanley Gillmar. *How to be an Importer and Pay for Your World Travel.* Berkeley: Ten Speed Press, 1993.

James, Jack D. *Starting a Successful Business in Canada.* Vancouver: Self-Counsel Press, 1995.

Management Systems Resources. *A Practical Guide to Importing and Exporting in Canada.* Toronto: Management Systems Resources, 1991. (looseleaf)

Ogden, Frank. *The Last Book You'll Ever Read: (and Other Lessons From the Future).* Toronto: Macfarlane, Walter and Ross, 1993.

Popcorn, Faith. *The Popcorn Report.* New York: HarperCollins, 1992.

Touchie, Rodger D. *Preparing a Successful Business Plan.* Vancouver: Self-Counsel Press, 1993.

WORKSHEET #1
QUESTIONNAIRE FOR THE NOVICE IMPORTER

1. Products you'd like to handle:_____
2. Where do they come from? _____
3. Disadvantages of trading with this country *(Include currency exchange rate, political problems, export regulations, if any. Be as complete as possible.)*:
   _____
   _____

   Advantages: _____
   _____

4. Product composition:_____
   Canadian requirements for admissibility *(if any)*:_____
   _____

5. Estimated cost per item once landed *(What tariff treatments, if any, is it eligible for? Will you have to pay additional costs for treatment or extra processing before it can enter Canada?)*: _____
   _____

6. Consumer appeal *(Is the product unique? What products would it compete against and how would it compare in terms of cost, quality, etc.?)*:_____
   _____

7. Expected profit per item:_____
8. Expected income annually: _____
9. Who would be your supplier?_____
   _____

   If relatives, what arrangements do you want to make with them?
   _____
   _____

10. Would you process the goods yourself through Customs or retain a customs broker? If you plan to do the work yourself, what time do you have available? Any other commitments that might intervene? _____
    _____
    _____
    _____

WORKSHEET #1 — Continued

11. Business/trade organizations you belong to: _____
    _____
    _____

    Organizations you'd join *(and annual fees)*: _____
    _____

12. Are you interested in operating a retail business? _____
          itinerant retail? _____
          wholesale? _____
          other? _____
    Specify why: _____
    _____

    Previous selling experience: _____
    _____

13. Do you see the business as full time? _____ part time? _____
    Estimated time commitment:
        daily: _____ hours   weekly: _____ hours
    If full time, how do you plan to support yourself in the early stages?
    _____

14. Do you have savings set aside for start up? If so, how much? _____
    _____

15. Estimate your set-up costs:

Incorporation and other legal fees	$ _____
Business premises	_____
Office supplies	_____
Customs broker	_____
Packaging materials	_____
Transportation (not shipment costs)	_____
Promotion	_____
TOTAL	$ _____

2
PAYING FOR YOUR GOODS

This chapter contains a review of the most common shipping terms, descriptions of the documents commonly used in import financing, an explanation of basic payment alternatives available to new importers, and advice on minimizing foreign exchange risk.

No aspect of the importing business is more important than a sound understanding of how to pay for the products you buy abroad — by the most efficient, profitable, and risk-free means available through the international banking system. Of these three adjectives, "risk-free" is perhaps the most important since it's only by minimizing your risk in each transaction that you're assured of getting the products you ordered.

More than domestic business managers, importers must monitor and respond to the factors that influence relations with their suppliers and with the countries in which these suppliers live. Domestic businesses rely on their associates to adhere to business principles and practices that are known and acceptable to all parties and generally enforceable under Canadian law.

Outside Canada, however, business is often conducted very differently. And as an importer, you will find yourself subject to different regulations and policies, a different legal system, different business customs, and very different political and economic realities. There will be times when your control of a business transaction is very limited and when fate intervenes to alter your business plans. It all depends on the country you're doing business with and your relationship with your supplier. In turn, these two factors determine the method of payment you choose to buy your goods.

a. ESTABLISH YOUR BASE

It is important, first of all, to open your business account at a financial institution that has well-established international ties and reliable international services for its business customers. Most of Canada's major banks fall into this category, and several have offices in larger urban centres that specialize in "trade finance." Obviously it would be to your advantage to establish your account in one of these. A quick survey of the institutions in your area, and a meeting in person or by telephone with a trade finance manager, should give you the information on services and charges you need to make a good choice.

Next, establishing a sound relationship with your suppliers also helps minimize the risk of financing problems. If you are fortunate enough to have known your suppliers before doing business with them — perhaps they are relatives or friends — then you are in a position to deal informally with them, making financial arrangements that are mutually advantageous. If they are unknown to you, however, then it is important, first of all, to obtain a credit report on them from your international banker (usually at no charge), and then to meet with them "on the ground" (i.e., in their own country) as soon as possible, to assess their business and build a relationship of mutual trust. This is vital to your business — so vital, in fact, that the cost of a trip for this express purpose should be included in your projected budget for the first year of operation.

Finally, you also simplify the financing process when you take the time to familiarize yourself with your products and develop a realistic marketing plan for them in advance of importing. By this we mean knowing how you are going to transport your goods and to where, what Customs' requirements they must meet and what tariffs, if any, they will be subject to. With this knowledge you can make an informed decision about how best to pay for them.

b. COMMON SHIPPING TERMS

A major portion of import expenses is derived from transportation charges. Today goods are transported by sea, land, or air, or by some combination of these three, depending on where you're importing from and the nature of your goods. Shipping and insurance fees are generally uniform worldwide, although there can be differences that you should take advantage of whenever you can.

Before you place your order with a supplier, you should ask him or her for a quotation on the cost. Cost means not only the basic cost of the goods, but also the cost of using one shipping method or another, plus the insurance coverage. As purchaser, you eventually must pay for all three — goods, transportation charges, and insurance — but how and when depends on the shipping arrangements you make with your supplier. You have several alternatives, as the following list of shipping terms demonstrates. These terms (our list is by no means complete) are standardized in international trade under a set of rules called INCOTERMS. INCOTERMS were first published in 1936 by the International Chamber of Commerce and are periodically updated. Essentially, the terms establish who assumes what risk and what cost in your contract with your supplier, and your obligations to each other. By choosing the right term, you can keep your freight and insurance costs to a minimum.

(a) *CIF (cost, insurance, freight) + name of destination.* When goods are sent CIF Vancouver, for example (represented as "CIF YVR"), the supplier pays for all costs, including the basic cost of the goods, insurance while they're in transit, and transport charges. Similarly, when you ask for a quote "CIF" from a supplier, it means that you want the supplier to give you costs for transport and insurance in addition to product costs. This can be very advantageous when the rate of exchange favors the Canadian dollar, but you must have confidence in your supplier and his or her shipping agent. Many importers use their own forwarding agents in the countries where they do business as a means of keeping transport costs down.

(b) *C & F (cost and freight), may also appear as CFR (cost, freight).* In this case, the supplier is quoting the cost of the goods and freight, while you pick up the insurance costs. This arrangement is often made by companies that import in quantity and have a blanket insurance policy for all their shipping. In such instances, the importer is responsible for advising his or her insurer of the orders made and the shipping arrangements for them, and for giving the supplier the insurer's name. Some suppliers, as a precautionary measure, may carry separate insurance over and above what the importer has taken out.

(c) *C & I (cost and insurance).* Here the supplier is quoting the basic cost of the goods plus insurance while you pick up the shipping charges. Again, this is the sort of arrangement made by importers who have a blanket agreement with a specific shipping company to handle all their shipping.

(d) *FOB (free on board)*. When you receive a quote that's FOB, the supplier is giving you the cost of the goods plus the cost, including loading charges, of putting them "on board" a ship or plane. The supplier also looks after all customs export formalities before they're loaded. This figure does not include insurance or freight, usually paid by the importer when the goods arrive at their destination. FOB is commonly used in importing and is particularly attractive to the supplier because it means less capital outlay for him or her.

(e) *FAS (free alongside ship)*. In this case, the supplier's quote includes the cost of getting the goods to their export point and through customs formalities. Everything else, including loading charges, is the responsibility of the importer.

(f) *EXW (ex warehouse, ex works, or ex factory)*. A quote of this sort represents the cost of the goods at their point of origin, nothing else — no transportation from factory to export point and beyond, no loading, no insurance.

(g) *DDP (delivered duty paid or free domicile)*. This is a very comprehensive quote including all costs, even import duties, to the doorstep of the purchaser. This approach is popular with non-resident importers (NRIs). Generally, charges against DDP shipments made subsequent to the point of direct shipment to Canada are not subject to duty.

A typical NRI would be an American manufacturer who ships in quantity to Canadian retailers, using a customs broker to process the goods through Canada Customs. Charges beyond the point of direct shipment of the goods would include shipping costs, GST, and brokerage fees, none of which is dutiable. One advantage of conducting business in this manner is that the customer knows exactly how much the shipment is going to cost.

c. DOCUMENTS USED IN IMPORTING

All the papers you receive in the course of completing a shipment, from the supplier's invoice to the shipper's bill of lading or air waybill, to the shipment packing list, invariably play an important role in the payment of your suppliers. Letters of credit, discussed later under section **d.**, are processed entirely on the basis of documentation.

Some documents are more common than others, and these are listed below as a prelude to our in-depth discussion of letters of credit. There are several types that may be categorized generally as transport, commercial, financial, and insurance documents.

1. Transport documents

(a) Bill of lading

A bill of lading (b/l) is a transport document representing the contract of carriage between the shipper and a shipping company. (Full contract details are usually printed on the back of the document.) There are several kinds of bills of lading: truck bills of lading, air bills of lading, rail bills of lading and, of course, bills of lading for shipment by sea.

A bill of lading contains the name of the shipping company (also called the carrier), the name of the shipper (your supplier or his or her agent), the consignee (that's you or the party who will be receiving the shipment), the name of the party the shipping company must notify once the shipment has arrived (your customs broker, for example) and the train, vehicle, vessel by which the goods are being shipped. There is also space for a brief description of the goods, their weight and cubic measurement, and how they're packed; a notation stating whether or not the shipment charges have already been paid; and, for ocean bills of lading, a reference to the number of originals being issued and the date your shipment is actually stowed on board with a further stamp that confirms "laden on board."

If you are paying your supplier by means of a letter of credit (l/c), and a clean bill of lading is one of the conditions in your letter of credit, then the bill of lading is called an "order bill of lading."

A clean bill of lading is one that contains no reference to goods or their packing being defective. If the shipping company spots any defects, it will note them on the bill, at which moment it becomes unclean or "claused." Letters of credit usually call for a clean bill of lading.

Once your shipment is actually in transit, the shipping company will send you at least two original bills of lading. These are usually airmailed separately on different days, in case one goes astray. (This practice dates from the old days of shipping by sea when the mails were less reliable.) You normally receive them well before the shipment's arrival and are then contacted by the shipping company's agent just a few days before the shipment is actually due. To collect your goods, you must present the company with an original endorsed bill of lading.

An original bill of lading, then, serves as a receipt of goods from the shipping company to your supplier and as a document of title for you. It is also an enforceable contract of carriage should your goods disappear in transit.

(b) Air waybill

An air waybill (AWB) is provided by an airline to your supplier or his or her agent when your goods are turned over for air transport. This document is not as formal as the ocean bill of lading, and airlines do not issue originals or demand that you present the waybill when you pick up your goods. Instead, they provide copies for the consignor (your supplier), the carrier, and the consignee (you). There is no requirement that the goods be "on board" before a bill is issued, and the date on the bill represents the day when the airline takes possession of the goods, not when they are sent.

(c) Other transport documents

Other transport documents include rail and truck bills of lading, and parcel post and courier receipts. Like the air waybill, these are not as formal as the ocean bill of lading, nor do they have as many functions. They do, however, serve as a receipt for your goods from the carrier and give proof of a contract of carriage should your goods be lost in transit. They are not documents of title and are not negotiable. (The phrase "non negotiable" may be printed right on them.) But the practice of all carriers (as they usually state on their documents also) is to release goods to the consignee named in the document.

(d) Drayage cartage receipt

A drayage receipt is an interim transport document and is issued, for example, to your supplier by the transport company responsible for taking your shipment to the dock or airport. When the shipment is loaded, the receipt is exchanged for a bill of lading, air waybill, or other transport document.

(e) Cargo receipt

A cargo receipt is issued by the receiving agent acting on your behalf once the goods have arrived at their destination. As in the case of the other interim transport documents, a cargo receipt is not a document of title and is not transferable; it merely acknowledges that your shipment has been received.

2. Commercial documents

(a) Commercial invoice

A commercial invoice is issued to you by your supplier when you place an order. The invoice is a form with the supplier's name and address at the top and space for information on the goods, including quantity, description, unit price, and extension. It also names you as the purchaser, gives your address, and provides information about the payment and shipping terms you've arranged. All other documents are prepared from the information contained in the commercial invoice and should be consistent with it.

(b) Pro forma invoice

A pro forma invoice is issued to you by your supplier as a quotation, an "invitation to buy," and it is clearly stamped "pro forma." It contains the same information as a commercial invoice and becomes a formal order once you accept and sign it. In countries where foreign funds are limited and foreign payments controlled, the banking authorities sometimes require a pro forma invoice before approving release of funds to pay for imported goods. In some cases, a pro forma invoice can also be used in lieu of a commercial invoice or Customs' invoice for Customs' entry purposes.

(c) Packing list

As its name suggests, a packing list provides information on how your goods have been packed — which products in what box — for your convenience and for the convenience of inspection authorities who wish to examine the shipment. The packing list is produced by your supplier.

(d) Certificate of Origin

Certificates of Origin certify the origin of your goods. For importations into Canada, Certificates of Origin are required for entry under the U.S. Tariff (UST), Mexico Tariff (MT), and the Mexico-U.S. Tariff (MUST) established under NAFTA; the General Preferential Tariff (GPT); the Least Developed Developing Country Tariff Treatment (LDDC); and the Commonwealth Caribbean Countries Tariff Treatment (CARIBCAN). The certificates generally establish the percentage of the product produced in the country of origin. In the case of GPT, LDDC, and CARIBCAN, the original Certificate of Origin (form A) must be presented to Canada Customs at the time of release. For the three NAFTA tariff treatments, however, the original certificate (form B-232E from Canada Customs) only must be in the hands of the importer at time of release, and be available to Customs on request. Form A certificates are provided by certifying bodies, as named in the list of Authorized Certifying Authorities contained in Schedule II of the Harmonized System Tariff (HS Tariff). (For more on this important subject, see the relevant sections in chapter 4 on the HS Tariff and chapter 5 on NAFTA.)

(e) Third-party inspection certificate

Sometimes an importer requests a third-party inspection certificate as part of the sales contract with the supplier. When you are unable to inspect the goods you're ordering before accepting them, you can request that they be inspected by an independent third party before they leave their country of origin. There are several companies, with offices in many countries, that perform this function. Once their inspection is complete, they provide your supplier with a certificate which he or she then forwards to you or your bank, depending on the payment arrangements you have made with the supplier.

3. Insurance documents

An insurance certificate is usually provided by the supplier, although some importers carry blanket insurance policies to cover the period their imports are in transit, or they decide to look after the insurance themselves. It all depends on the transport and payment arrangements that the supplier and importer have made with each other (see the earlier discussion of CIF and C & I under section **b.** above). A typical insurance certificate contains the name and signature of the insurer, a description of the goods, details of the risks covered, and information on how to make a claim.

4. Financial documents

Depending on your financial arrangements, your supplier may be required to provide you with a bill of exchange. A bill of exchange or draft is an order made by the drawee (your supplier) to the drawer (you, the importer), for payment, requiring that you pay him or her a specified sum of money.

Two types of bills of exchange or drafts are commonly used in importing transactions: a "sight draft," which must be paid as soon as it is presented, and a "term draft," which is payable after a fixed period (90 days after acceptance of the goods, for example), as specified right on the draft.

d. PAYMENT ALTERNATIVES

The method you use to pay for your goods should always be negotiated with your supplier as part of your sales agreement or contract.

The size of your order and your supplier's requirements (or the requirements of the export authority of his or her country) may well influence your choice of payment. But in the end your decision is also based on the degree of risk you're prepared to accept in completing a particular transaction.

Different methods of payment carry different degrees of risk and, as depicted in our chart of payment terms (see Figure #1), the method most attractive to an importer is the least palatable to a supplier or exporter. Your negotiations with your supplier may result in a compromise which provides a measure of protection to you both. Let's look now at a few of your alternatives.

1. Open account

In an open account arrangement, your supplier sends you goods "on account" to be paid after a period of time (30, 60, or 90 days) in a set amount at set intervals (e.g., on a monthly basis), or as the goods sell ("on consignment"). This alternative is almost wholly to your advantage as the importer, and a supplier will usually agree to it only if the market elsewhere for the goods is slow, and it gives him or her an opportunity to move products that would otherwise be taking up costly storage space. If you can arrange it, it is an excellent way for you, as a new importer, to build up your inventory without making a major cash outlay. All you really need, aside from adequate storage space, is a reliable accounting system to keep track of the sales of each consignee's products. This alternative works best when you know your suppliers well.

2. Documentary collections

(a) Documents against acceptance

When you agree to documents against acceptance (D/A), you receive your shipment against a bill of exchange that has been arranged with your supplier through your respective banks. The documents for the shipment are processed through the banks, and you then sell the goods and pay for them on a specific date, as previously agreed between you and your supplier and noted on the bill of exchange.

Another word for a bill of exchange is a draft. It looks like a cheque and, like a cheque, it is an order for payment that requires one person (the drawer — that's you as importer) to pay another (the drawee, your supplier) a certain sum of money at a specified time. In effect, it is a form of credit made available to you by your bank for a set period.

FIGURE #1
PAYMENT TERMS AND RISK

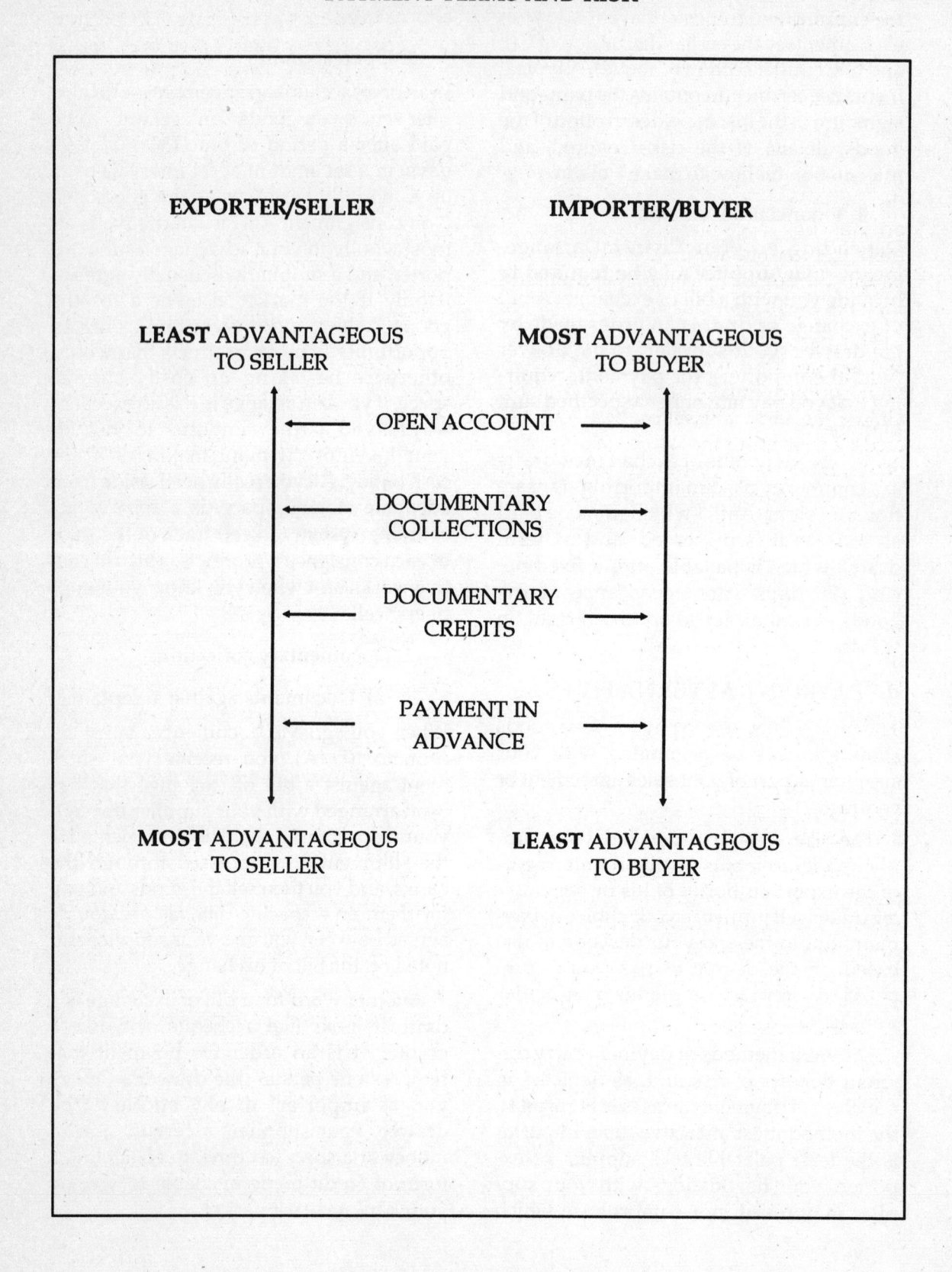

EXPORTER/SELLER   **IMPORTER/BUYER**

LEAST ADVANTAGEOUS TO SELLER   **MOST** ADVANTAGEOUS TO BUYER

←——— OPEN ACCOUNT ———→

←——— DOCUMENTARY COLLECTIONS ———→

←——— DOCUMENTARY CREDITS ———→

←——— PAYMENT IN ADVANCE ———→

MOST ADVANTAGEOUS TO SELLER   **LEAST** ADVANTAGEOUS TO BUYER

D/As are most favorable to the importer and are most successful when both parties are well known to each other.

(b) Documents against payment

If you arrange for documents against payment (D/P), your supplier sends all the documents you've asked for through his or her bank to yours, usually by mail or via the shipping agent responsible for transporting your goods once they've arrived. If these documents are in good order, you pay at your convenience, and the goods are then released to you.

This particular arrangement favors you as importer since you don't have to pay your supplier immediately. It also offers almost the same protection as a letter of credit, but without the service fee. As with D/As, D/Ps work best when both parties know each other well.

3. Documentary credits (letters of credit)

A letter of credit (l/c) is a written undertaking for payment, or a guarantee of payment, made by your bank at your request as an importer. You actually apply for an letter of credit and are therefore called the "applicant" while your supplier, the person you intend to pay, is called the "beneficiary." Once your credit is approved and your application is accepted, your bank becomes the "issuing bank."

A letter of credit is a conditional undertaking — that is, payment is made provided the beneficiary meets certain conditions, as listed in the letter of credit. You specify those conditions when you apply for your letter of credit. They often include the following:

(a) Provision of certain transport, commercial, and insurance documents

(b) Shipment of the goods and presentation of documents within a specified period of time

(c) A brief description of the goods

(d) Any other conditions you might consider necessary, such as provision of a third-party certificate of inspection completed within a certain period of time, or provision of a Certificate of Origin (form A or B-232E).

The purpose of all these conditions is to ensure that your shipment arrives in good time and without defects and is packaged and labelled according to the requirements of Consumer and Corporate Affairs Canada. You will note that various documents from different sources may be required to confirm that the conditions have been met — hence, letters of credit are also called "documentary credits." In fact, letters of credit are transacted purely through documentation since that's the only way your banker can determine if all your requirements have been satisfied.

Letters of credit are either freely negotiable or restricted. In the case of a freely negotiated letter of credit, the beneficiary may present documents for payment to any bank. Under a restricted letter of credit, the documents must be presented to the designated bank. Whatever arrangement is made, the bank that ultimately pays the supplier under the letter of credit is called the "negotiating bank."

You can make your letter of credit revocable or irrevocable. An irrevocable letter of credit cannot be changed without the agreement of all parties. A revocable letter of credit, on the other hand, can be amended or even cancelled without the beneficiary's consent. Needless to say, most letters of credit are irrevocable.

Once the issuing bank (your bank) accepts your letter of credit application, it contacts a bank in your supplier's country, known as the "advising bank," and asks it to advise your supplier of the terms and conditions of the letter of credit.

Your supplier goes through the letter of credit and either accepts it as is or requests changes. Once the conditions are acceptable to all parties, the supplier completes packaging and shipping arrangements for your order, collects all the required documents, and sends them to the negotiating bank within the time limit set. The bank reviews the documents and, if they're satisfactory, it pays the supplier according to the instructions contained in the letter of credit. The supplier may be paid within 48 hours or up to two weeks later, depending on the relationship between the issuing bank and the negotiating bank.

To expedite payment under a letter of credit, the issuing bank may ask the negotiating bank to pay a supplier as soon as he or she has presented all documents required. Such bank-to-bank arrangements can speed up payment to the supplier and should be discussed with your international banker. Should your supplier request a "confirmed" letter of credit, the issuing bank must request the advising bank to "add its confirmation." This is the negotiating bank's "guarantee" of payment to the supplier. Confirmation charges should be reviewed beforehand and discussed with your supplier as part of your price negotiation. Again, your international banker should be in a position to advise you.

As this short explanation demonstrates, an letter of credit transaction is not a simple process and can entail contractual arrangements between as many as five or six banks. It is a well-established payment alternative, however, recognized by financial institutions around the world and governed by a set of specific rules (Policy #500 Uniform Custom and Practice for Documentary Credits) developed and administered by the International Chamber of Commerce (ICC), an informal regulatory body based in Paris. Virtually all trading nations, save China, subscribe to these rules and when problems over documentary credits arise, the disputing parties refer to the ICC for an interpretation.

You will likely pay a fee of over $100 to the bank for your letter of credit (one-time use), so you may hesitate to use this approach unless it's absolutely necessary, although there are times when it will be. If you are doing business in a third-world nation, for example, you may be required by the country's export authorities to pay by letter of credit because it's one way the government can access valuable foreign currency. Many foreign suppliers also make payment by letter of credit a condition of doing business, especially when the purchaser is unknown to them. Sample #3 shows an application for a letter of credit.

4. Payment in advance

Payment in advance means you send your payment in full before receiving the goods. In this case, your shipment is probably small and your investment minimal. Obviously, this alternative is to your supplier's advantage and leaves you with virtually no options if you are dissatisfied with the goods when they arrive.

Another way to handle the situation is to make a partial payment beforehand, sending the remainder of the payment only after you have received the goods and are satisfied with them. This gives you more leverage in the transaction and encourages your supplier to fill the order exactly as requested. In general, paying in advance is only recommended if you know your supplier well.

e. REIMBURSEMENT METHODS

If you are paying on an open account or in advance, how do you actually send your payment to your foreign supplier? You have several choices:

(a) *By cheque*: Cheaper for you because you then have more time to use your money; you can also stop payment if problems arise between you and your supplier. More expensive for

SAMPLE #3
LETTER OF CREDIT

Application for Documentary Credit
Demande de crédit documentaire

1. Reference Number / N° de référence: _____
   Date of expiry / Date de validité extrême: **May 21, 1993**

2. Please Issue / Veuillez émettre un:
   - [X] Irrevocable / irrévocable
   - [ ] Revocable / révocable
   - [ ] Transferable / transférable
   Documentary Credit / crédit documentaire
   - [ ] By Airmail / par courrier aérien
   - [X] By cable / par câble — Full Particulars which will be the operative credit instrument

3. For Account of (Applicant) - Full name and address:
   Ace Sports Limited
   1010 West Georgia Street
   Vancouver, B.C.

4. In Favour of (Beneficiary) - Full name and address:
   Royal Rubbers Supplies
   10 Appian Way
   Hong Kong.

5. Advising Bank:
   Standard Chartered Bank
   52 High Street
   Hong Kong.

6. Currency and Amount: Canadian $50,000.
   - [X] Maximum
   - [ ] Approximately

8. Available by:
   - [X] drafts
   - [X] at sight
   - [ ] days sight
   - [ ] deferred payment

7. Partial shipments: [X] Allowed [ ] Not Allowed
   Transhipment: [X] Allowed [ ] Not Allowed

9. For 100% of invoice value (unless otherwise indicated) drawn at your option on you or your correspondent.

10. Shipment/Despatch/Taking in charge from/At: Hong Kong
    No later than: April 30, 1993

11. For Transportation to: Vancouver, B.C.

Accompanied by the following documents. (In duplicate unless otherwise indicated.) Indicate by an "X".

12. [X] Commercial Invoice
13. [X] Canadian Customs Invoice, if required, in Quintuplicate or ___ copies
14. a) [X] Full set clean "ON BOARD" Marine Bills of Lading, made out to order, blank endorsed and marked
    - [ ] Freight prepaid
    - [ ] Freight collect
    - [X] Notify applicant
    b) [ ] Combined Transport/Forwarder's Cargo Receipt/Forwarder's Bill of Lading/House Bill of Lading
15. [ ] Air Waybill marked
16. [X] Insurance Policy/Certificate in negotiable form, covering Institute Cargo clauses "ALL RISKS", Institute war, S.R.C.C. and T.P.N.D. clauses for **110** % of invoice value
17. [X] Packing List
18. [ ] Certificate of origin indicating _____ origin

Other Documents:
- [X] Certificate of Inspection signed by A.W.S. Services verifying quality, quantity, colour, and shipping specifications.
- [ ]
- [ ]

19. [X] Covering (Brief description of merchandise): 24,000 Boxes of "Grand Smash" tennis balls.

20. Terms of delivery:
    - [ ] F.O.B.
    - [ ] C and F
    - [X] C.I.F / CAF
    - [ ] C. & I.
    - [ ] Exfactory
    - [ ] Other (specify)

21. Special conditions: _____

All Banking charges outside of Canada for:
- [X] Beneficiary
- [ ] Applicant's Account

22. Documents to be presented within **10** days after the date of issuance of the shipping document(s) but within validity of the credit.

23. [X] Please forward the credit to the beneficiary through your correspondents.
24. [X] Return original credit to this branch for delivery to ourselves.

I/We fully understand that the documentary credit to be issued in response to this application will be subject to the "Uniform Customs and Practice for Documentary Credits (1983 Revision)", International Chamber of Commerce Publication No. 400, and documents presented and conforming to these provisions will be acceptable unless the terms of this application specifically detail otherwise.

Ace Sports Limited

IMPORTANT: The agreement on the reverse of this form must be signed.

Applicant(s) Signature

Date: April 1, 1993

your supplier who will probably pay a bank fee for processing the cheque.

(b) *By bank draft (money order)*: In the form of an international bank draft, readily available from your financial institution. More expensive for you because the bank charges a fee for this service and the funds are taken out of your account immediately. Also risky, particularly if you're sending it to a country with an unreliable postal system.

(c) *By money transfer (MT)*: Normally done by mail through banking channels. Not as fast as an electronic transfer but very safe. Expect a service fee.

(d) *By telegraphic/teletransmission (TT)*: Fast and safe, but the service fee is more expensive.

(e) *By SWIFT (Society for Worldwide Interbank Financial Telecommunications)*: An electronic transfer through the banking system. Virtually instantaneous and very safe, but again, you pay for it.

f. MANAGING THE RISK OF FOREIGN EXCHANGE

Foreign exchange rates are fundamentally important to the import/export business. If you are placing only small orders, you will be less affected by fluctuations in the currencies of the countries you're buying from. But once your business begins to grow and shipments increase, you will see the benefit of keeping a close watch on these fluctuations and planning ahead with your payment schedules. So important is this aspect of the business, in fact, that larger companies employ financial experts in house to analyze the money market and recommend payment strategies.

What is a foreign exchange rate exactly? According to Alasdair Watson, author of *Finance of International Trade* (see Recommended Reading at the end of this chapter), "a rate of exchange is the price of one currency in terms of another."

In Canada, for example, the rates for various currencies are quoted in terms of the Canadian dollar. When you go into a bank to buy foreign currency, you will see that two rates are normally advertised: one for buying a currency and one for selling it. The buying rate is generally higher because of the way free markets work.

Fluctuations in foreign exchange rates are caused by many factors, from catastrophic political or environmental crises within a country to the country's GNP, inflation rate, and interest rates. An actual or anticipated change in leadership can also affect currency ratings, as can major government policy changes and industrial relations. Influences outside the country also play an important role: changes in consumer spending, boycotts, the dealings of large multi-national companies. They can all cause a currency to fluctuate, sometimes by as much as 20% to 30% in a matter of weeks or months.

Companies use several strategies to benefit from currency fluctuations — or, at least, to minimize their negative impact on profits — some of which are discussed in this section. As you read through our list, bear in mind that it is incomplete and is intended only to inform you of the importance of foreign exchange fluctuations in your import dealings. Suffice it to say, this subject is complex, and for more information you must read one of the many authoritative books already written on it.

1. Forward rate contract

Just as its name suggests, a forward rate contract is a type of contract you make with your bank to purchase or sell a specified sum of foreign currency on a specific date or within a specific period of time in the future. When the transaction is to take place on a specific date, the contract is said to be "fixed." When it is scheduled for a specific period, it is called an "option" contract —

you have the option, that is, to choose the exact transaction day within the period specified. Forward rate contracts permit you to calculate the exact cost of a foreign currency payment when it comes due and thus to reduce the risk of loss from currency fluctuations.

2. Foreign exchange options from your bank

In this instance, you make an agreement with your bank to buy or sell foreign currency at a specific rate up to a specified date, in return for which you agree to pay a premium. You are not obliged to follow through with the purchase or sale; this approach merely gives you the option to. The premium you pay is determined by the probability of the option being exercised. This method is much more flexible than the forward rate contract. Having paid the premium, you are protected on the downside but can participate in favorable movements in the currency.

3. Foreign exchange options and futures on the stock market

You can always invest spare dollars in currency options and futures on the stock exchange. This is a very fast-moving and complex market, however, and unless you're intimately familiar with it, or are represented by a broker who is, you risk losing your shirt, as well as your original investment. Larger companies with in-house financial experts might well opt for this strategy.

4. Foreign currency account

If you have a large sum to deposit (more than $25 000), you can open a foreign currency account at your bank which frees you of bank charges and commissions on foreign currency payments and may give you the opportunity to borrow in foreign currency as well. For this type of account to be beneficial, however, you should have both revenue and expenses in the foreign currency.

5. Back-to-back financing

Back-to-back financing refers to the practice of both buying and selling in foreign dollars. You might ask your Japanese supplier to quote in American or Canadian dollars, for example, and settle the transaction in the same currency. By using a single currency throughout, you eliminate the effects of fluctuations in the exchange rate.

6. Leads and lags

These are terms that refer to the practice of delaying a foreign currency transaction (lagging) when currency rates are falling and speeding up settlement (leading) when they're on the rise. This can easily be done between two subsidiaries with the same parent company. But when the two companies are separate, they are bound by their contractual agreement and must negotiate separately if the purchaser wants to lead or lag.

RECOMMENDED READING

Watson, Alasdair. *Finance of International Trade.* London: Bankers Books, 1990.

3
CANADA CUSTOMS AND *CUSTOMS 2000*

This chapter provides a general description of the structure of Revenue Canada, Customs, Excise and Taxation, and information on changes that the department has already made or is planning to make over the 1990s as a result of the trend to computerization and an increase in the number of commercial imports and travellers.

a. THE CHANGING LANDSCAPE

Where once it was unusual to see imported goods on grocery and department store shelves in Canada, today it is commonplace. Indeed, today's consumer expects to be able to buy imports from all over the world and would feel deprived if they suddenly disappeared from the marketplace.

Commercial shipments into Canada have been increasing steadily over the past decade — from around seven million in 1980 to more than ten million in recent years. Most of this growth has occurred since the 1980s when Canada began using the General Agreement for Trade and Tariffs (GATT) transaction value system of valuation and started to move away from protectionist trade policies. At the time, Canada was being pressured on many fronts, not the least of them being the negotiations then under way for a free trade agreement with the United States. Today that pressure continues as Mexico joins our free trade pact, and other bilateral and multi-lateral trading agreements are reached between nations around the world.

In the late 1980s, these events, together with increases in cross-border shopping, began to put considerable strain on Canada Customs, making apparent the need to review and completely reset its underlying philosophy and operations. The result was a detailed, large-scale policy document, *Customs 2000: A Blueprint for the Future*, which provided a general overhaul and realignment of the department to meet Canada's expanding role in international trade into the 21st century.

The document itself had no absolute goals or deadlines. It was essentially a ten-year plan with objectives written loosely enough to accommodate for new developments in the industry and electronic communications over the same period. More than an plan, it also contained a vision of an efficient and economical electronic processing system that permitted immediate release of low-risk shipments, protected the Canadian public from dangerous and illegal shipments, and incorporated major government initiatives, like the GST and NAFTA. Today that vision is gradually becoming reality as import/export activities continue to grow and Customs pursues further initiatives like the *New Business Relationship*.

The *New Business Relationship* was launched in September 1992, after extensive consultation with the business community. Developed expressly to improve the administrative procedures underlying commercial imports, it has encouraged the establishment of such new programs as the Business Number (BN). The BN numbering system assigns a single number to individual businesses that replaces all the other numbers they've previously acquired to deal with the federal government.

During the same period, Customs has also adopted a simplified release policy, eliminating the delayed release of shipments with minor documentation errors, and established the National Customs Rulings (NCR) program to ensure consistency in the tariff classification of imported goods country wide. For a more detailed discussion of NCRs, see chapter 4.

b. OVERVIEW OF CANADA CUSTOMS

Canada Customs is actually a component of the Department of National Revenue, formally known as Revenue Canada, Customs, Excise and Taxation (see introduction for more details). The customs and excise functions of the department are well established, having first come into being at confederation, and are administered by many thousands of staff across the country. Figure #2 shows the different program branches within Revenue Canada.

Canada Customs is headquartered in Ottawa and has six regions, each broken down into several divisions. Within each region, Customs Border Services is responsible for administering the various stations (also called "ports") where imported goods may be cleared. The six regions are:

(a) Atlantic

(b) Quebec

(c) Northern Ontario

(d) Southern Ontario

(e) Prairies

(f) Pacific

The elected Minister of National Revenue, Customs, Excise and Taxation, assisted by a Deputy Minister, heads the department while an Assistant Deputy Minister (ADM) handles the administration of each region. Under the ADM are several regional directors, including a director, Customs Border Services in charge of customs activities. A full list of the Customs Border Services offices with their addresses and phone numbers is provided in Appendix 1 at the end of this manual.

Most Canadians know Canada Customs only by the inspectors they talk to briefly at the primary inspection line (PIL) at border crossings or coming home from a flight abroad. If you're an importer, however, the inspector is just one of several Customs professionals with whom you have occasional dealings. Others you or your representatives are likely to speak to include the following:

(a) *Commercial inspectors*, who are generally responsible for inspecting and releasing commercial shipments, ensuring that the shipments are as described on the accompanying invoice and meet all relevant regulations under the Customs Act and other federal acts administered by Canada Customs.

(b) *Commodity specialists*, who are responsible for examining accounting documents after the release of a shipment to ensure that the tariff status of the goods, the goods' value, and the taxes paid are all in order.

(c) *Tariff and values administrators*, who are responsible for determining (verifying) the tariff classification and value for duty of goods, on request from a customs broker or the public, or during the routine review of an entry. (An entry is the accounting document completed by an importer or customs broker; see chapter 11.)

(d) *Inspectors*, who work out of several divisions and are involved in different types of investigations, ranging from investigations of drawback claims to post-audit investigations of specific shipments of imported goods.

FIGURE #2
REVENUE CANADA, CUSTOMS, EXCISE AND TAXATION PROGRAM BRANCHES

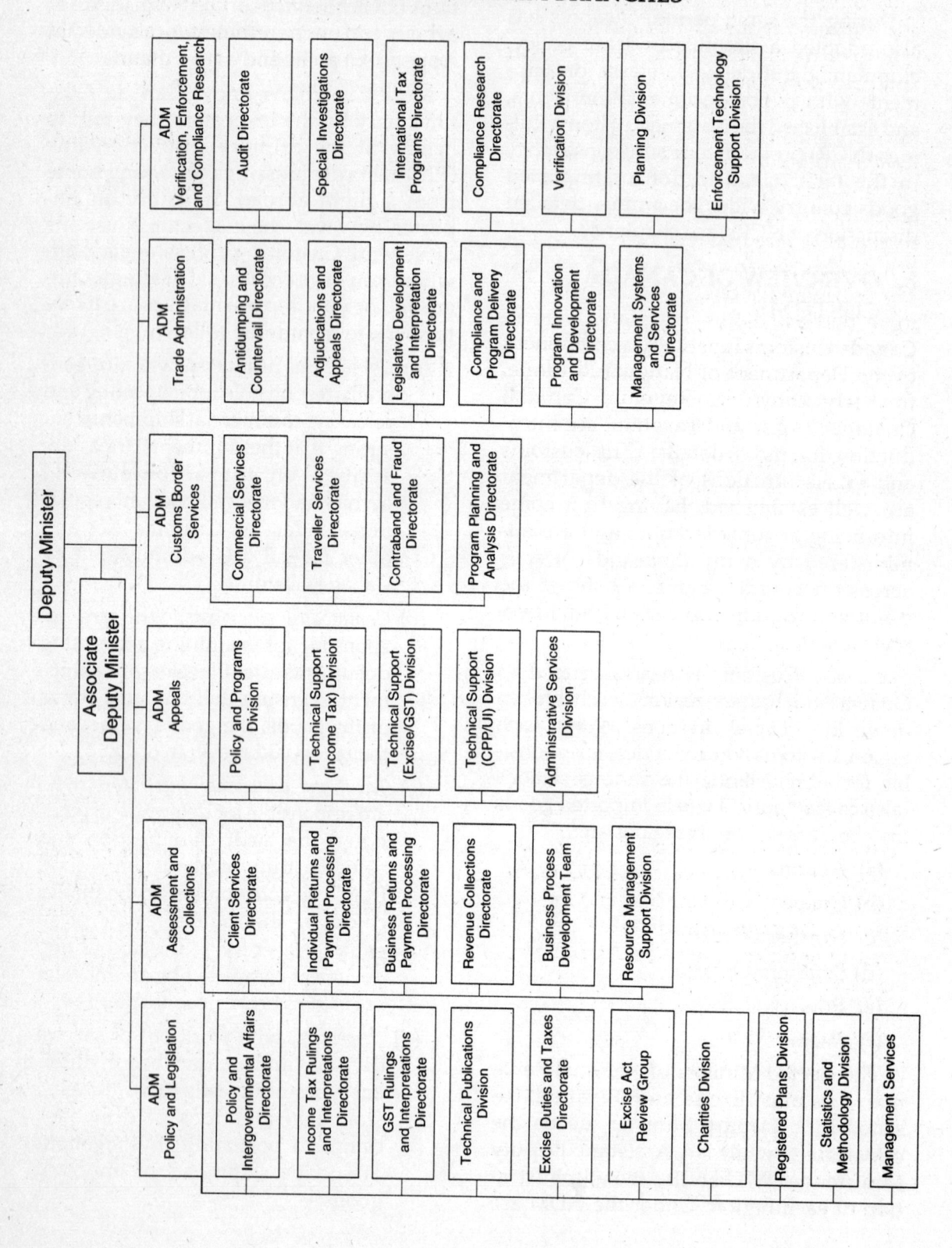

Deputy Minister
Associate Deputy Minister

- **ADM Verification, Enforcement, and Compliance Research**
  - Audit Directorate
  - Special Investigations Directorate
  - International Tax Programs Directorate
  - Compliance Research Directorate
  - Verification Division
  - Planning Division
  - Enforcement Technology Support Division

- **ADM Trade Administration**
  - Antidumping and Countervail Directorate
  - Adjudications and Appeals Directorate
  - Legislative Development and Interpretation Directorate
  - Compliance and Program Delivery Directorate
  - Program Innovation and Development Directorate
  - Management Systems and Services Directorate

- **ADM Customs Border Services**
  - Commercial Services Directorate
  - Traveller Services Directorate
  - Contraband and Fraud Directorate
  - Program Planning and Analysis Directorate

- **ADM Appeals**
  - Policy and Programs Division
  - Technical Support (Income Tax) Division
  - Technical Support (Excise/GST) Division
  - Technical Support (CPP/UI) Division
  - Administrative Services Division

- **ADM Assessment and Collections**
  - Client Services Directorate
  - Individual Returns and Payment Processing Directorate
  - Business Returns and Payment Processing Directorate
  - Revenue Collections Directorate
  - Business Process Development Team
  - Resource Management Support Division

- **ADM Policy and Legislation**
  - Policy and Intergovernmental Affairs Directorate
  - Income Tax Rulings and Interpretations Directorate
  - GST Rulings and Interpretations Directorate
  - Technical Publications Division
  - Excise Duties and Taxes Directorate
  - Excise Act Review Group
  - Charities Division
  - Registered Plans Division
  - Statistics and Methodology Division
  - Management Services

c. ACTS ADMINISTERED BY CANADA CUSTOMS

Chief among the acts administered by Canada Customs is the Customs Act and its extensive regulations, completely revised and passed by Parliament in 1986. One of the most powerful pieces of legislation in force in Canada today, the act gives Canada Customs officers authority to search travellers and seize goods (and/or the conveyances they're being carried in) if they have reason to believe that the law is being broken. It also carries severe penalties in the case of contraventions. (See chapter 13 for a more detailed discussion of the enforcement provisions of this legislation.) A list of the regulations, referred to as the "D" series or Departmental Memoranda, is provided in Appendix 2 at the back of this book.

Several other acts and accompanying regulations are also interpreted and administered by Canada Customs, including the Customs Tariff Act, Excise Tax Act, Excise Act, Special Import Measures Act, and the Export and Import Permits Act. The department administers legislation on behalf of several other government departments as well — an estimated 70 acts in all — as listed in Appendix 3.

d. ELECTRONIC DATA INTERCHANGE (EDI) SYSTEMS

Today's society-wide trend to computerization has been an obvious catalyst in the development of *Customs 2000* and the *New Business Relationship* initiatives. In fact, were it not for the computer revolution of the past 25 years, it would be hard to imagine some of the changes now taking place at Canada Customs.

One direct result of this trend, back in the 1980s, was Customs' adoption of Electronic Data Interchange (EDI) as a means of transmitting and receiving information. Thanks largely to EDI, the department was able to develop the Customs Automated Data Exchange System (CADEX) for transmitting entry data. CADEX, implemented in 1988, linked Customs to brokers and large-scale importers, allowing them to submit data over telecommunications lines instead of completing a paper entry form. Customs currently uses CADEX in the processing of 85% of all the entry forms it receives and is now planning to implement a complete electronic release system in December 1995, eliminating the need for paper altogether.

As an adjunct to CADEX, Customs has also developed the Technical Reference System to assist its commodity specialists in reviewing entries and making better classification and valuation decisions. A virtual compendium of Customs information, from recent valuation decisions to the latest exchange rates, the system may also become available to brokers and importers via computer linkup.

EDI has spawned several other time- and cost-saving systems as well, including the following:

(a) *Customs Declaration (CUSDEC)*, which is another means of electronically transmitting entry data, similar to CADEX but done through an international format that uses the United Nations Electronic Data Interchange.

(b) *External Affairs/Customs automated permit system (EXCAPS)*, which accelerates the import permit process by electronically transmitting permits issued by Foreign Affairs and International Trade Canada; it is currently being piloted in Ontario for application Canada-wide.

(c) *Electronic Funds Transfer (EFT)*, which enables importers to remit duties and taxes by electronic transmission rather than by cheque at a Customs office; recently piloted in the Toronto area for application throughout Canada.

(d) *Release Notification System (RNS)*, which provides importers/customs brokers, warehouse operators, and carriers with electronic notification of a Customs release within 30 minutes of the release decision

(e) *EDI cargo system*, which allows marine and rail carriers to transmit cargo and transport data to Customs before actually arriving at a Customs office; carriers no longer need present paper copies of cargo and transport reports

As well, a departmental line release program is now in operation, primarily to streamline truck imports from the United States and Mexico. The concept of line release was first described in *Customs 2000*, and its establishment represents the fulfillment of a major *Blueprint* objective.

"Line release" is the term for a computer-assisted set of operations that facilitates the clearance of commercial goods through primary inspection lines at the border. Participants in the program provide Customs with the required documents before their shipment arrives at border offices, giving Customs staff a chance to process the shipment ahead of time. Most carriers of line-release goods now spend less than a minute in Customs, a vast improvement from the hour or more spent in Customs before the program went into operation.

There are one or two interesting, if predictable, outcomes of Customs' trend to computerization. As electronic systems have proliferated, several brokerage firms have developed software packages for use in their own businesses. These programs are also offered for sale to client importers with sufficient purchase volumes to warrant the investment. Many brokerage companies have also sized down and no longer maintain separate office space in key locations like airports; computerization has simply eliminated the need.

e. VOLUNTARY COMPLIANCE AND ENFORCEMENT

Central to Customs' *Blueprint*, and the more recent *New Business Relationship*, is the concept of voluntary compliance — the willingness of importers to abide by Customs' policies and decisions. Customs believes that most Canadians are law abiding and should not be made to pay for the actions of a few. By instituting a policy of voluntary compliance, in accordance with the underlying philosophy of the Customs Act itself, the department can eliminate or streamline many procedures, saving the honest importer time and tax dollars.

At the same time, Customs also endorses enforcement procedures that are clear, fair, and vigorously pursued, in the belief that compliance is greater when the penalties for noncompliance are stringent. To this end, its plans provide for staff training, improved facilities and equipment, and the development of a strict penalty structure. No doubt, new developments in technology are going to play a role here as well, providing the department with equipment that simplifies and speeds the examination of high-risk shipments.

f. PROCEDURES TODAY AND TOMORROW

While some shipments must still be processed by hand because of their relative complexity, electronic release, as mentioned earlier, is just a few months away. A strong EDI network is evolving to link Customs with virtually all participants in international trading operations, including carriers, brokers, exporters, importers, banks, and insurance companies. Data detailing cargo, release, and invoicing is being carried via telecommunications lines, along with entry information. Paper, except in the case of traditional hand-processed entries, has been all but eliminated.

Many brokers and large-scale importers are also now participating in a new accounting system for low-value shipments (LVS) — shipments worth less than C $1 200. Under this new system, accounting data on the shipments is held for some weeks after the shipments are released. The data is then "batched" to Customs on a once-monthly basis — an approach that will eventually be extended to all shipments, regardless of value. Eventually participants will also be invoiced for all duties and taxes, and will pay via electronic funds transfer, as some in the Toronto area are already doing.

Thanks again to EDI, Customs is accumulating data on shipments and will continue to do so as part of its screening and enforcement activities. This data collection took an interesting form under the FTA where Canadian and American authorities agreed to share the collection function: Canada collecting information on American imports in exchange for the United States maintaining statistics on Canadian imports. Today the same system continues under NAFTA and may well be extended to include Mexico. As Customs data accumulates, it will be shared with other government departments and customs agencies around the world as a means of ensuring compliance and spotting illegal import activities.

Of course, not everyone — and especially not the novice importer — will be in a position to purchase EDI technology and software or take immediate advantage of the system's many benefits. For this group, Customs will continue to administer the traditional entry and accounting systems now in place.

g. RESPONDING TO BUSINESS

When you consider the size of Customs staff — an estimated 40 000 Canada-wide — and the fact that most of its traditional systems were still in place in 1989 when Blueprint was published, it is nothing short of a miracle that the department has successfully computerized its services in the six years since. Even more amazing, however, is the change in its general approach to business to a new openness and responsiveness to business needs. This is exemplified, of course, in its New Business Relationship initiative. But it is also evident in the internal restructuring of the department that has gone on in recent years, in the publication of brochures such as *Your Opinion Counts* (an invitation to the public to comment on Revenue Canada services), and in the very demeanor of Customs staff.

Unforeseeable developments in trade and technology will doubtless continue to affect the department's evolution and efficiency. But it has made a solid start in the right direction and, in the process, is aiding the cause of Canadian business in the international marketplace. It is an exciting time for aspiring importers, and you should take advantage of the situation by offering your comments and suggestions regarding the Customs services you use.

RECOMMENDED READING

Canada. Revenue Canada, Customs and Excise. *Customs 2000: A Blueprint for the Future.* [Ottawa]: Government of Canada, 1990.

Canada. Revenue Canada, Customs, Excise and Taxation. *A Guide to Importing Commercial Goods: April 1995.* [Ottawa]: Government of Canada, 1995.

Canada. Revenue Canada, Customs, Excise and Taxation. *Index to Revenue Canada Services.* [Ottawa]: Government of Canada, 1994.

4
THE HARMONIZED SYSTEM TARIFF

This chapter provides a brief history and introduction to the Harmonized System Tariff used by Canada Customs and most other GATT member countries to classify imported items and determine the tariff treatment and duty payable on them.

On January 1, 1988, Revenue Canada, Customs and Excise, adopted the Harmonized Commodity Description and Coding System, or HS, Tariff, as provided under the Customs Tariff Act. This tariff was developed by the Customs Co-operation Council in Brussels, Belgium, for use by members of GATT and represents a major step toward the standardization of international trade.

Canada's reputation as a trading partner has suffered over the years as a result of our bilingual labelling policies, our quota systems, and our previous valuation system (fair market value) and Customs Tariff. The government's adoption of the HS Tariff and a new valuation system represents a basic shift in attitude and promises increased trade in international markets. The United States, our largest trading partner, implemented the same valuation and tariff system on January 1, 1989, the day the FTA went into effect.

a. THE TARIFF'S SEVEN SCHEDULES

The HS Tariff may seem an intimidating document at first glance, with more than 8 000 different tariff classifications and as many as 20 000 if you also consider the special concessionary rates of duty offered in its Schedule II. But with an understanding of its basic format and the General Interpretive Rules, it soon becomes more user friendly.

The HS Tariff consists of seven schedules, each dealing with a different aspect of the classification process.

1. Schedule I

Schedule I is the most significant of the seven in terms of usage. It deals with the general rules for the interpretation of the HS and with the approximately 8 000 tariff items contained in 21 sections and 98 chapters.

2. Schedule II

Schedule II contains the special concessionary rates of duty that apply when certain specific requirements are met. Under certain circumstances, usually owing to the end use of the goods or perhaps the end user of the goods, a lower than normal rate of duty applies. Concessionary rates take effect when the four-digit Schedule II code is applied to the tariff classification number on a customs entry. The codes are itemized according to industry sector.

Schedule II is also referred to as the Consolidation of Concessionary Provisions or the Annex.

3. Schedule III

Schedule III sets out the five columns of tariff treatment accorded to Canada's trading partners (countries with which we have a formal trade agreement). These tariff treatments are the following:

(a) *Most Favoured Nations Tariff Treatment (MFN)*, which applies to all countries listed in the Schedule

(b) *General Preferential Tariff Treatment (GPT)*, which applies to certain developing countries. Goods must be shipped directly to Canada, with or without transhipment (shipment through another country without entering the commerce of that country), and an Original Certificate of Origin (form A) is required.

(c) *United States Tariff Treatment (UST)*, as established under NAFTA. A Certificate of Origin (Canada Customs form B-232E) is required.

(d) *Mexico Tariff Treatment (MT)*, as established under NAFTA. A Certificate of Origin (Canada Customs form B-232E) is required.

(e) *Mexico-United States Tariff Treatment (MUST)*, as established under NAFTA. A Certificate of Origin (Canada Customs form B-232E) is required.

As well, three other tariff treatments are discussed in the Customs Tariff Act:

(a) *British Preferential Tariff Treatment (BPT)*, which applies to developing countries that are members of the British Commonwealth and to Australia and New Zealand.

(b) *Least Developed Developing Country Tariff Treatment (LDDC)*, which applies to certain countries that, according to the United Nations, are deserving of special treatment. Goods must be shipped directly to Canada, with or without transhipment, and an original Certificate of Origin is required.

(c) *Commonwealth Caribbean Countries Tariff Treatment (CARIBCAN)*, which applies to Commonwealth Caribbean countries. Goods must be shipped directly to Canada, with or without transhipment, and an original Certificate of Origin (form A) is required.

There is also one other tariff treatment of significance — the General Tariff. The General Tariff applies to all countries not listed in Schedule III. Because there is no trade agreement in place with these countries, the duty rates are significantly higher.

4. Schedule IV

Schedule IV provides for duty recovery by drawback on imported goods that undergo some further manufacture in Canada and are then consumed here. "Drawback" is the process of filing a claim for recovery of duty already paid (discussed in more detail in chapter 12). A common example is "Products of Steel" (listed in chapter 72 of the HS Tariff); if used in the manufacture of cutlery or files for Canadian consumption, it becomes eligible for a 100% drawback on duty paid.

5. Schedule V

Schedule V provides for duty recovery, by drawback, on imported goods used for certain purposes, as in the case, for example, of billiard table slate of at least 19 mm thickness (tariff item No. 6803.00.90). This product becomes eligible for 100% drawback when at least 50% of the factory cost of producing the finished table is incurred in Canada.

6. Schedule VI

Schedule VI lists tariff items, specifically machinery and equipment, that qualify for entry into Canada duty free because they are "of a class or kind not available from production in Canada." Importers of these items must first apply for a remission — that is, for all duty to be remitted on entry of the goods into Canada.

7. Schedule VII

Schedule VII lists certain goods that are prohibited entry into Canada — white phosphorus matches, for example.

b. THE TARIFF FORMAT

Each product or group of products described in the tariff is preceded by a number or series of digit groupings. Each of these numbers or groupings tells you something about the level of the classification. For example —

45.03: Articles of natural cork

4503.10.00.00: Corks and stoppers

Obviously we are dealing here with corks and stoppers of natural cork. But what else do these numbers tell us?

- 45 — indicates that the item falls within chapter 45 of the HS Nomenclature (classification system)

- 45.03 — is the heading (always four numbers) with a decimal inserted for ease of reading

- 4503.10 — is the subheading (six digits). Subheadings are consistent internationally, and all GATT countries that use the HS recognize the same goods to the six-digit level.

- 4503.10.00 — is the tariff classification number. The seventh and eighth digits are unique to Canada. These digits dictate the rate of duty assessed for specified goods under a particular tariff treatment. When certain goods within a subheading are given tariff protection, they are "broken out" or assigned separate tariff classification numbers and a separate duty rate.

- 4503.10.00.00 — the ninth and tenth digits are for statistical purposes only and are also unique to Canada. These are used in identifying types and quantities of foreign goods entering Canada. Additional "breakouts" are used as needed.

Goods are classified in the tariff according to their "essential character" — that is, by what they are, not by what they are going to be used for, or who the end user will be. The tariff's table of contents shows that the system is set up in a hierarchical manner, as you can see from the pages shown in Sample #4. In both sections and chapters the goods are listed in raw form first, then in semi-manufactured or processed form, and last, in fully manufactured or processed form. By keeping the "essential character" of an item in mind, as well as the hierarchical setup of the tariff, you should find the classification process a little easier to understand.

There are two common methods of reading the tariff — the numerical method, by digit grouping, and the dash method.

If you use the numerical method, start the classification process by going to the table of contents. There you'll see that the HS has 21 sections consisting of 99 chapters. (A section is a group of chapters representing similar or related products.) Find the appropriate chapter (two digits). Then move along to the proper heading (four digits). Then identify the subheading (six digits) and the tariff item (eight digits), and, finally, the statistical level (ten digits).

It is important to classify in this order without taking shortcuts. As each set of two digits is added to a number, the description of the item becomes more precise. Were you to start at the subheading level, you might miss something in the heading that excludes the item you're classifying. Remember also that the chapters are generally laid out according to degree of manufacture, starting with items of lesser manufacture.

The second approach is the dash method, which is based on the number of dashes preceding the description of goods listed in the HS. Look for a single dash preceding a subheading. This dash reflects a change in the fifth digit of the ten-digit classification number. Two dashes reflect a change at the sixth-digit level, three a change in the seventh digit, and so on, to ten digits.

SAMPLE #4
HS TARIFF — TABLE OF CONTENTS

TABLE OF CONTENTS

GENERAL INFORMATION   PAGE NO.

- General Information — i
- Administrative Guidelines — iii
- List of Countries with Applicable Tariff Treatments (Schedule III) — vii

THE CUSTOMS TARIFF

- An Act respecting the imposition of, and providing relief against the imposition of, duties of customs and other charges, and to give effect to the International Convention on the Harmonized Commodity Description and Coding System
- General Rules for the Interpretation of the Harmonized System
- Sections and Chapters (Schedule I)

SECTION I — I - 1
LIVE ANIMALS; ANIMAL PRODUCTS

1	Live animals	01 - i
2	Meat and edible meat offal	02 - i
3	Fish and crustaceans, molluscs and other aquatic invertebrates	03 - i
4	Dairy produce; birds' eggs; natural honey; edible products of animal origin, not elsewhere specified or included	04 - i
5	Products of animal origin, not elsewhere specified or included.	05 - i

SECTION II — II - 1
VEGETABLE PRODUCTS

6	Live trees and other plants; bulbs, roots and the like; cut flowers and ornamental foliage	06 - i
7	Edible vegetables and certain roots and tubers	07 - i
8	Edible fruit and nuts; peel of citrus fruit or melons	08 - i
9	Coffee, tea, maté and spices	09 - i
10	Cereals	10 - i
11	Products of the milling industry; malt; starches; inulin; wheat gluten	11 - i
12	Oil seeds and oleaginous fruits; miscellaneous grains, seeds and fruit; industrial or medicinal plants; straw and fodder	12 - i
13	Lac; gums, resins and other vegetable saps and extracts	13 - i
14	Vegetable plaiting materials; vegetable products not elsewhere specified or included	14 - i

SECTION III — III - 1
ANIMAL OR VEGETABLE FATS AND OILS AND THEIR CLEAVAGE PRODUCTS; PREPARED EDIBLE FATS; ANIMAL OR VEGETABLE WAXES

15	Animal or vegetable fats and oils and their cleavage products; prepared edible fats; animal or vegetable waxes	15 - i

Issued January 1, 1995

SAMPLE #4 — Continued

	PAGE NO.
SECTION IV	IV - 1
PREPARED FOODSTUFFS; **BEVERAGES, SPIRITS AND VINEGAR; TOBACCO** **AND MANUFACTURED TOBACCO SUBSTITUTES**	
16 Preparations of meat, of fish or of crustaceans, molluscs or other aquatic invertebrates	16 - i
17 Sugars and sugar confectionery	17 - i
18 Cocoa and cocoa preparations	18 - i
19 Preparations of cereals, flour, starch or milk; pastrycooks' products	19 - i
20 Preparations of vegetables, fruit, nuts or other parts of plants	20 - i
21 Miscellaneous edible preparations	21 - i
22 Beverages, spirits and vinegar	22 - i
23 Residues and waste from the food industries; prepared animal fodder	23 - i
24 Tobacco and manufactured tobacco substitutes	24 - i
SECTION V	V - 1
MINERAL PRODUCTS	
25 Salt; sulphur; earths and stone; plastering materials, lime and cement	25 - i
26 Ores, slag and ash	26 - i
27 Mineral fuels, mineral oils and products of their distillation; bituminous substances; mineral waxes	27 - i
SECTION VI	VI - 1
PRODUCTS OF THE CHEMICAL OR ALLIED INDUSTRIES	
28 Inorganic chemicals; organic or inorganic compounds of precious metals, of rare-earth metals, of radioactive elements or of isotopes	28 - i
I. - Chemical elements	28 - 1
II. - Inorganic acids and inorganic oxygen compounds of non-metals	28 - 2
III. - Halogen or sulphur compounds of non-metals	28 - 4
IV. - Inorganic bases and oxydes, hydroxydes and peroxydes of metals	28 - 4
V. - Salts and peroxysalts, of inorganic acids and metals	28 - 7
VI. - Miscellaneous	28 - 16
29 Organic chemicals	29 - i
I. - Hydrocarbons and their halogenated, sulphonated, nitrated or nitrosated derivatives	29 - 1
II. - Alcohols and their halogenated, sulphonated, nitrated or nitrosated derivatives	29 - 5
III. - Phenols, phenol-alcohols and their halogenated, sulphonated, nitrated or nitrosated derivatives	29 - 7
IV. - Ethers, alcohol peroxides, ether peroxides, ketone peroxides, epoxides with a three-membered ring, acetals and hemiacetals, and their halogenated, sulphonated, nitrated or nitrosated derivatives	29 - 9
V. - Aldehyde-function compounds	29 - 10

Issued January 1, 1995

SAMPLE #4 — Continued

			PAGE NO.
	VI.	- Ketone-function compounds and quinone-function compounds	29 - 11
	VII.	- Carboxylic acids and their anhydrides, halides, peroxides and peroxyacids and their halogenated, sulphonated, nitrated or nitrosated derivatives	29 - 13
	VIII.	- Esters of inorganic acids and their salts, and their halogenated, sulphonated, nitrated or nitrosated derivatives	29 - 20
	IX.	- Nitrogen-function compounds	29 - 21
	X.	- Organo-inorganic compounds, heterocyclic compounds, nucleic acids and their salts, and sulphonamides	29 - 26
	XI.	- Provitamins, vitamins and hormones	29 - 31
	XII.	- Glycosides and vegetable alkaloids, natural or reproduced by synthesis, and their salts, ethers, esters and other derivatives	29 - 33
	XIII.	- Other organic compounds	29 - 34
30		Pharmaceutical products	30 - i
31		Fertilizers	31 - i
32		Tanning or dyeing extracts; tannins and their derivatives; dyes, pigments and other colouring matter; paints and varnishes; putty and other mastics; inks	32 - i
33		Essential oils and resinoids; perfumery, cosmetic or toilet preparations	33 - i
34		Soap, organic surface-active agents, washing preparations, lubricating preparations, artificial waxes, prepared waxes, polishing or scouring preparations, candles and similar articles, modelling pastes, ``dental waxes'' and dental preparations with a basis of plaster	34 - i
35		Albuminoidal substances; modified starches; glues; enzymes	35 - i
36		Explosives; pyrotechnic products; matches; pyrophoric alloys; certain combustible preparations	36 - i
37		Photographic or cinematographic goods	37 - i
38		Miscellaneous chemical products	38 - i

SECTION VII — VII - 1

**PLASTICS AND ARTICLES THEREOF;
RUBBER AND ARTICLES THEREOF**

39		Plastics and articles thereof	39 - i
	I.	- Primary forms	39 - 1
	II.	- Waste, parings and scrap; semi-manufactures; articles	39 - 6
40		Rubber and articles thereof	40 - i

SECTION VIII — VIII - 1

**RAW HIDES AND SKINS, LEATHER, FURSKINS AND ARTICLES
THEREOF; SADDLERY AND HARNESS; TRAVEL GOODS,
HANDBAGS AND SIMILAR CONTAINERS; ARTICLES OF ANIMAL GUT
(OTHER THAN SILK-WORM GUT)**

41	Raw hides and skins (other than furskins) and leather	41 - i
42	Articles of leather; saddlery and harness; travel goods, handbags and similar containers; articles of animal gut (other than silk-worm gut)	42 - i
43	Furskins and artificial fur; manufactures thereof	43 - i

Issued January 1, 1995

SAMPLE #4 — Continued

		PAGE NO.
	SECTION IX	IX - 1
	WOOD AND ARTICLES OF WOOD; WOOD CHARCOAL; CORK AND ARTICLES OF CORK; MANUFACTURES OF STRAW, OF ESPARTO OR OF OTHER PLAITING MATERIALS; BASKETWARE AND WICKERWORK	
44	Wood and articles of wood; wood charcoal	44 - i
45	Cork and articles of cork	45 - i
46	Manufactures of straw, of esparto or of other plaiting materials; basketware and wickerwork	46 - i
	SECTION X	X - 1
	PULP OF WOOD OR OF OTHER FIBROUS CELLULOSIC MATERIAL; WASTE AND SCRAP OF PAPER OR PAPERBOARD; PAPER AND PAPERBOARD AND ARTICLES THEREOF	
47	Pulp of wood or of other fibrous cellulosic material; waste and scrap of paper or paperboard	47 - i
48	Paper and paperboard; articles of paper pulp, of paper or of paperboard	48 - i
49	Printed books, newspapers, pictures and other products of the printing industry; manuscripts, typescripts and plans	49 - i
	SECTION XI	XI - 1
	TEXTILES AND TEXTILE ARTICLES	
50	Silk	50 - i
51	Wool, fine or coarse animal hair; horsehair yarn and woven fabric	51 - i
52	Cotton	52 - i
53	Other vegetable textile fibres; paper yarn and woven fabrics of paper yarn	53 - i
54	Man-made filaments	54 - i
55	Man-made staple fibres	55 - i
56	Wadding, felt and nonwovens; special yarns; twine, cordage, ropes and cables and articles thereof	56 - i
57	Carpets and other textile floor coverings	57 - i
58	Special woven fabrics; tufted textile fabrics; lace; tapestries; trimmings; embroidery	58 - i
59	Impregnated, coated, covered or laminated textile fabrics; textile articles of a kind suitable for industrial use	59 - i
60	Knitted or crocheted fabrics	60 - i
61	Articles of apparel and clothing accessories, knitted or crocheted	61 - i
62	Articles of apparel and clothing accessories, not knitted or crocheted	62 - i
63	Other made up textile articles; sets; worn clothing and worn textile acticles; rags	63 - i
	I. - Other made up textile articles	63 - 1
	II. - Sets	63 - 7
	III. - Worn clothing and worn textile articles; rags	63 - 7

Issued January 1, 1995

SAMPLE #4 — Continued

		PAGE NO.
	SECTION XII	XII - 1
	FOOTWEAR, HEADGEAR, UMBRELLAS, SUN UMBRELLAS, WALKING-STICKS, SEAT-STICKS, WHIPS, RIDING-CROPS AND PARTS THEREOF; PREPARED FEATHERS AND ARTICLES MADE THEREWITH; ARTIFICIAL FLOWERS; ARTICLES OF HUMAN HAIR	
64	Footwear, gaiters and the like; parts of such articles	64 - i
65	Headgear and parts thereof	65 - i
66	Umbrellas, sun umbrellas, walking-sticks, seat-sticks, whips, riding-crops and parts thereof	66 - i
67	Prepared feathers and down and articles made of feathers or of down; artificial flowers; articles of human hair	67 - i
	SECTION XIII	XIII - 1
	ARTICLES OF STONE, PLASTER, CEMENT, ASBESTOS, MICA OR SIMILAR MATERIALS; CERAMIC PRODUCTS; GLASS AND GLASSWARE	
68	Articles of stone, plaster, cement, asbestos, mica or similar materials	68 - i
69	Ceramic products	69 - i
	I. - Goods of siliceous fossil meals or of similar siliceous earths, and refractory goods	69 - 1
	II. - Other ceramic products	69 - 2
70	Glass and glassware	70 - i
	SECTION XIV	XIV - 1
	NATURAL OR CULTURED PEARLS, PRECIOUS OR SEMI-PRECIOUS STONES, PRECIOUS METALS, METALS CLAD WITH PRECIOUS METAL, AND ARTICLES THEREOF; IMITATION JEWELLERY; COIN	
71	Natural or cultured pearls, precious or semi-precious stones, precious metals, metals clad with precious metal, and articles thereof; imitation jewellery; coin	71 - i
	I. - Natural or cultured pearls and precious or semi-precious stones	71 - 1
	II. - Precious metals and metals clad with precious metal	71 - 2
	III. - Jewellery, goldsmiths' and silversmiths' wares and other articles	71 - 5
	SECTION XV	XV - 1
	BASE METALS AND ARTICLES OF BASE METAL	
72	Iron and steel	72 - i
	I. - Primary materials; products in granular or powder form	72 - 1
	II. - Iron and non-alloy steel	72 - 4
	III. - Stainless steel	72 - 21
	IV. - Other alloy steel; hollow drill bars and rods, of alloy or non-alloy steel	72 - 25
73	Articles of iron or steel	73 - i
74	Copper and articles thereof	74 - i

Issued January 1, 1995

SAMPLE #4 — Continued

		PAGE NO.
75	Nickel and articles thereof	75 - i
76	Aluminum and articles thereof	76 - i
77	(Reserved for possible future use in the Harmonized System)	77 - i
78	Lead and articles thereof	78 - i
79	Zinc and articles thereof	79 - i
80	Tin and articles thereof	80 - i
81	Other base metals; cermets; articles thereof	81 - i
82	Tools, implements, cutlery, spoons and forks, of base metal; parts thereof of base metal	82 - i
83	Miscellaneous articles of base metal	83 - i

SECTION XVI

XVI - 1

MACHINERY AND MECHANICAL APPLIANCES: ELECTRICAL EQUIPMENT; PARTS THEREOF; SOUND RECORDERS AND REPRODUCERS, TELEVISION IMAGE AND SOUND RECORDERS AND REPRODUCERS, AND PARTS AND ACCESSORIES OF SUCH ARTICLES

84	Nuclear reactors, boilers, machinery and mechanical appliances; parts thereof	84 - i
85	Electrical machinery and equipment and parts thereof; sound recorders and reproducers, television image and sound recorders and reproducers, and parts and accessories of such articles	85 - i

SECTION XVII

XVII - 1

VEHICLES, AIRCRAFT, VESSELS AND ASSOCIATED TRANSPORT EQUIPMENT

86	Railway or tramway locomotives, rolling-stock and parts thereof; railway or tramway track fixtures and fittings and parts thereof; mechanical (including electro-mechanical) traffic signalling equipment of all kinds	86 - i
87	Vehicles other than railway or tramway rolling-stock, and parts and accessories thereof	87 - i
88	Aircraft, spacecraft and parts therof	88 - i
89	Ships, boats and floating structures	89 - i

SECTION XVIII

XVIII - 1

OPTICAL, PHOTOGRAPHIC, CINEMATOGRAPHIC, MEASURING, CHECKING, PRECISION, MEDICAL OR SURGICAL INSTRUMENTS AND APPARATUS; CLOCKS AND WATCHES; MUSICAL INSTRUMENTS; PARTS AND ACCESSORIES THEREOF

90	Optical, photographic, cinematographic, measuring, checking, precision, medical or surgical instruments and apparatus; parts and accessories thereof	90 - i
91	Clocks and watches and parts thereof	91 - i
92	Musical instruments; parts and accessories of such articles	92 - i

Issued January 1, 1995

SAMPLE #4 — Continued

		PAGE NO.
	SECTION XIX	XIX - 1
	ARMS AND AMMUNITION; PARTS AND ACCESSORIES THEREOF	
93	Arms and ammunition; parts and accessories thereof	93 - i
	SECTION XX	XX - 1
	MISCELLANEOUS MANUFACTURED ARTICLES	
94	Furniture; bedding, mattresses, mattress supports, cushions and similar stuffed furnishings; lamps and lighting fittings, not elsewhere specified or included; illuminated signs, illuminated name-plates and the like; prefabricated buildings	94 - i
95	Toys, games and sports requisites; parts and accessories thereof	95 - i
96	Miscellaneous manufactured articles	96 - i
	SECTION XXI	XXI - 1
	WORKS OF ART, COLLECTORS' PIECES AND ANTIQUES	
97	Works of art, collectors' pieces and antiques	97 - i
98	Special classification provisions	98 - i
99	(Reserved for special uses by Contracting Parties)	99 - i
•	Statutory Concessionary Provisions (Schedule II) - Codes 0005 to 2999	A - 1
•	Customs Duties Reduction or Removal Order - Codes 3005 to 6965	B - 1
•	Chemicals and Plastics Duties Reduction or Removal Order - Codes 7005 to 7982	C - 1
•	Goods Subject to Drawback for Home Consumption (Schedule IV) - Codes 9000 to 9095	D - 1
•	Goods Subject to Drawback when used for certain purposes (Schedule V) - Codes 9200 to 9240	E - 1
•	Agreement on Trade in Civil Aircraft (Schedule II) - Codes 9300 to 9350	F - 1
•	Automotive Products Trade Agreement provisions - Codes 9400 to 9450	G - 1
•	After-market Automotive Parts (Schedule II) - Codes 9600 to 9645	H - 1
•	Customs Duties Accelerated Reduction Order - Codes 9650 to 9688	I - 1
•	Prohibited Goods (Schedule VII) - Codes 9950 to 9967	J - 1
•	Machinery and Equipment provisions (Schedule VI) - Code MACH	K - 1

Issued January 1, 1995

When you are going through the classification process, remember that the first level of description with legal significance is the heading. If you are certain the goods qualify under a particular heading, consider the various subheadings under that heading. Read only the subheadings (one dash). Determine which subheading is most appropriate and proceed to the next level (two dashes) and so on, to the sixth dash. Once again, being systematic is essential to this classification technique. Comparing all the items at the same dash level soon becomes second nature if you do it regularly.

One other classification method, the electronic-based tariff method, is not yet in use. Recently developed by Canada Customs, this method will provide a faster, more efficient means of determining tariff classification. Now being reviewed and tested by selected industry members, it operates on the basis of text retrieval, not unlike the computer systems developed for libraries.

c. PUNCTUATION AND WORDING

Because the tariff contains industry-specific terminology, the proper interpretation of tariff items can be complicated. Understanding the use of commas, semicolons, colons, and the words "and" and "or" makes the process easier.

1. Commas

Commas are generally used to list commodities as in the case of Heading 0101 "live horses, asses, mules, and hinnies."

2. Semicolons

Semicolons are used in a tariff item to indicate a full stop. Items separated by a semicolon should be considered as separate and distinct from each other. Tariff item 0508.00.00, for example, reads: "Coral and similar materials, unworked or simply prepared but not otherwise worked; shells of molluscs, crustaceans, or echinoderms and cuttle-bone, unworked or simply prepared but not cut to shape, powder and waste thereof."

When you read this item, it's important to recognize the products and descriptive phrases on either side of the semicolon and keep them separate. In our excerpt, the product is "coral and similar materials" and the descriptive phrase is "unworked or simply prepared but not otherwise worked."

3. Colons

Colons indicate that there is additional information to follow on the items specified. For example:

1209	Seeds, fruit and spores, of a kind used for sowing.
	– Beet seed:
1209.11	- - Sugar beet seed
1209.19	- - Other

The colon after "beet seed" tells you that there is more information to come on this item. In this case, the beet seed is broken down into two subcategories: sugar beet seed and other beet seed.

4. "And," "or," and some unusual terms

The words "and" and "or" have probably caused more problems and confusion than any other two words in the English language. In the HS, the word "and" is used in a series — for example, "pictures, designs, and photographs"; and is also used to join descriptive phrases or conditions.

The word "or" is also used in a series, but to suggest alternatives. Heading 6404, for example, reads "footwear with outer soles of rubber, plastics, leather or composition leather and uppers of textile materials." This means that the footwear can have outer soles of rubber, plastics, leather or composition leather (these are the alternatives), but must have uppers of textile materials.

While we're on the subject of editorial format and word usage, it's probably a good time to comment briefly on some of the more unusual terms used to describe items classified in the HS Tariff. A truck may be referred to as a lorry; a battery as an accumulator. Why these uncommon words — uncommon in Canada, at least — are used can probably be explained by the fact that the tariff was developed over a period of years for use mainly in Europe, where most of GATT's member nations were at one time concentrated. It's a good idea to keep this in mind when you go through the classification process and, if you're having trouble finding the item you want, to consider other terms it might be known by.

d. THE GENERAL INTERPRETIVE RULES

The General Interpretive Rules of the HS Tariff, found in Schedule I, are the rules that govern its use. There are two types of rules: General Rules and Canadian Rules. The six General Rules apply internationally to all users of the tariff; the three Canadian Rules are unique to Canada. Rules one through four must always be considered and applied in sequence. Rules five and six can be applied independently.

1. International rules

(a) Rule one

Rule one informs you that the tariff is divided into sections, chapters, and subchapters for your convenience only. These divisions have no basis in law. The legal classification process begins at the heading level and is subject to the provisions of any section or chapter notes. Both section and chapter notes have legal significance and are discussed in more detail later.

Knowing the legal status of the various parts of the tariff is especially important in matters of dispute. If you feel, for example, that a product should be classified under one tariff item and Customs has a different opinion, it helps to know what part of the tariff is legally enforceable and what part quasi-judicial, representing GATT's interpretation. Many tariff disputes are settled through the appeal process, with settlement eventually reached by the Canadian International Trade Tribunal or, in some cases, the Federal Court.

(b) Rule two

Rule two is divided into two parts. The first part states that goods that are incomplete, unfinished, unassembled, or disassembled must be classified as complete (or finished or assembled) as long as they have the essential character of the complete or finished article and are not excluded from that heading in any of the legal notes.

The second part states that any reference to a material or substance includes mixtures or combinations of that material or substance, providing that what is added does not change the essential character of the initial substance. If, for example, you were to add some grains of rice to bulk table salt to prevent moisture agglomeration, the mixture would be classified as table salt under heading 2501 because the grains of rice do not alter the essential character of the mixture. Also, there are no legal notes that would exclude the mixture from classification under that heading.

The same principle also applies to goods. A leather jacket, for example, is not usually made entirely of leather. But the lining, buttons, zipper, and other non-leather articles do not change its essential character and so it is classified under tariff item 4203.10.00 as "articles of apparel, leather."

(c) Rule three

Goods that consist of more than one material or substance are sometimes classifiable under more than one tariff item. When this occurs, rule three is applied. The first part of the rule states that the heading that provides the most specific description is preferred.

Consider the classification of an electric shaver, for example:

(a) Heading 85.08 reads "Electro-mechanical tools for working in the hand, with a self-contained motor."

(b) Heading 85.09 reads "Electro-mechanical domestic appliances, with self-contained electric motor."

(c) Heading 85.10 reads "Shavers and hair clippers, with self-contained electric motor."

Electric shavers could be classified under any of these headings. Heading 85.10, however, specifically mentions "shavers... with self-contained electric motor" and, by virtue of rule three, shavers are classified under this heading.

The second part of rule three states that goods made up of different components, and goods put up in sets for retail sale, that cannot be classified by reference to rule three (a), should be classified as if they consisted of the material or component that gives them their "essential character."

While determining the essential character of an item is usually easy, you'd be surprised at how complicated it can become at times. Take the example of pre-packaged spaghetti dinner. The package consists of loose, uncooked spaghetti, a tin of tomato or meat sauce, and some cheese. Most of us would say that the essential character of the set is the spaghetti. But ask an Italian and he or she will tell you that the essential character is the sauce!

Finally, rule three says that when goods cannot be classified by reference to the earlier parts of this rule, "they shall be classified under the heading that occurs last in numerical order among those that equally merit consideration."

For example, a mixture of 50% table salt (Heading 2501) and 50% pepper (Heading 0904) would be better classified as salt because 2501 occurs after 0904 in the tariff.

(d) Rule four

Rule four says that when no classification for a specific item is apparent, then it should be classified under the same heading as the item it most resembles. This same principle was applied under the old Tariff when computers were first imported into Canada. Since there was no heading for computers per se, computer keyboards were classified as typewriters and monitors as television sets.

(e) Rule five

Rule five deals with two issues. First, camera cases, musical instrument cases, gun cases, drawing instrument cases, necklace containers and similar containers, are classified with the items they contain, provided they are —

(a) specifically shaped or fitted to contain a specific article,

(b) suitable for long-term use, and

(c) imported with the articles they contain.

The one exception to this rule is cases that give items their essential character. A gold case designed for and containing business cards, for example, would be classified by its case, not by its business cards.

Rule five also says that if packing materials or containers are not re-usable, they are classified with the goods they contain. When they can be re-used, they're classified according to their essential character and are liable for duty and taxes.

(f) Rule six

Rules one through five deal with classification at the heading level only. Rule six states that the previous five rules also apply at the subheading level. Rules one through four continue to be applied in sequence. Rule five stands alone.

2. Canadian rules

(a) Rule one (Canadian)

Rule one of the Canadian rules is similar to rule six (international), only it extends the level of comparison beyond the subheading to the tariff item. Tariff items at the same level are comparable, subject to the relative section and chapter notes.

(b) Rule two (Canadian)

Because the tariff is an international document, the meaning of certain words or phrases may vary according to the interpreting country. Recognizing this as a potential problem, Canada has implemented rule two, which gives precedence to the international meaning of a disputed term.

(c) Rule three (Canadian)

Under rule six, the principles of the General Rules were extended to the subheading level. Under rule one (Canadian), they were extended to the tariff item level. This rule now extends them to the statistical level. Since it is beyond the tariff level and has no monetary significance, the statistical level is not part of Customs Tariff legislation.

e. ESSENTIAL CHARACTER

We have referred several times to the term "essential character" in our discussion on the tariff, and it appears in three of the six General Interpretive Rules. Its meaning is fundamental to the classification process, although no appeals over its interpretation have yet reached the Canadian International Trade Tribunal (at least, not as of the writing of this book).

If we look at rule two (a) again, the question of whether a component of an article has the essential character of the finished article is purely subjective. Would you say, for example, that a vehicle engine has the essential character of a vehicle? What about a vehicle chassis? Or a vehicle body? It all depends on how you interpret the function and importance of the item being classified.

Let's look at another example, drawn this time from a real-life classification problem — parking meters. A parking meter consists of a supporting pole, a single housing (which contains a vault and housing assembly), and a mechanism assembly. The mechanism assembly consists of a coin-handling device affixed to a timer. Importers of mechanism assemblies must determine whether the assemblies have the essential character of a finished parking meter or should be classified under "other watch or clock parts" or "other articles of iron or steel." By looking at the three alternatives and their respective rates of duty, we see that parking meters have a much higher duty rate than the other two. (Customs' position, however, is that the mechanisms have the essential character of parking meters and are to be classified as such.)

Different classifications can have very different duty rates, so the question of essential character can have a tremendous impact on your cost. Furthermore, if you make an error in classification, you must be prepared for Customs to change the classification and charge you for any resulting shortfall of duty and GST. They are also empowered to issue a penalty, depending on the circumstances (see chapter 13 for more).

f. TARIFF CLASSIFICATION AND OTHER RULINGS

If you have any doubt as to the correct HS Tariff classification of a particular item, you can request a National Customs Ruling (NCR). As its name suggests, once an NCR has been issued, it becomes public information and applies on a national basis. Regardless of who imports the item, or where it enters Canada, its classification remains the same. Each NCR is given a ruling number, more properly called a Technical Reference System number, which must then appear on the importer's B-3 entry form (the standard consumption entry used in the importing process, discussed in more detail in chapter 11) or in field K160 if the importer is making a CADEX electronic entry (described in chapter 3).

NCRs are issued on request to importers (both resident and non-resident) and their agents or customs brokers. They are not issued to exporters. Also, their application is not limited to tariff classification — a National Customs Ruling also applies when the valuation and origin of goods are being determined (valuation, the process of determining the value for duty of an imported item, is discussed in chapter 6). The main purpose of the NCR program is to promote consistency, clarity, and voluntary compliance among importers across Canada. It does not handle questions concerning the classification of goods imported under NAFTA. These should be made to NAFTA's Advance Ruling program.

In order for Canada Customs to issue binding customs rulings, it must have complete and accurate information about the items being classified. This is usually supplied by the importer or the agent or customs broker acting for the importer. If the information is incomplete, the NCR becomes null and void. While there is no formal appeal process for NCRs, an appeal can be filed under the appeal provisions of the Customs Act, once the goods in question have been imported. Where Customs is provided with confidential and/or proprietary information in order to make a ruling, it "sanitizes" — removes all confidential information — before making the ruling public.

NCRs are binding on both the importer and Canada Customs so long as all conditions respecting the classified item remain unchanged. When changes do occur, the onus is on the importer to advise Customs so the ruling can be modified or revoked. Customs will consider retroactive assessments if an importer has failed to classify a particular item according to a published NCR and the item is imported after the ruling has been made.

Regulations governing National Customs Rulings are contained in the regulations of the Customs Act (Memoranda D11-11-1 and D11-11-2), available at your local public library. Also provided in the regulations is a compendium of the NCRs published to date.

g. PARTS AND ACCESSORIES

Whether an item is a part of something else or an accessory has created classification problems for many years. There is nothing in the tariff that provides a definition of either term. However, both terms are used as if they have quite different and distinct meanings. For classification purposes, the General Interpretive Rules apply equally to whole goods, parts, and accessories.

Nuts, bolts, screws, washers, bearings, transistors, capacitors, and electric motors are all examples of items that generally form a part of something else. Yet these items are all specifically named in the tariff and are classified according to their own heading. They are never classified as part of something else.

By comparison, Heading 84.54 reads "Converters, ladles, ingot mould and casting machines, of a kind used in metallurgy or in metal foundries" and is followed by four subheadings:

(a) 8454.10 - - Converters

(b) 8454.20 - - Ingot mould and ladles

(c) 8454.30 - - Casting machines

(d) 8454.90 - - Parts

The tariff items listed under the last subheading are referred to as "parts tariff items." Under this subheading are classified parts for converters, ingot mould and ladles, and casting machines, provided they are not specifically named elsewhere in the tariff.

h. NOTES

Two types of notes play a role in the classification process: legal notes and explanatory notes.

1. Legal notes

Legal notes are found at the beginning of each chapter and section of the tariff. Have a look again at the table of contents in Sample #4 for the format. Chapter notes pertain to all the tariff items in the chapter; section notes, to all the items in the section. Once you have identified a particular tariff classification number for an item, always verify that there are no legal notes that preclude you from using that number. If you have classified an item under chapter 88, for example, refer to the chapter notes at the beginning of that chapter, and to the section notes just prior to chapter 86.

Legal notes are legally enforceable and have international significance. They perform three functions:

(a) they define the limits of a heading, subheading, or subdivision;

(b) they provide lists of goods that are specifically included; and

(c) they provide lists of goods that are specifically excluded, directing the user to the correct classification area.

Supplementary notes, also legally enforceable, apply only to Canada.

2. Explanatory notes

Explanatory notes are designed to go hand in hand with the tariff. Although they're only quasi-judicial, they are still a very important part of the classification process.

Basically, the explanatory notes are a compilation of information to assist in the classification process. Like section and chapter notes, they list inclusions and exclusions, and provide some insight into methods of production, industry terminology, item appearance and properties, etc.

i. SCHEDULE II CODES

At the beginning of this chapter, we discussed the seven schedules of the tariff and indicated that Schedule II contains special concessionary rates of duty. Under this schedule, for example, commodities encompassed by a particular tariff rate qualify for a lower rate of duty, as do items designed for a particular end use.

While importers applaud the lower rate of duty, the truth is that Schedule II, with its additional coding requirements, adds to the complexity of the tariff. For this reason, Customs has recently formed a Tariff Simplification Task Force to determine if the schedule should be eliminated. The schedule could be eliminated if certain existing duty rates were adjusted and several new tariff items created. It hasn't happened yet, however, and until it does, importers should continue to review Schedule II concessions carefully and discuss them with their customs broker.

j. CLASSIFICATION WORKSHEET

As a means of getting you started on using the HS Tariff, we've developed a Classification Worksheet that identifies each step you take in the course of classifying or rating an item (see Worksheet #2). Take a photocopy of it with you whenever you're planning to determine a classification, and use it as a checklist until you are familiar with the tariff and more proficient in rating your goods. You must rate your invoice — identify the tariff classification of each product — before you can complete your entry for submission to Customs.

Most public libraries have a copy of the HS Tariff, or you can use the copy available at the Canada Customs office nearest you. When in doubt about a classification, remember that it's best to make a written request to Customs for an NRC, providing as much information as you can on the item in question.

RECOMMENDED READING

Amendment Service to Explanatory Notes
   Alpha Index (Catalogue 12-579E)
   Harmonized Commodity Description and Coding System (Catalogue RV55-2/1992E)

Amendment Service to HS
   Explanatory Notes (Catalogue RV51-20/1-1992E)

Note: All of these are available, by mail, from:

   Canada Communications Group — Publishing
   Ottawa, Canada
   K1A 0S9

or

   McMullin Publishers Ltd.
   417 Rue St. Pierre
   Montreal, Quebec
   H2Y 2M4

WORKSHEET #2
CLASSIFICATION WORKSHEET FOR
THE HS TARIFF

1. Product to be classified: _____

   Other names it might be known by: _____

   Detailed description: _____
   _____

   Properties/components: _____
   _____

   Proposed application(s): _____

   End user(s): _____

   Disposition: _____
   _____

   Value: _____

2. Chapter *(refer to the Table of Contents, the Alpha Index, any classification software developed for this purpose, etc.)*: _____
   _____

3. Heading *(refer to the General Interpretive Rules, as required; the heading is the first category with legal significance in the classification process)*: ____
   _____

4. Dash levels *(refer to explanatory notes for assistance, particularly if there are two or more classification possibilities)*:

   One-dash   _____

   Two-dash   _____

   Three-dash _____

   Four-dash _____

   Five-dash _____

   Six-dash   _____

5. Review chapter notes and section notes to ensure that you've considered every reference.

6. Schedule II code (where applicable): _____

7. Refer to the appropriate tariff treatment for the duty rate: _____

5
THE NORTH AMERICAN FREE TRADE AGREEMENT

This chapter provides a brief discussion of the North American Free Trade Agreement (NAFTA) which came into effect on January 1, 1994. A trilateral agreement with Mexico as the third signatory, NAFTA replaces the Free Trade Agreement (FTA) instituted between Canada and the United States in 1989.

The recent implementation of NAFTA by Canada, the United States, and Mexico has laid the groundwork for the development of the largest free trade zone in the world. With a trading population of 360 million consumers and a combined gross national product in excess of seven trillion dollars, the long-term impact of the agreement on its three signatories is likely to be considerable. Like the FTA, NAFTA will be phased in over several years during which time entire industries will be restructured and repositioned. This is expected to have a domino effect on manufacturers and their suppliers in all three countries — affecting, in turn, the exporters and importers doing business with them.

An accession clause in NAFTA permits other countries to join the agreement. During the past year, for example, Chile has expressed interest in becoming a member if the process can be accelerated as it was for Mexico. Japan may follow. World trading blocs are emerging as the direction of future international trade, with political and cultural differences among participants being perhaps the most difficult obstacle to overcome.

NAFTA is a trilateral agreement, consistent with Article XXIV of GATT which specifically provides for the establishment of free trade agreements among member countries. It covers a broad range of topics — government procurement, services, investment and temporary entry, financial services, and institutional and other provisions. In this chapter we discuss only those aspects of NAFTA that have a direct impact on the importation process: tariff elimination and marking, rules of origin, and customs procedures.

First, a word of caution. NAFTA differs from its predecessor, the FTA, in one important respect: it's more precise and, as a result, more complex. For a full understanding of the document, you have no alternative but to read it. And even then you may have difficulty. Unless you're planning to acquire an in-depth knowledge of this subject, you would probably find it easier (and more economical timewise) to retain a customs consultant or other expert to give you periodic advice and assistance. There's a lot of information available on NAFTA today, but it falls into one of two distinct categories — it's either too simple or too technical for the needs of most importers. We've tried to bridge the gap with our approach in the discussion below, but are only too aware of its inadequacies.

a. TARIFF ELIMINATION UNDER NAFTA

Under the FTA, tariffs were eliminated in accordance with three rate reduction schedules: immediately (January 1, 1989);

over a five-year program; or over a ten-year program. Had we continued with it, 1994 would have been year six under the agreement. Instead, we are now in our first year of NAFTA.

NAFTA has not had much affect on the old rate reduction schedules. Generally, goods scheduled to become duty free over five years under the FTA are now free and will remain so under the new agreement.

At the same time, tariffs on goods scheduled to become duty free over ten years will continue to be eliminated, more or less as established under the old agreement. The rate reduction schedules under both agreements are generally referred to as "staging categories."

Canada has released a tariff schedule in conjunction with NAFTA. Entitled the North American Agreement Tariff Schedule of Canada, it sets out tariff item numbers, corresponding article descriptions, the staging categories, and the base rates for all goods under the new agreement. The base rates are the rates of duty from which reductions are to be made under each staging category.

In all, there are six staging categories under the new agreement:

(a) *Staging Category A tariffs* — duty free effective January 1, 1994, the date of reduction implementation. Includes items such as ceramic tiles and cameras with their parts and accessories.

(b) *Staging Category B tariffs* — duty free as of January 1, 1998, after five equal annual reductions, beginning January 1, 1994. Includes items such as certain types of fruit and/or vegetable juices and microwave popping corn.

(c) *Staging Category C tariffs* — duty free as of January 1, 2003, after ten equal annual reductions, beginning January 1, 1994. Includes items such as candles and wire made from iron or non-alloy steel.

(d) *Staging Category D tariffs* — duty free to begin with and still duty free.

(e) *Staging Category B1 tariffs* — duty free as of January 1, 1999, after six equal annual reductions, beginning January 1, 1994. Includes certain textile and apparel goods as listed in Appendix 300-B.1.1.

(f) *Staging Category B+ tariffs* — duty free as of January 1, 2001, after eight annual reductions as set out below, beginning January 1, 1994. Includes certain textile and apparel goods as listed in Appendix 300-B.1.1.

January 1, 1994	20%
January 1, 1995	0%
January 1, 1996	10%
January 1, 1997	10%
January 1, 1998	10%
January 1, 1999	10%
January 1, 2000	10%
January 1, 2001	30%

As in the FTA, NAFTA contains provisions to accelerate the deductions of specified goods or services when all three countries are in agreement with the acceleration. Also, where two of the three agree, those two may implement a rate reduction while the third retains its tariff protection.

b. NAFTA'S TARIFF TREATMENTS

Under NAFTA there are three tariff treatments — the United States Tariff (UST); the Mexico Tariff (MT); and finally, the Mexico-United States Tariff (MUST). Each of these occupies a column in the HS Tariff, as described in chapter 4.

1. The United States Tariff

This is a carry-over from the FTA, where it was first introduced. Thus, the base rate for the UST is actually the year five rate of the UST under the FTA.

The UST applies to goods that originate in the United States, even though they may have some non-NAFTA content. Should the goods then be exported to Mexico for further processing, they would still qualify for UST, providing the value added does not exceed 7%. This content cannot exceed 7% of the total value of the goods. Take the case, for example, of a U.S. manufacturer of ceramic pots who exports them to Mexico for painting and then ships them to Canadian customers. As long as the value of the painting does not exceed 7% of the value of the finished painted pots, the pots may enter Canada under the UST.

2. The Mexico Tariff

This is based mainly on the General Preferential Tariff rates. This tariff applies to goods that originate in Mexico or incorporate some non-NAFTA content but still qualify as Mexican goods. Should the goods then be exported to the United States for further processing, they would still qualify for MT, providing the value added does not exceed 7%. In other words, goods that originate in Mexico and are subsequently exported to the United States for further processing still qualify for the MT when they enter Canada, so long as the value added in the United States does not exceed 7% of the value of the finished item.

3. The Mexico–United States Tariff

This generally carries the highest duty rates of the three NAFTA tariff treatments. MUST applies to those products that qualify for NAFTA preferential treatment but, for one reason or another, do not qualify for the UST or MT.

c. MARKING RULES UNDER NAFTA

Implementation of NAFTA brought about a new Country of Origin Marking program for goods exported from NAFTA countries.

The federal government actually established marking requirements for certain specified commodities many years ago. These requirements are in Departmental Memorandum D11-3-1 of the Customs regulations, and all goods imported from other than NAFTA countries are still subject to them. The requirements list 60 classes of goods that must be marked, including items such as dishes, twine, bicycles, toys, textiles, wearing apparel, and iron or steel pipes and tubes. (A copy of the D11-3-1 Marking Requirements is provided in chapter 8 in relation to our discussion of non-tariff barriers.)

The country of origin of non-NAFTA goods is the country where they were substantially manufactured and took their final form before being imported into Canada. The new marking rules under the Country of Origin Marking program determine the country of origin of goods imported from a NAFTA country.

The methodology of the marking rules parallels the NAFTA Rules of Origin. That is, the rules are based on a change in the HS classification.

Three sets of regulations, all listed in Appendix 1 of Customs Departmental Memorandum D11-3-1, are used to administer the marking program:

(a) Determination of Country of Origin for the Purpose of Marking Goods (NAFTA countries) Regulations

(b) Determination of Country of Origin for the Purpose of Marking Goods (non-NAFTA countries) Regulations

(c) Marking of Imported Goods Regulations

The regulations are based on two fundamental principles established under NAFTA. First, no goods requiring marking can be imported unless they're properly marked. Second, failure to comply with the regulations will result in a penalty being assessed against the importer. When goods are not marked, Customs issues a notice to the importer, giving him or her a time limit in which to meet the requirements before the goods are released. Penalties are not assessed for first-time offences, but can range from $250 to $2 000 for subsequent offences, depending on their severity.

With the implementation of NAFTA, a Customs officer in each region is now designated to make marking determinations and issue advance marking rulings. These determinations and rulings are both subject to appeal.

d. HS CLASSIFICATION AND THE DEFINITIONS OF TERMS

Before we move on to our discussion of the Rules of Origin, we'd like to note two considerations of fundamental importance to their understanding: HS classification and the definitions of the terms applied in the agreement.

To determine if a product qualifies for entry into Canada under one of NAFTA's three preferential tariff treatments, you must establish its correct HS classification. Then you must determine if it contains any non-NAFTA material and, if so, what the HS classification of that material was on entry into North America. Only after that can you proceed to the Rules of Origin — and only, we reiterate, if you're sure your classification is correct. All the work you're about to embark on will be meaningless otherwise.

Also necessary to a full understanding of the rules are the definitions of the terms applied in the agreement, as provided in chapter 2. These include key terms such as:

- *originating* — qualifying under the Rules of Origin set out in chapter 4 of NAFTA.

- *territory* — the territory of a party as set out in Annex 201.1; that is, the territory of Canada, the United States, or Mexico. The actual definition is much more precise and refers to territorial specifics such as islands, seabeds, territorial seas, and even the space above the national territory.

- *party* — this term refers to Canada, the United States, or Mexico.

- *material* — a good that's used in the production of another good, and includes a part or an ingredient. Under the NAFTA definition, a material can be a part, a component or a sub-assembly as long as it's used in the production of another good.

e. THE RULES OF ORIGIN

NAFTA contains only one set of Rules of Origin that apply equally, regardless of which NAFTA country the goods originate from or are moving to. Articles 401 (a),(b),(c), and (d) of the agreement relate specifically to the rules and are summarized below.

1. Article 401(a)

Article 401(a) of NAFTA tells us that if a good is wholly obtained or produced entirely within the territory of one or more of the parties, as defined in Article 415, it qualifies. To be "wholly obtained or produced," however, the good must be made exclusively from North American materials and can have no foreign (non-North American) content whatsoever.

Obviously, foreign goods — goods produced entirely outside of North America — do not qualify for the benefits of NAFTA. But what about goods that are partially produced here and partially made up of foreign content? In such a case you must apply the rules for the correct determination.

2. Article 401(b)

Article 401(b) reads "Each of the non-originating materials used in the production of the good undergoes an applicable change in tariff classification set out in Annex 401 as a result of production occurring entirely in the territory of one or more of the parties, or the good otherwise satisfies the applicable requirements of that Annex where no change in tariff classification is required, and the good satisfies all other applicable requirements of this chapter."

Generally speaking, there are only three kinds of rules. The first requires a tariff shift; the second, a tariff shift plus "regional value content" (value added); and the third, regional value content only.

(a) Tariff shift

A tariff shift is a change in tariff classification. Let's say, for example, that an American firm imports paint from Italy for application to the ceramic pots it manufactures. The paint enters the United States under HS chapter 32. The finished pots are then sold to a customer in Canada and enter here under HS Tariff item 6913.90.90. If we look up the Rule of Origin for this tariff item (Annex 401 of NAFTA), we find that it reads, "a change to heading 69.01 to 69.14 from any other chapter." The imported paint from HS chapter 32 has been changed into a painted pot of heading 69.13 and the pots have met the requirements set out in the Rule of Origin. Thus they now qualify for the UST preferential tariff under NAFTA. A tariff shift, then, means that a good has undergone sufficient transformation in one NAFTA country before being exported to another NAFTA country.

(b) Tariff shift plus regional value content

The term "regional value content" refers to a calculation made to establish what percentage of an item originates in the NAFTA territory. North American regional content is calculated by one of two methods — the transaction value method or the net cost method, as follows:

(a) Transaction value method:

$$RVC = \frac{TV - VNM}{TV} \times 100$$

(b) Net cost method:

$$RCV = \frac{NC - VNM}{NC} \times 100$$

RVC = regional value content

TV = transaction value

NC = net cost of good

VNM = value of non-originating materials used by the producer in the production of the good

An item is considered to have originated in a particular NAFTA country when the tariff-shift requirement is met and the regional value content or RVC is not less than 60% according to the transaction value method of valuation, and not less than 50% under the net cost method.

(c) Regional value content only

Typically, the type of rule that requires RVC only reads:

> No required change in tariff classification to Canadian tariff item 8529.90.60, U.S. tariff item 8529.90.30C or Mexican tariff item 8529.90.22, provided there is regional value content of not less than:
>
> (a) 60 percent where the transaction value method is used, or
>
> (b) 50 percent where the net cost method is used.

To demonstrate how this might work, let's use the example of an American manufacturer who imports brackets into the United States from Japan under HS classification 8529.90 and then incorporates them into panels for color television cameras. The bracket is thus a part of the panel which is part of the camera. When the manufacturer sells the panel to a Canadian customer, it enters our country under the provisions of HS item 8529.90, exactly the same classification as that of the bracket on entering the United States. In other words, there has been no tariff shift. And if we then examine the particular Rule of Origin governing the importation of color television camera parts, we see that it requires only regional value content or RVC — there is no requirement for a tariff shift.

3. Article 401(c)

Article 401(c) of NAFTA states that a good originates where "the good is produced entirely in the territory of one or more of the parties exclusively from originating materials." This means that a good qualifies as long as it is made up of any combination of originating materials (through a tariff shift, for example) and materials wholly obtained or produced in a NAFTA country.

This type of rule would come into play where, for example, iron ore is imported into the United States by a manufacturer of furniture door handles. The iron ore is manufactured into a door handle for a wooden desk. A tariff shift occurs (from iron ore to furniture parts) and, with this shift, the door handle is considered as originating within the United States. The door handle is then attached to a finished wooden desk made from Canadian pine. Since the pine comes from a NAFTA country and, as we've just mentioned, the handles are considered as originating within the United States, the finished desk is also considered as originating within the United States.

4. Article 401(d)

Article 401(d) states that a good is considered as originating where

> except for a good provided for in Chapters 61 through 63 of the Harmonized System, the good is produced entirely in the territory of one or more of the parties but one or more of the non-originating materials that are used in the production of the good does not undergo a change in tariff classification because
>
> (i) the good was imported into the territory of a Party in an unassembled or a disassembled form, but was classified as an assembled good pursuant to General Rule of Interpretation 2(a) of the Harmonized System, or
>
> (ii) the heading for the good provides for and specifically describes both the good itself and its parts and is not further subdivided into subheadings, or the subheading for the good provides for and specifically describes both the good itself and its parts, provided that the regional content of the good, determined in accordance with Article 402, is not less than 60 percent where the transaction value method is used, or is not less than 50 percent where the net cost method is used, and that the good satisfies all other applicable requirements of this chapter.

If we examine this rule more carefully, we can see that it's divided into four parts. The first part begins with an exclusion of goods covered in chapters 61 through 63 (generally articles of apparel and other textile products). Then it states that, where an item is made up of one or more non-originating materials which do not undergo a tariff shift because of either of two special circumstances, the item will still qualify, provided the regional value content requirements have been met. These two special circumstances exist under the following conditions:

(a) *When an item is disassembled or unassembled.* Were someone to import a bicycle in kit form (unassembled) into the United States, for example, it would have to be classified under the tariff as an entity rather than as a collection of individual bicycle parts. And provided the cost of assembling the bike or its regional value content constituted not less than 60% (using the transaction value method) or 50% (under the net cost method) of the full value of the assembled item, it would qualify for preferential tariff treatment under NAFTA.

(b) *When an item and its parts are covered in the same HS classification.* HS Tariff item 9402.10.90 provides for barbers' chairs and parts. Were an American manufacturer of this type of chair to import parts from Italy, they would be classified under the same tariff classification as the finished product. And if the manufacturer sold a chair to a Canadian customer, it would enter Canada under the same classification. There is no tariff shift because the tariff item provides for both the chair and its parts. Under NAFTA Article 401(d), the barbers' chairs qualify for preferential tariff treatment, provided the regional value content requirement is met.

f. THE DE MINIMIS RULE

Not found in the FTA, this new rule states that where an item contains a minimal amount of non-originating material (less than 7% of the transaction value FOB), it will be considered as originating in the NAFTA country. There are ten exceptions, however, as listed in Article 405.

g. THE NAFTA CERTIFICATE OF ORIGIN

The NAFTA Certificate of Origin (see Sample #5) replaces the FTA Exporter's Certificate of Origin and is perhaps the single most important trade document for transborder shipments within North America. It allows goods that qualify to enter Canada (or the United States or Mexico) under the preferential NAFTA duty rates and must be completed in accordance with the instructions on its reverse side. Not to complete it correctly can result in fines being levied against both exporter and importer by their respective governments.

NAFTA, like the FTA, requires that the importer be in possession of a properly completed Certificate of Origin before the preferential duty rate can be claimed. There is no requirement to actually furnish Customs officials with a copy at the time of import, unless they specifically request it.

A separate certificate should be completed for every qualifying commercial shipment valued at US $1 000 or more. In the case of goods of lesser value, an informal declaration is sufficient. Certificates can be completed in English, French, or Spanish, but Customs may ask for a translation.

Multiple shipments of the same goods can be accommodated by blanket certification, valid for a period not exceeding 12 months. As the importer, you are obligated to retain the original certificates and related documentation for these shipments for six years. NAFTA certificates may be completed by either the producer of the goods or the actual exporter.

As we warned at the beginning of this chapter, NAFTA is not a simple document, and it takes some experience to understand the procedures established under it. You would be well advised to contact a customs consultant or other international trade professional before embarking on any NAFTA-related importing activities. To help clarify our discussion of the subject, see Worksheet #3 that identifies the main steps in determining whether or not a product is eligible for a NAFTA tariff treatment.

RECOMMENDED READING LIST

Canada. External Affairs and International Trade Canada. *NAFTA What's it all about?* Ottawa: Government of Canada, 1993.

North American Free Trade Agreement, 1992 (about 3 000 pages).

The North American Free Trade Agreement — Errata, 1993 (39 pages).

Canada. Foreign Affairs and International Trade Canada. *The North American Free Trade Agreement at a Glance.* Ottawa: Government of Canada, 1993.

All of the above are available free of charge from:
   Info Ex
   Foreign Affairs and International
   Trade Canada
   Lester B. Pearson Building
   125 Sussex Drive
   Ottawa, Ontario
   K1A 0G2

Tel: (613) 944-4000 (Ottawa area)
1-800-267-8376 (toll-free)
Fax: (613) 996-9709

WORKSHEET #3
THE NAFTA WORKSHEET

Use this worksheet for potential qualifying products.

1. Product:_____
   Other names it may be known by: _____
   HS classification number:_____
   Tariff treatments/duty rates:_____

2. If the product is subject to duty, is the product wholly obtained or produced outside North America?
   yes____   no____
   If yes, it does not qualify for the NAFTA preferential tariff rate. It may still qualify for the General Preferential Tariff (GPT) or the Most Favoured Nations Tariff (MFN).

3. Is the product wholly obtained or produced within North America?
   yes____   no____
   If yes, it qualifies for the preferential NAFTA rates.

4. Does the product contain some NAFTA and some non-NAFTA material?
   yes____   no____
   If yes, determine the HS classification of the non-NAFTA material as it entered the first NAFTA country.

5. Consult the NAFTA Rules of Origin and establish the type of rule that applies to the item being imported (see 1. above).
   Tariff shift only: _____ Tariff shift plus RVC:_____ RVC only:_____

6. Does all of the non-NAFTA material qualify as originating?
   yes____   no____
   If yes, it qualifies for the preferential NAFTA rates. If no, list the materials and HS classification of those goods that don't qualify.

7. Determine if NAFTA Article 401(d)(i) (unassembled/disassembled goods) or (ii) (goods and parts in same classifications) can be applied to any of the materials considered to be non-originating.

8. Determine if the De Minimis rule can be applied to the balance of the list of non-originating goods. (Does it represent less than 7% of the FOB value?) *If yes, it qualifies. If no, it doesn't.*

9. Once you establish that the product qualifies for the benefits of NAFTA, the Certificate of Origin can be completed.

SAMPLE #5
NAFTA CERTIFICATE OF ORIGIN
(form B-232E)

J.B. ELLIS & CO. LTD.

P.O. Box 12100
Suite 2730 Harbour Centre
555 West Hastings Street
Vancouver, B.C. Canada V6B 4N5

Phone: (604) 684-1254
Fax: (604) 684-3342
International Trade Services

PROTECTED (when completed)

NAFTA CERTIFICATE OF ORIGIN

Please Print or Type

1 Exporter's Name and Address:

Tax Identification Number:

2 Blanket Period:

From DD MM YY   To DD MM YY

3 Producer's Name and Address:

Tax Identification Number:

4 Importer's Name and Address:

Tax Identification Number:

5 Description of Good(s)	6 HS Tariff Classification Number	7 Preference Criterion	8 Producer	9 Net Cost	10 Country of Origin

11 I certify that:

- the information on this document is true and accurate and I assume the responsibility for proving such representations. I understand that I am liable for any false statements or material omissions made on or in connection with this document;
- I agree to maintain, and present upon request, documentation necessary to support this Certificate, and to inform, in writing, all persons to whom the Certificate was given of any changes that would affect the accuracy or validity of this Certificate;
- the goods originated in the territory of one or more of the Parties, and comply with the origin requirements specified for those goods in the North American Free Trade Agreement, and unless specifically exempted in Article 411 or Annex 401, there has been no further production or any other operation outside the territories of the parties; and
- this Certificate consists of _____ page(s), including all attachments.

Authorized Signature:

Name:

Date (DD/MM/YY):   Telephone:

Company:

Title:

FAX:

SAMPLE #5
(Back)

NORTH AMERICAN FREE TRADE AGREEMENT
CERTIFICATE OF ORIGIN INSTRUCTIONS

For purposes of obtaining preferential tariff treatment, this document must be completed legibly and in full by the exporter and be in the possession of the importer at the time the declaration is made. This document may also be completed voluntarily by the producer for use by the exporter. Please print or type.

Field 1: State the full legal name, address (including country) and legal tax identification number of the exporter. Legal tax identification number is: in Canada, employer number or importer/exporter number assigned by Revenue Canada; in Mexico, federal taxpayer's registry number (RFC); and in the United States, employer's identification number or Social Security Number.

Field 2: Complete field if the Certificate covers multiple shipments of identical goods as described in Field 5 that are imported into a NAFTA country for a specified period of up to one year (blanket period). "FROM" is the date upon which the Certificate becomes applicable to the good covered by the blanket Certificate (it may be prior to the date of signing this Certificate). "TO" is the date upon which the blanket period expires. The importation of a good for which preferential tariff treatment is claimed based on this Certificate must occur between these dates.

Field 3: State the full legal name, address (including country) and legal tax identification number, as defined in Field 1, of the producer. If more than one producer's good is included on the Certificate, attach a list of the additional producers, including the legal name, address (including country) and legal tax identification number, cross referenced to the good described in Field 5. If you wish this information to be confidential, it is acceptable to state "Available to Customs upon request". If the producer and the exporter are the same, complete field with "SAME". If the producer is unknown, it is acceptable to state "UNKNOWN".

Field 4: State the full legal name, address (including country) and legal tax identification number, as defined in Field 1, of the importer. If importer is not known, state "UNKNOWN"; if multiple importers, state "VARIOUS".

Field 5: Provide a full description of each good. The description should be sufficient to relate it to the invoice description and to the Harmonized System (HS) description of the good. If the Certificate covers a single shipment of a good, include the invoice number as shown on the commercial invoice. If not known, indicate another unique reference number, such as the shipping order number.

Field 6: For each good described in Field 5, identify the HS tariff classification to six digits. If the good is subject to a specific rule of origin in Annex 401 that requires eight digits, identify to eight digits, using the HS tariff classification of the country into whose territory the good is imported.

Field 7: For each good described in Field 5, state which criterion (A through F) is applicable. The rules of origin are contained in Chapter Four and Annex 401. Additional rules are described in Annex 703.2 (certain agricultural goods), Annex 300-B, Appendix 6A (certain textile goods) and Annex 308.1 (certain automatic data processing goods and their parts). **NOTE: In order to be entitled to preferential tariff treatment, each good must meet at least one of the criteria below.**

PREFERENCE CRITERIA

A The good is "wholly obtained or produced entirely" in the territory of one or more of the NAFTA countries, as referred to in Article 415. **NOTE:** The purchase of a good in the territory does not necessarily render it "wholly obtained or produced". If the good is an agricultural good, see also criterion F and Annex 703.2. *[Reference: Article 401(a) and 415]*

B The good is produced entirely in the territory of one or more of the NAFTA countries and satisfies the specific rule of origin, set out in Annex 401, that applies to its tariff classification. The rule may include a tariff classification change, regional value-content requirement or a combination thereof. The good must also satisfy all other applicable requirements of Chapter Four. If the good is an agricultural good, see also criterion F and Annex 703.2. *[Reference: Article 401(b)]*

C The good is produced entirely in the territory of one or more of the NAFTA countries exclusively from originating materials. Under this criterion, one or more of the materials may not fall within the definition of "wholly produced or obtained", as set out in Article 415. All materials used in the production of the good must qualify as "originating" by meeting the rules of Article 401(a) through (d). If the good is an agricultural good, see also criterion F and Annex 703.2. *[Reference: Article 401(c)]*

D Goods are produced in the territory of one or more of the NAFTA countries but do not meet the applicable rule of origin, set out in Annex 401, because certain non-originating materials do not undergo the required change in tariff classification. The goods do nonetheless meet the regional value-content requirement specified in Article 401(d). This criterion is limited to the following two circumstances:
1. the good was imported into the territory of a NAFTA country in an unassembled or disassembled form but was classified as an assembled good, pursuant to HS General Rule of Interpretation 2(a); or
2. the good incorporated one or more non-originating materials, provided for as parts under the HS, which could not undergo a change in tariff classification because the heading provided for both the good and its parts and was not further subdivided into subheadings, or the subheading provided for both the good and its parts and was not further subdivided.

NOTE: This criterion does not apply to Chapters 61 through 63 of the HS. *[Reference: Article 401(d)]*

E Certain automatic date processing goods and their parts, specified in Annex 308.1, that do not originate in the territory are considered originating upon importation into the territory of a NAFTA country from the territory of another NAFTA country when the Most-Favoured-Nation Tariff rate of the good conforms to the rate established in Annex 308.1 and is common to all NAFTA countries. *[Reference: Annex 308.1]*

F The good is an originating agricultural good under preference criterion A, B or C above and is not subject to a quantitative restriction in the importing NAFTA country because it is a "qualifying good" as defined in Annex 703.2, Section A or B (please specify). A good listed in Appendix 703.2.B.7 is also exempt from quantitative restrictions and is eligible for NAFTA preferential tariff treatment if it meets the definition of "qualifying good" in Section A of Annex 703.2. **NOTE 1: This criterion does not apply to goods that wholly originate in Canada or the United States and are imported into either country. NOTE 2: A tariff rate quota is not a quantitative restriction.**

Field 8: For each good described in Field 5, state "YES" if you are the producer of the good. If you are not the producer of the good, state "NO" followed by (1), (2), or (3), depending on whether this certificate was based upon: (1) your knowledge of whether the good qualifies as an originating good; (2) your reliance on the producer's written representation (other than a Certificate of Origin) that the good qualifies as an originating good; or (3) a completed and signed Certificate for the good, voluntarily provided to the exporter by the producer.

Field 9: For each good described in Field 5, where the good is subject to a regional value content (RVC) requirement, indicate "NC" if the RVC is calculated according to the net cost method; otherwise, indicate "NO". If the RVC is calculated according to the net cost method over a period of time, further identify the beginning and ending dates (DD/MM/YY) of that period. *[Reference: Articles 402.1, 402.5]*

Field 10: Identify the name of the country ("MX" or "US" for agricultural and textile goods exported to Canada; "US" or "CA" for all goods exported to Mexico; or "CA" or "MX" for all goods exported to the United States) to which the preferential rate of customs duty applies, as set out in Annex 302.2, in accordance with the Marking Rules or in each Party's schedule of tariff elimination.

For all other originating goods exported to Canada, indicate appropriately "MX" or "US" if the goods originate in that NAFTA country, within the meaning of the NAFTA Rules of Origin Regulations, and any subsequent processing in the other NAFTA country does not increase the transaction value of the goods by more than 7%; otherwise indicate as "JNT" for joint production. *[Reference: Annex 302.2]*

Field 11: This field must be completed, signed and dated by the exporter. When the Certificate is completed by the producer for use by the exporter, it must be completed, signed and dated by the producer. The date must be the date the Certificate was completed and signed.

6
VALUATION: DETERMINING VALUE FOR DUTY

This chapter provides a general introduction to the methods and regulations applied by Canada Customs in determining the value of your imported goods for Customs' purposes. Use it as an introduction and a supplement to more detailed reference works listed at the end of this chapter.

As a member of GATT, Canada joined most other trading nations in 1979 in adopting the "transaction value system" of customs valuation at GATT's Tokyo Round of Trade Negotiations. It did not implement this new system until January 1, 1985, however, using the intervening years to assess and study it, particularly in relation to its potential impact on tariff protection.

Prior to the introduction of the transaction value system, Canada had used the "fair market value" system of valuation, reflecting its protectionist approach to international trade and making it a less than popular trading partner among nations worldwide. Its adoption of the new approach signalled the beginning of a more open and tolerant attitude in these matters and has since stimulated the myriad of organizational and administrative changes now transforming Canada Customs.

a. WHAT IS VALUATION?

Canada Customs uses the phrase "determining value for duty or VFD" in describing valuation. We might expand on this slightly to define it as the process of determining the transaction value of imported goods in order to calculate the duty owing on them. And what is transaction value? According to the Customs Act and its regulations, it is:

> the price paid or payable for goods, as adjusted, when sold for export to Canada. It represents the aggregate of all payments made or to be made by the purchaser in Canada, whether directly or indirectly, to the benefit of the vendor.

In other words, it is the price you pay for your goods.

1. Point of direct shipment

To determine your VFD, you must first establish when and at what point your shipment was forwarded directly to you; that is, the date and the place at which it began its continuous journey to Canada. The value for duty is based on the amount you paid from the place of direct shipment, expressed in Canadian dollars, calculated according to the exchange rate on that day.

It sounds simple enough, but what does this approach actually mean in terms of dollars and cents? Let's look at an example.

Suppose you're buying 25 000 inflatable plastic rubber rafts from a Taiwanese factory and have ordered your goods directly from the factory itself to be paid in American funds. In a situation like this, the price you pay for your goods at the factory door becomes the value for currency conversion (VFCC) — or the value for duty once the conversion to Canadian dollars has been made.

Freight and other charges made after the point of direct shipment to Canada (in this case the factory) are not dutiable. But what if the Taiwanese company has no storage space at its factory and routinely stores its finished product at a dockside warehouse, 40 miles away? This makes the warehouse the point of direct shipment to Canada. Included in your invoice from the company is a charge of US $225 for shipment of the goods to the warehouse. Is this dutiable? Yes, it is because only charges made subsequent to the point of direct shipment to Canada are not dutiable. So the final value for duty of your goods, after conversion to Canadian dollars, is the cost of the goods plus domestic freight charges.

Now let's add a further twist. Let's say that it is part of your agreement with the vendor to package your rafts before they leave Taiwan via the same dockside warehouse. Here we must determine what the supplier does on a routine basis. If the supplier routinely sends all products for packaging and then ships them to the dockside warehouse for storage, then the point of direct shipment for your goods is the warehouse. If, on the other hand, the supplier does not ordinarily package goods and must obtain specific labels and packaging for your order, the point of direct shipment for the goods becomes the packaging facility.

You then pay duty on any shipping charges for transporting your order from the factory to the packaging facility, but not from the facility to the dockside warehouse. Again, charges made subsequent to the point of direct shipment to Canada are not dutiable. Sometimes the easiest way to understand this process is to depict it in a figure, as we have done in Figure #3.

Other costs besides domestic freight may also affect the final transaction value of imported goods (see section **e.** later in this chapter). First, let's take a look at the various valuation methods currently applied by Canada Customs.

b. METHODS OF DETERMINING VALUE FOR DUTY

There are six methods of determining value for duty under the Customs Act, sections 47 to 55. The methods are arranged in order of applicability and must always be used in sequence (except in the case of sections 51 and 52 which can be used interchangeably, as the circumstances require). You start, then, by applying section 48 and, if it cannot be used, you go on to section 49 — and so on, until you identify a method that's suitable.

The six methods are —

(a) Transaction value method (section 48)

(b) Transaction value of identical goods (section 49)

(c) Transaction value of similar goods (section 50)

(d) Deductive value method (section 51)

(e) Computed value method (section 52)

(f) Residual value method (section 53)

Most purchases of goods from abroad are without complication, making the calculation of duty a simple matter for the importer. Company A in Canada buys goods from Company B in Taiwan. The two companies are unrelated and, based on the commercial invoice provided by the vendor to the purchaser, the importer establishes the value for currency conversion (VFCC) of his or her goods and makes the conversion to Canadian dollars (using the exchange rate on the date of direct shipment). This gives him or her the value for duty (VFD). He or she applies the duty rate to get the amount of duty and adds it to the VFD to get the value for tax (VFT). Then he or she calculates the GST and any other applicable taxes. Sample #6 is an example of a calculation of duty owing.

It is important to remember that it is the importer, not Canada Customs, who accounts for the shipment by establishing the

FIGURE #3
ESTABLISHING THE POINT OF DIRECT SHIPMENT

A
Manufacturer routinely prepackages

B
Manufacturer does not prepackage

Factory A

Factory B

Packaging Plant

X Packaging Plant

X Dockside Warehouse

Dockside Warehouse

X = point of direct shipment

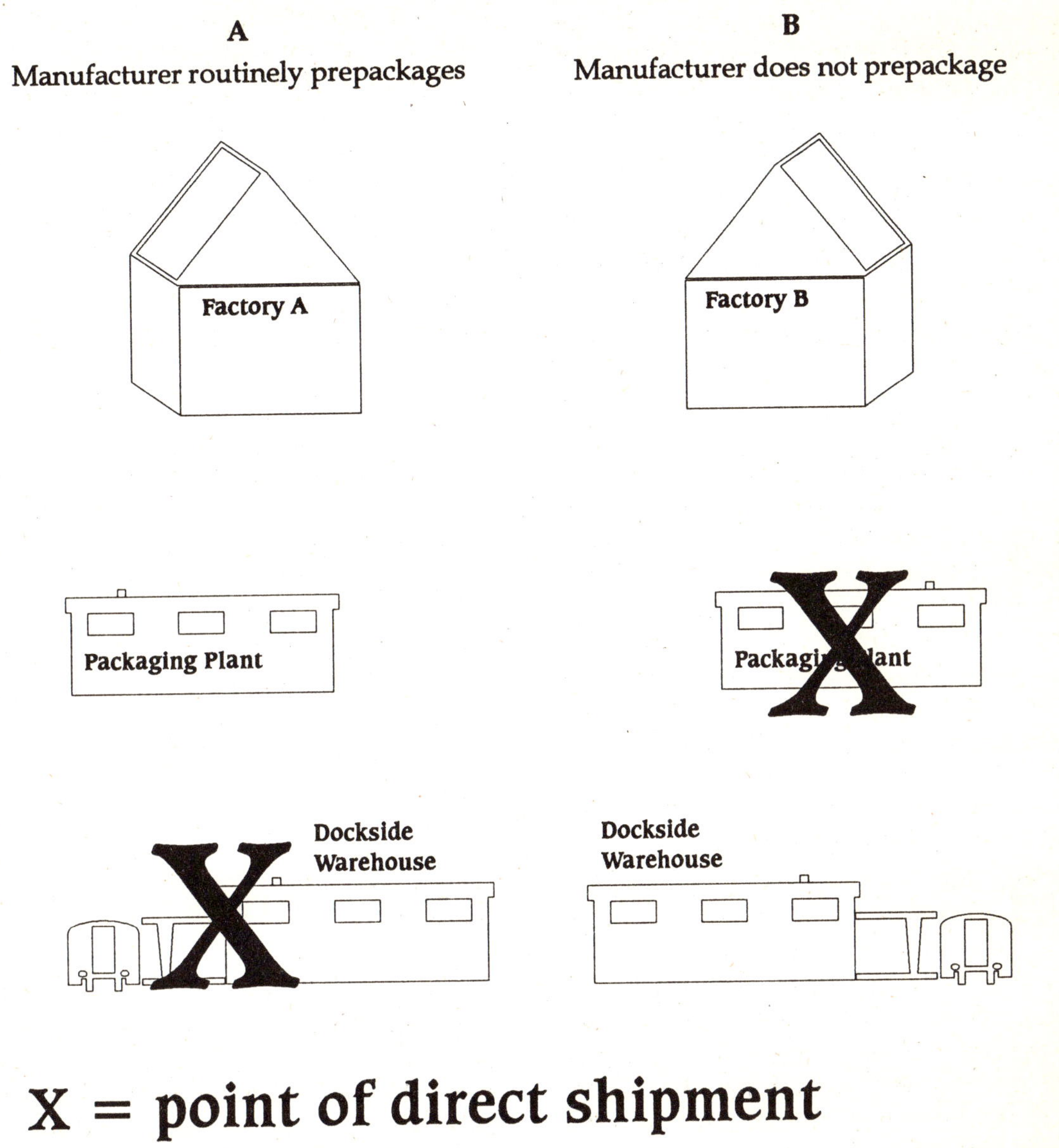

In **A**, the importer pays no duty on inland freight because the manufacturer routinely stores all goods at the dockside warehouse.

In **B**, the importer pays duty on the inland freight from factory to packaging plant.

SAMPLE #6
CALCULATION OF DUTY

DUTY AND TAX OWING ON TAIWANESE GOODS

Value for currency conversion (VFCC):	Taiwan $15 000.00
Exchange rate:	C $.05*
Value for duty (VFD):	
(T $15 000 x .05)	C $750.00
Duty rate: 5%*	
Duty owing:	
(C $750.00 x .05)	C $37.50
Value for Tax (VFT):	
(C $750.00 + C $37.50)	C $787.50
Tax rate: 7% (GST)	
(C $787.50 x .07)	C $55.13
Total duty and tax owing:	
(C $37.50 + C $55.13)	C $92.63

*These figures are not a true representation of current exchange and duty rates and have been chosen simply for demonstration purposes.

VFD, then determining the duty and taxes payable. Customs, in the form of a commodity specialist, verifies the importer's entry information, including the VFD, when it conducts its routine review of the entry. Customs will assist a new importer with the first entry but discourages the practice on an ongoing basis. If you're having difficulty determining the VFD of your goods, you might consult a customs broker or customs consultant.

There are, of course, exceptions to and variations on the simple process just described as detailed in the "D" series Customs regulations relating to valuation. However, for the purposes of the following discussion, we are dealing only in generalities and refer the interested reader to the Recommended Reading list at the end of this chapter for sources that provide a more in-depth explanation.

c. APPLYING THE TRANSACTION VALUE METHOD

As you will have seen from the six methods of valuation listed above, the transaction value method can't always be used. Certain conditions must be met and these can be generally determined by answering three questions:

(a) Have the goods been "sold for export" to Canada?

(b) Are the vendor and the purchaser related?

(c) If the answer to question (b) is yes, has the price of the goods been influenced by the relationship?

Let's look at each of these questions individually.

1. Have the goods been "sold for export" to Canada?

The transaction value method of valuation can be used only when goods have been "sold for export" to Canada. Obviously, goods that have been consigned, leased, or given away do not fall into this category. Customs Act regulations offer several examples of what exactly is meant by "sold for export" and generally it refers to goods sent by a vendor living in the same country where the goods are produced, to a Canadian purchaser or a purchaser resident in Canada. But this doesn't have to be the case — and sometimes it isn't.

Take, for example, a major engineering firm in Canada which issues a purchase order to an American company for an electronic pump manufactured in Japan. The American company places the order and has the pump shipped directly from Japan to the company's headquarters in Nova Scotia. Is duty going to be based on the invoice from the Japanese vendor to the American purchaser, or on the invoice from the American supplier to the Canadian purchaser? In this case, it is on the American supplier's invoice.

The actual country of export is not a relevant factor in this matter; nor is the supplier's country of residence. What is relevant are the terms of the original agreement made between vendor and purchaser — in our example, the Canadian company's purchase order — initiating the chain of events that has resulted in the goods being sold for export to Canada.

2. Are the purchaser and vendor related?

The term "related parties" is taken from the definition contained in the federal Income Tax Act, and applies not only to blood relatives or those connected by marriage but also to business partners and others who are directors or employees in the same companies. Under the act, persons are related to each other if —

(a) they are individuals connected by blood relationship, marriage, or adoption within the meaning of subsection 251(6) of the Income Tax Act;

(b) one is an officer or director of the other;

(c) each such person is an officer or director of the same two corporations, associations, partnerships, or other organizations;

(d) they are partners;

(e) one is the employer of the other;

(f) they directly or indirectly control or are controlled by the same person;

(g) one directly or indirectly controls or is controlled by the other;

(h) any other person directly or indirectly owns, holds, or controls 5% or more of the outstanding voting stock or shares of each such person; or

(i) one directly or indirectly owns, holds or controls 5% or more of the outstanding voting stock or shares of the other.

3. If the answer to the second question is "yes, they are related," has the price of the goods been influenced by the relationship?

There are several ways that vendor and purchaser might demonstrate that their transaction has been conducted "at arm's length." For example, they might cite other transactions that the vendor has conducted with unrelated purchasers in Canada; his or her sale of similar products in the domestic market; or his or her export of similar products to related parties in a third country that uses the same (GATT approved) valuation methods. Canada Customs is willing to entertain any reasonable evidence from the importer to show that he or she has not received a price advantage. If there is a relationship between purchaser and vendor, but the relationship has not influenced the selling price of the goods, the transaction value can still be used as the basis for value of duty.

d. APPLYING THE OTHER FIVE VALUATION METHODS

If your goods are not considered to have been "sold for export" to Canada or were provided to you at a price advantage because of your relationship with the vendor or for some other reason, bypass the first of the valuation methods listed above and move on to the second — the "transaction value of identical goods" — as described in section 49 of the Customs Act.

1. Transaction value of identical goods

If there is no transaction value, establish if other shipments of identical goods have been sold by the vendor "at arm's length" to unrelated purchasers in Canada. "Identical" in this context means exactly the same goods; if you bought inflatable rafts in January of this year, then look for an example of the same inflatable rafts being sold to another party in Canada at the same level of trade (under the same market conditions) and at relatively the same time.

2. Transaction value of similar goods

If there are no examples of exactly the same product being sold, move on to the third method of valuation, the transaction value of similar goods method, as described in section 50 of the Customs Act.

Here, look for imports of a similar type, manufactured in the same country and sold by the same vendor to another party in Canada under the same market conditions and at relatively the same time. Then make adjustments for any subtle differences.

3. Deductive value method

If there are no examples of similar products, turn to the fourth method, the deductive value method, as described in section 51 of the act. This method of valuation, as its name suggests, involves deducing the transaction value of imported goods by going to the first "arm's length" sale after importation of the same or similar goods (sold under the same market conditions) and deducting certain charges. Your intention here is to obtain the price per unit of the goods. The charges you subtract may include the sales commission earned on a per unit basis, profit and expenses per unit, international freight and insurance costs, transportation and insurance costs once the goods are in Canada, and duties and taxes paid at the time of import.

Obviously, sales where the vendor and purchaser are related cannot be used here, nor can sales where the importer has provided his or her foreign supplier with any assistance in the production or export of the goods.

4. Computed value method

Where the deductive method is not applicable, you may next consider the computed value method of establishing the transaction value of goods, as described in section 52 of the Customs Act. The two need not be considered in order: sections 51 and 52 are interchangeable.

This method applies when the vendor is also the manufacturer of the goods and is selling them under circumstances that cannot be interpreted according to any of the previous valuation methods up to section 52. As a result, it is not often used.

Put very simply, the computed method involves establishing the cost of materials and production, then adding other dutiable charges (such as the manufacturer's profit and general expenses). As in all the other methods, the purpose here is to arrive at the equivalent to the transaction value of the goods — the price paid in an ordinary transaction between an unrelated vendor and purchaser under the same market conditions.

5. Residual value method

The last of the various valuation methods, the residual method, can best be described as "making your best effort" to arrive at an appropriate value for duty by applying one or more of the other five methods in a flexible manner. In general, the practice here is to choose the method or methods that need the least adjustment, then strive to avoid distortion in the value derived.

e. SOME COMMONLY ASKED QUESTIONS ABOUT VALUATION

A general introduction to a subject of this nature, such as we have just provided, often provokes more questions than answers as you begin to consider some of the real-life valuation scenarios. Following are some of the more common questions which should help increase your understanding of valuation without necessarily taking the discussion to a new level of complexity. At the end of each question and answer we provide the reference in the Customs Act or regulations that the particular issue relates to. You might also want to consult Appendix 2 for a full list of valuation issues in the "D" series Customs regulations.

Q: We want to use an agent to inspect and pay for the goods we are planning to import. Is the agent's fee included in calculating the transaction value of our goods?

A: As you will recall from chapter 1, established importers often retain a purchasing agent in the country they're importing from to locate and purchase goods on their behalf. The agent's fee for this service, paid by the importer, is not dutiable. In the case of all shipments forwarded by agents, however, Customs still needs to know who is paying the agent and exactly what service he or she is performing. Some services, such as the selling commission paid to an agent by the vendor, are dutiable (see Customs Memorandum D 13-4-7 for examples).

Q: What about our customs broker's fees?
A: The fees charged by customs brokers to process shipments through Customs are not dutiable (see Customs Memorandum D 13-4-7 for a discussion of the term "brokerage").

Q: How are the "special deals" or discounts offered by our supplier interpreted by Canada Customs in establishing the transaction value of our goods?
A: "Buy ten and get one free." "Pay cash within 21 days and deduct a further 3% from the bill." These examples represent a price advantage to the purchaser that affects the value of the goods being purchased. Identical goods provided free as part of a package deal are not dutiable. Importers may also take advantage of cash discounts, but they must be taken and earned in order to be deducted for VFD purposes (Customs Memorandum D13-4-10).

Q: Are the packing costs and charges for our goods dutiable?
A: Any cartons and containers, etc., generally considered to be part of the imported goods, together with the cost of packing the goods for shipment to Canada, are dutiable at the same rate as the goods they contain (see General Interpretive Rule Five in chapter 4). Usually these costs are incurred by the vendor and itemized in the purchaser's invoice (section 48(5)(a)(i), Customs Act).

Q: We're providing our vendor, free of charge, with a component part of the product we're purchasing from him. How does this affect calculation of the transaction value?
A: Where is the part made and how much does it cost? Generally speaking, the cost of parts, materials, tools, moulds, artwork, etc., provided to the vendor, and commonly referred to as "assists," is added to the transaction value of the goods. This is

a complex subject, however, and much space is devoted to it in Customs Memoranda D13-3-12 and D13-4-8.

Q: Can we deduct our costs from the price of goods that were sent to us incorrectly marked and required some sorting by our staff?

A: Importers who receive goods that require some correction or change may deduct costs and expenses incurred in putting the goods to right, so long as these costs and expenses are deemed eligible (non-dutiable) in Memorandum D13-4-7 of the Customs regulations. Take the fast food chain, for example, that has ordered a large number of plastic trinkets as giveaways to customers during an upcoming promotion, only to discover that the trinkets have been incorrectly boxed. They must now incur the unanticipated expense of having the entire shipment examined and re-boxed, and are entitled to deduct most of this expense from the transaction value of the goods before duty is calculated. We say "most" because some expenses may not be named in the Customs regulations. You can deduct hotel expenses for the individual who's been brought in from Toronto to investigate the problem, for example, but not the beverages she ordered in her hotel room on the three nights she was in town (section 48(5)(b), Customs Act).

Q: I would like to establish a warehouse in the United States where I can store the American goods I buy in bulk for export to my Canadian wholesale outlet. How would this affect the amount of duty I pay?

A: When you establish a warehouse on the American side of the border for holding goods you intend to sell on the Canadian side, you become both a vendor and a purchaser: your American operation sells the goods to your Canadian operation, making them "related parties" under the Customs Act. In such a situation, you must examine the questions of price influence, discussed earlier. If the selling price is influenced by the relationship, you must use an alternate means of valuation. You cannot, as a means of avoiding duty, charge your Canadian arm less than the transaction value of the same goods sold "at arm's length." (Memorandum D13-4-5.)

Q: What is meant by the phrase "generally accepted accounting principles"?

A: This phrase is used throughout sections 48 to 53 of the Customs Act and refers to the accounting principles established by the Canadian Institute of Chartered Accountants in accordance with principles generally accepted by professional chartered accountancy organizations worldwide. Generally accepted accounting principles are applied by Canada Customs in their review of value for duty and indirectly encourage a certain level of professionalism and uniformity in the maintenance of accounting records among Canadian importers and their foreign suppliers. Concern for uniform accounting is valid; in some countries exporters maintain three or four separate sets of books, providing the appropriate set in response to the questions being asked and the authority making the inquiries (Memorandum D13-3-8).

f. THE CUSTOMS VALUATION QUESTIONNAIRE

By now we hope you have a reasonably clear idea of what valuation means and a general sense of Canada Customs' current valuation procedures and policies. But you're probably still wondering what information and documentation you'll have to provide if Customs decides to investigate your valuation.

The Canadian Trade Law Reports has provided a Customs Valuation Questionnaire at the end of its discussion of customs valuation on page 9001 of its publication (cited in Recommended Reading at the end of the chapter). That questionnaire is reproduced in full in Appendix 4 at the back of this book, and we encourage you to review it thoroughly. Not all of the questions will apply to you, especially if you are just starting your import business. But you may find that it helps to clear away any remaining confusion about the subject of valuation as a whole.

RECOMMENDED READING

Dearden, Richard G. "Customs Valuation," *Canadian Trade Law Reports*, CCH Canadian (1989).

Gottlieb, Richard and Darrel H. Pearson. *Transaction Value in Canada*. Montreal: Gottlieb, Kaylor & Stocks, 1985.

Irish, Maureen. *Customs Valuation in Canada*. Ottawa: CCH Canadian, 1985.

7
CALCULATING THE GST AND OTHER TAXES

This chapter provides information on the goods and services tax as it applies to goods imported for resale, on excise taxes and duties, and on obtaining a refund.

The GST and other taxes represent separate, additional costs that you must include in calculating the landed cost of your goods. We look first at the GST, then briefly review the excise tax and how you might apply for a refund in the event you return your goods to your foreign supplier.

a. THE GST

Only a very few items escape the GST, as we all know now, having lived with the tax for over three years. Basic groceries, which you may well "import" as you drive over the border from a vacation in the United States, are among this grouping. You are otherwise required to pay the tax on most other goods coming into the country, based on their value after duty and excise — their value, that is, including transaction value, duty, duty under the Special Import Measures Act (SIMA), and excise tax, if applicable.

It is important to note that packing charges, including the materials and containers provided for this purpose (reusable or otherwise), are also subject to the GST, unless their cost is already included in the cost of your goods. Customs broker's fees are taxable under the GST as well, but not the international freight charges you may pay your broker at the same time, as a matter of convenience. A typical brokerage invoice is shown in Sample #7.

Of course, we are speaking here of goods for resale, items you have bought in quantity for your new import wholesale or retail business. Imported services are not taxable (except if you happen to be a financial institution), along with some other kinds of imports (e.g., if you are returning from a posting abroad, for example, your goods are not subject to the GST). **Note:** The government's current policy on imported services is based on its belief that goods or services produced with the help of an imported service will themselves be GST taxable.

Other goods that are not taxable include the goods of settlers arriving in this country for the first time and goods returned to you after having been repaired outside Canada under warranty. A full list of GST exempt goods and services is contained in the Excise Tax Act.

If you anticipate doing at least $30 000 worth of business annually and have registered your business with the government, you should be able to recover the GST you've paid out by collecting it from your own customers and submitting regular GST tax returns. The GST is a consumer-paid tax and is not supposed to cost Canadian businesses anything (although there is certainly a cost to you in the time taken to calculate your GST return and complete the appropriate forms). This makes the whole procedure sound simple when, in fact, it can be quite complicated, depending on the nature of your business and the complexities of accommodating your accounting system to the various rules and regulations governing the tax.

Businesses that have not registered with the government recover the tax informally, by including it in the price tag of their imported goods.

If you decide to return your goods to your foreign supplier, you can apply for a refund of the duty you paid on them but not for the GST unless you're a non-registrant of the GST program. As a non-registrant, you apply for a rebate by completing a B-2R form to accompany your refund claim (as you will see in chapter 12).

There are several excellent books available on the goods and services tax. We recommend that you keep one of these on hand as a general reference for your everyday business affairs. As an importer you are not subject to any special considerations or limits under the tax, but as a business person you should be familiar with its various applications and ramifications for your operating costs.

You may want to refer, for example, to *The GST Handbook,* another title in the Self-Counsel Series. (See Recommended Reading at the end of this chapter.)

b. EXCISE TAXES AND DUTIES

While the GST applies to all goods and services, save those zero rated under the Excise Tax Act, the excise tax is specific, limited mainly to goods that are considered luxuries such as jewellery, top-of-the-line watches and clocks, precious and semi-precious stones (and items made from them), automobile air conditioning systems, and even cigarettes, gasoline, and diesel fuel.

Certificates of exemption from paying this tax are available for those who purchase excisable goods with the intention of incorporating them into finished excisable products, as in the case of a goldsmith setting a watch into a handcast gold pendant. Wholesalers of excisable goods may also avoid paying this tax at time of purchase. The regulations that apply to these situations are long standing and well set out. In neither instance, however, is the importer exempt from paying GST.

If you mistakenly pay excise tax — you've purchased items, for example, on behalf of someone who holds a certificate of exemption — you may apply for a refund by completing a refund claim (form B-2) within two years of the items being entered into Canada (see chapter 12).

c. THE EXCISE ACT

The Excise Act is separate and distinct from the Excise Tax Act. While the Excise Tax Act regulates the GST and excise tax on luxuries, the Excise Act authorizes the collection of excise duties on alcohol, spirits, beer, tobacco, and products made from these goods.

RECOMMENDED READING

Appel, Robert S. *The GST Handbook: A Practical Guide for Small Business.* Vancouver: Self-Counsel Press, 1990.

Canada. Revenue Canada, Customs, Excise and Taxation. *Index to Revenue Canada Services.* [Ottawa]: Government of Canada, 1994.

SAMPLE #7
CUSTOMS BROKERAGE INVOICE

JBE

J.B. ELLIS & CO. LTD.
CUSTOMS BROKERS, CONSULTANTS & FREIGHT FORWARDERS

HEAD OFFICE: P.O. BOX 12100
SUITE 2730 - 555 WEST HASTINGS STREET
VANCOUVER, B.C., CANADA V6B 4N5
TEL: (604) 684-1254 FAX: (604) 684-3342

INVOICE

DATE	INVOICE NO.	CLIENT NO.
28 SEP 1995	114820	1792

SAMALEX ENTERPRISES
P.O. BOX 999999
1234 ANYWHERE AVENUE
YOURTOWN, BC
A1A 1A1

GST REGISTRATION NO: R102597200

YOUR ORDER NO.	VENDOR	TRANSACTION NO.	OUR FILE NO.
082195	ZIRO DESIGN INC	13540-00099294-3	839173

SHIPPED VIA	LOCATION	CAR/CONT/TRAILER NO.	BILL OF LADING/AWB NO.	EXCH. RATE
	PACIFIC HIGHWAY			1.345100

```
DESCRIPTION OF CHARGES:                           AMOUNT
   DUTY                                            64.92
   CUSTOMS GST                                     72.37
   BROKERAGE FEES                                  29.50 *
                                                 --------
   SUB TOTAL                                      166.79
 * GST ON SERVICES                                   2.07
                                                 --------
   INVOICE TOTAL      (GST $74.44)               $168.86
```

TERMS: PAYABLE UPON RECEIPT   TOTAL DUE IN CAD FUNDS

ENTRY SUMMARY

LINE	DESCRIPTION	CLASSIFICATION NO.	TAR CODE	TT	SA	DUTY RATE	ET RATE	GST RATE
	VALUE FOR DUTY	DUTY	SIMA	EXCISE TAX		VALUE FOR TAX	GST	
1	DESK ALARM CLOCKS	9105.11.00.00		10		6.7		7.0
	968.96	64.92				1,033.88	72.37	

TOTAL VALUE FOR DUTY: $968.96   TOTAL VALUE FOR TAX: $1,033.88

OUR GOAL IS TO BE THE BEST CUSTOMS BROKER IN CANADA. WE ARE ENTHUSIASTIC, AUTOMATED, AND INNOVATIVE. HOW CAN WE BE OF ASSISTANCE?

IMPORTANT: WRITTEN NOTIFICATION OF ERRORS OMMISSIONS, SHORTAGES AND/OR DAMAGE MUST BE RECEIVED BY US WITHING 90 DAYS OF RELEASE DATE

8
THE SPECIAL IMPORT MEASURES ACT AND OTHER NON-TARIFF BARRIERS

This chapter provides a description of the Special Import Measures Act (SIMA), the federal legislation established to protect Canadian producers from unfair competition by foreign companies, and other non-tariff barriers that discourage international trade. Students of this interesting area should review the recommended reading list at the end of the chapter for references that provide further information on the subject.

As we have already remarked in other chapters, Canada's protective policies toward its domestic industries have made it a less-than-ideal trading partner in the international marketplace. The Special Import Measures Act (SIMA) is an apt demonstration of these policies in action. Originally called the Anti-Dumping Act, this legislation has been protecting Canadian producers against their foreign competitors for more than 50 years in conformity with Canada's rights and obligations under Article VI of the (GATT).

a. THE SPECIAL IMPORT MEASURES ACT (SIMA)

Importers of trinket baskets handwoven from local grasses in the highlands of Ethiopia will have no need to concern themselves with this act. But if you're interested in importing goods from the United States or other industrialized nations, you should generally be aware of SIMA and its purpose.

Under SIMA, domestic producers can seek protection against two forms of "unfair and injurious" foreign competition —

(a) *dumping*, or the importing and sale of goods in Canada at prices lower than what they would sell for in their own domestic market, and

(b) *subsidizing*, or the importing of goods produced in their country of origin with the aid of government grants or other assistance.

Although the term implies otherwise, goods "dumped" on the Canadian market are usually acceptable and even desirable to Canadian consumers — especially if they keep consumer prices down. They become a only problem when they compete successfully against similar products already manufactured in Canada, thus threatening domestic production, sales, profits, and employment. In fact, imported goods cannot become the subject of anti-dumping duties until they've been investigated by the federal government under the auspices of SIMA, and that won't happen until a complaint is lodged with the government by a local producer.

The complaint and investigation process is clearly laid out in the act. Two authorities are involved in ruling on complaints: the Deputy Minister of National Revenue, Customs and Excise, and the Canadian International Trade Tribunal (formerly the Anti-Dumping Tribunal), comprising nine members appointed to provide a balance in the regions, professional interests, and personal backgrounds they represent.

Now let's take a look at the process itself. (Most of the following information is drawn from *Dumping and Subsidizing Injury Inquiries,* one of several publications available from the tribunal.)

1. The six steps of the complaint process under SIMA

(a) The complaint

The investigation process of an alleged dumping begins when a Canadian producer or producers (or an association representing their interests) lodges a complaint with the deputy minister.

Let's say, for example, that the Canadian manufacturers of a particular electronic device for radios have reason to believe that the same device manufactured in the Philippines is currently being dumped on the Canadian market. If there is sufficient evidence that the dumping has occurred and has caused material injury to the Canadian producer, the deputy minister authorizes a formal investigation. The relevant parties — namely, the Filipino exporters and Canadian importers of the device — are advised and their transactions investigated.

The investigation is usually completed within 90 days (up to 135 days in the case of a complex transaction), after which the deputy minister has three options:

(a) formally end the investigation,

(b) accept an undertaking by the exporters to adjust their prices upwards so that the goods are no longer dumped (in effect, suspending any further investigation, or

(c) issue an initial judgment or "preliminary determination."

When the preliminary determination is announced, Canada Customs lists the item in its monthly SIMA Index and begins levying provisional duties on it. Sample #8 shows the SIMA Index for June 1995.

(b) The inquiry

When the tribunal receives the deputy minister's preliminary determination, it begins an inquiry to determine if the dumping "has caused, is causing, or is likely to cause material injury" to Canadian producers of similar devices.

Material injury is not defined in SIMA, nor in the GATT Codes, and the tribunal thus makes its determination based on a series of criteria such as the effect of the presence of the imported goods on domestic prices, production, sales, employment, and profit.

Its first step, however, is to issue a notice of a public hearing in the *Canada Gazette* and forward copies of the notice to all interested parties. (The *Gazette* is a federal government publication, issued weekly, and lists all government notices, including regulations and advertisements.) The notice contains information on how parties may participate in the public hearing and gives deadline dates for submissions and the date and location of the hearing.

As this is happening, tribunal members are also obtaining information from the deputy minister and collecting other relevant data from manufacturers, importers and, occasionally, the end user of the goods in question.

(c) The final determination

Within 90 days of making the preliminary determination, the deputy minister issues a final determination based on any further evidence accumulated in the interim. This is at about the same time that the tribunal's public hearing is held.

(d) The public hearing

The tribunal holds a public hearing to provide the complainants — that is, Canadian producers — with an opportunity to demonstrate how their industry has

SAMPLE #8
SIMA INDEX

SIMA Index for June 1995

SYMBOLS + Addition to last posting   # Change from last posting   * Anti-dumping and Countervailing Duties   ** Countervailing Duty   *** Surtax Only   pd Provisional Duty

Countries:
- AR - Argentine
- AT - Austria
- BE - Belgium
- BR - Brazil
- CN - China
- CS - Czechoslovakia
- DD - German Democratic Republic
- DE - Federal Republic of Germany
- DK - Denmark
- ES - Spain
- TW - Taiwan
- FR - France
- GB - United Kingdom
- GR - Greece
- HK - Hong Kong
- HU - Hungary
- ID - Indonesia
- IE - Ireland
- IN - India
- IT - Italy
- JP - Japan
- KR - Republic of Korea
- LU - Luxembourg
- MY - Malaysia
- MX - Mexico
- NL - Netherlands
- PL - Poland
- PT - Portugal
- SE - Sweden
- SG - Singapore
- SU - U.S.S.R.
- US - United States
- UCA - California
- UID - Idaho
- UOR - Oregon
- UWA - Washington
- YU - Yugoslavia
- ZA - South Africa

Items are listed in the following fashion:
Product
Country   HS Classification Opinion

ALBUMS, photo and leaves
KR   4820.50.90.10/4820.50.90.90/
                4820.90.90.90/3926.90.99.30

ALBUMS, photo & leaves
ID TH PH   4820.50.90.10/4820.50.90.90
                4820.90.90.90

ALBUMS, photo & leaves
CN   4820.50.90.10/4820.50.90.90/
                4820.90.90.90

ALBUMS, photo & leaves
SG MY TW   4820.50.90.10/4820.50.90.90/
                4820.90.90.90

ALBUMS, photo & leaves
HK KR   4820.50.90.10/4820.50.90.90/
                4820.90.90.90

ALBUMS, photo with pockets
JP KR CN   4820.50.90.10/4820.50.90.90/
HK TW SG   4820.90.90.90/3926.90.90.30
MY DE

APPLES   fresh, whole and delicious
US   0808.10.10.60

BALER TWINE, synthetic
US   5607.41.00.00

**BEEF, manufacturing, boneless
BE DK FR   0202.30
DE GR IE
IT LU NL
PT ES GB

BICYCLES   8712.00.00.10/8712.00.00.20/
TW, CN   8712.00.00.30/8712.00.00.40/
                8712.00.00.50/8712.00.00.90/
                8714.91.00.00

BRUSHES, paint, hogbristle
CN   9603.40.90/9603.40.10

CARPETS, machine tufted
US   5703.20.10.00/5703.30.10.10
                5703.30.10.20

COIL STOCK,   7216.90.90.90/7326.90.99.99/
aluminum   7606.11.20.11
SE   7606.11.20.13/7606.12.29.11/
                7607.19.99.00/7616.90.90.60
                7616.90.90.90/8302.49.90.90

COPPER PIPE FITTINGS
US   7412.10.00.11/7412.10.00.19/
                7412.10.00.20/7412.10.00.90/
                7412.20.00.11/7412.20.00.12/
                7412.20.00.19/7412.20.00.20/
                7412.20.00.90

FIBREGLASS PIPE INSULATION
US   7019.39.00.12

FOOTWEAR, ladies shoes and boots
BR PL RO   6402.91.00.22/6402.91.00.92/
YU CN TW   6402.99.00.92/6403.51.00.22/
HR ST BA MK   6403.51.00.92/6403.59.00.92/
                6403.91.00.22/6403.59.00.92/
                6403.91.00.92/6403.99.00.92/
                6404.19.90.92/6404.20.00.92/
                6405.10/6405.20/
                6405.90.00.90

FOOTWEAR, waterproof rubber
CZ PL KR   6401.10.10.00/6401.91.10.00/
TW SK   6401.92.11.00/6401.92.91.10/
                6401.92.91.20/6401.92.91.30/
                6401.99.91.00/4015.90.90.00

FOOTWEAR, waterproof rubber
YU HK MY   6401.10.10.00/6401.91.10.00/
CN HR SI BA   6401.92.11.00/6401.92.91.10/
MK   6401.92.91.20/6401.92.91.30/
                6401.99.91.00/4015.90.90.00
                4015.90.90.00

GYPSUM BOARD   6809.11.10.00/6809.11.90.00
US   6809.19.00.00

**HAM, canned
DK NL   1602.41.10.00

LETTUCE   0705.11.11.40/0705.11.11.00/
US   0705.11.90.00

**LUNCHEON MEAT, canned pork
DK NL BE   1602.49.91.10
FR DE GR
IE IT PT
ES GB LU

*MEMORIALS, black granite memorials and slabs
IN   6802.93.00.20/6802.23.00.20

METALS SEE BELOW

ONIONS, yellow
US (UID UCA
UOR UWA)   0703.10.91/0703.10.99

**PAPER, refill
BR   4820.10/4823.51/
                4823.59.00.90/4823.90.99.90

POTATOES, russet skins
US (UID UCA
UOR UWA)   0701.90.
POTATOES, whole
US (UID UCA
UOR UWA)   0701.90

ROPE, synthetic
KR   5607.49.10/5607.49.20/
                5607.50.10/5607.50.20/5609

SHOTSHELLS, 12 gauge
CZ, HU   9306.21.00

TOOLS, tillage
BR   8432.90.20.

TOOTHPICKS, wooden
US (UME)   4421.90.90.30/4421.90.90.99

METALS:
STEEL:
Pipe, carbon steel, welded
KR   7306.30.00.14/7306.30.00.19
                7306.30.00.24/7306.30.00.29

Pipe, carbon steel, welded
AR IN RO   7306.30.00.14/7306.30.00.19/
TH TW VE   7306.30.00.24/7306.30.00.29

Pipe, carbon steel welded
BR   7306.30.00.14/7306.30.00.19/
                7306.30.00.24/7306.30.00.29

Plate, carbon steel 7208.32.00.10/7208.32.00.95
BE BR CS DK DE 7208.33.00.94/7208.42.00.93
RC GB MK   7208.43.00.92/7208.32.00.94/
                7208.33.00.10/7208.33.00.95/
                7208.42.00.94/7208.43.00.93/
                7208.32.00.92/7208.33.00.91/
                7208.42.00.10/7208.42.00.95/
                7208.43.00.94/7208.32.00.93/
                7208.33.00.92/7208.42.00.91/
                7208.43.00.10/7208.43.00.95/
                7208.32.00.94/7208.33.00.93/
                7208.42.00.92/7208.43.00.91/
                7208.32.00.91

PLATE, carbon steel
IT, KR, ES,   7208.32.00.10/7208.32.00.91
UKRAINE   7208.32.00.92/208.32.00.93
                7208.32.00.94/7208.32.00.95
                7208.33.00.10/7208.33.00.91
                7208.33.00.92/7208.33.00.93
                7208.33.00.94/7208.33.00.95
                7208.42.00.10/7208.42.00.91
                7208.42.00.92/7208.42.00.93
                7208.42.00.94/7208.42.00.95
                7208.43.00.10/7208.43.00.91
                7208.43.00.92/7208.43.00.92
                7208.43.00.93/7208.43.00.94
                7208.43.00.95

SHEET, cold rolled steel
US FR DE GB IT 7209.11.00/7209.12.00/
                7209.13.00/7209.21.00/
                7209.22.00/7209.23.00/
                7209.24.00/7209.31.00/
                7209.32.00/7209.33.00/
                7209.34.00/7209.41.00/
                7209.42.00/7209.43.00/
                7209.44.00/7211.30.00/
                7211.41.00/7211.49.00

SHEET, corrosion resistant
AU BR DE ES FR 7210.31/7210.39/7210.49/
GB JP KR NZ SE US 7212.21/7212.29/7212.30/
                7225.90.00.10/7226.99.00.10

Well casing, oil & gas
US KR   7304.20.90.00/7305.20.00.00/
                7306.20.00.00/7306.20/
                7304.20.10.00

STAINLESS STEEL:
Pipe, welded
TW   7306.40.00.11/7306.40.00.12/
                7306.40.00.13

UNDERTAKINGS:
File Folders, hanging
US   4820.30.00.90

Frozen pot pies, dinners
US   1602.31.10/1602.39.10.99/
                1602.39.10/
1602.50.10/1602.49.10

Shrinkable bags, plastic
                3920.10.00.11, 3923.21.00.41,
                3923.21.00.42

Prefabricated metal sheds, residential steel storage
                9406.00.99.20, 9406.00.99.90

Wedge Clamps, Aluminum
US   7616.90.90.90

Well Casing, oil and gas
DE JP   7304.20.90/7305.20/
                7306.20./7304.20.10

79

been injured by competition from the imported goods on the Canadian market. Tribunal members do not rule on whether or not goods have been dumped; that issue has already been decided by the deputy minister. Importers and other parties adversely affected by the deputy minister's decision have a chance to challenge the complainants. The proceedings are conducted much as they would be in a courtroom and parties making a submission can opt to retain legal counsel for the purpose, although they are free to represent themselves.

(e) The finding

Tribunal members are required to issue their finding within 120 days of the deputy minister's preliminary determination, and then they have another 15 days to publish a statement of reasons for their decision. Both the finding and the statement of reasons are published in the *Canada Gazette* and sent to all hearing participants as soon as they're issued.

By this time in the complaint process, Revenue Canada has already assessed duties on the goods. Should the tribunal rule that material injury has occurred, then these duties serve to offset the unfair price advantage that the imported goods have previously enjoyed. If, on the other hand, the tribunal finds that no injury has been suffered, all duties collected to this date are refunded.

(f) Review of the findings

The tribunal can review its findings at any time, either on its own initiative or at the request of an interested party. An importer, for example, may apply for a review on the basis that certain domestic goods do not now need protection because they're no longer being manufactured in Canada. So might a Canadian producer who wants a particular finding to be continued. And so might the deputy minister, or any other person or government, if the circumstances surrounding the original finding have changed. The tribunal itself, however, decides whether or not a review is warranted.

The tribunal's findings otherwise lapse after five years, although it sends out a notice of expiry about eight months before the lapse date, giving those interested an opportunity to make submissions in support of a review.

Reviews are conducted along the same lines as injury inquiries with the tribunal placing a notice in the Gazette, making its own research with questionnaires, and holding a public hearing. The tribunal's finding and reasons are also published within the same time limits and can result in a previous finding being rescinded or altered.

All tribunal findings, whether made in the course of an injury inquiry or a review, are final and binding. They can be reviewed by the federal Court of Appeal, but only on points of law, not on the substance of the case itself. If it's not satisfied that the law was fully applied, the court can request that the tribunal re-hear a case. Judicial reviews involving goods imported from the United States may be conducted by a Canada-U.S. panel established under SIMA as a result of the formation of the FTA and continued under NAFTA.

Figure #4 shows the complaint process.

2. SIMA's other functions

SIMA incorporates other functions as well as the complaint procedure detailed above. At the request of the deputy minister or other interested parties, for example, the tribunal may review a case where evidence of dumping appears insufficient and advise the deputy minister to either re-open, proceed with, or terminate an investigation (without taking the matter to a public hearing). Similarly, the legislation provides for the tribunal to take action on behalf of the public, reporting to the Minister of Finance any instances where the imposition of anti-dumping duties would be detrimental to public interest.

We have given you only a very brief introduction to the act here and we urge you to read the legislation in its entirety, as well as our other references, if you want to make a more complete study of it.

b. OTHER NON-TARIFF BARRIERS

While they bear no direct relation to anti-dumping duties, other non-tariff barriers serve to discourage nations from trading with Canada and are representative of the same protectionist tendencies inherent in Canadian trading policies and practices since the turn of the century.

A barrier usually takes the form of a requirement that goods produced abroad must meet before they can be imported into Canada. Tariffs act as barriers by obliging importers to pay more for goods. Non-tariff barriers also force importers to pay more — by demanding that they meet bilingual labelling requirements if they're importing clothing for example or by limiting (imposing a quota on) or prohibiting the import of certain goods. They may not be termed "barriers" in the legislation where they appear, but that's still their main purpose.

Barriers are introduced for several reasons, chief among them the protection of Canadian industry, as we've already mentioned. But they are also used to enforce global environmental decisions, as in the case of the protection of endangered species under CITES (Convention on International Trade in Endangered Species), discussed in chapter 1. Sometimes they are used to make a political statement concerning the activities of another country. For several years, for example, Canada prohibited the importation of any foodstuffs from South Africa, in protest against that country's apartheid policies.

The D11-3-1 marking regulations are an excellent example of a non-tariff barrier in action. Under them many kinds of imports, from household items to clothing, must be stamped with the name of the country of origin before they're allowed to enter Canada (the label may be in English or French, but not in both). Each item is identified and a precise description of the marking requirement provided — so precise, in fact, that the importer is well advised to repeat the instructions verbatim on his or her purchase order and make satisfaction of them a condition of payment. See Figure #5 for a full listing of imports that must bear a country-of-origin label.

Other non-tariff barriers have also been established by the Department of External Affairs under the provisions of the Export and Import Permits Act and its regulations, passed in 1985 and administered by Canada Customs. The act encompasses several federal acts, listing a variety of goods (chiefly clothing) which are prohibited from entry to Canada or can be imported only with the issuance of an import permit, licence, or certificate. From time to time, the list is adjusted.

The procedures for obtaining permission to import controlled goods vary, depending on the nature of the goods and the purposes to which they are being put. They are clearly laid out in the regulations, and examples of the permit application and the permit itself can be found in chapter 9, Samples #15 and #16, respectively.

RECOMMENDED READING

Appeals from Customs and Excise Decisions
Dumping and Subsidizing Injury Inquiries
General Inquiries into Economic, Trade and Tariff Matters
Import Safeguard Complaints by Domestic Producers
Import Safeguard Complaints Concerning the General Preferential Tariff (GPT) or CARIBCAN
Introduction to the Canadian International Trade Tribunal

All of the above publications are published by and available, by mail and free of charge, from:

> The Canadian International Trade Tribunal
> 333 Laurier Avenue W.
> Ottawa, Ontario
> K1A 0G7

Canada. Special Trade Relations Bureau. *The Export and Import Permits Act Handbook.* [Ottawa]: Department of External Affairs, 1991.

Salembier, G.E., Andrew R. Moroz, and Frank Stone. *The Canadian Import File: Trade, Protection, and Adjustment.* Montreal: The Institute for Research on Public Policy, 1987.

FIGURE #4
THE COMPLAINT PROCESS — SPECIAL IMPORT MEASURES ACT (SIMA)

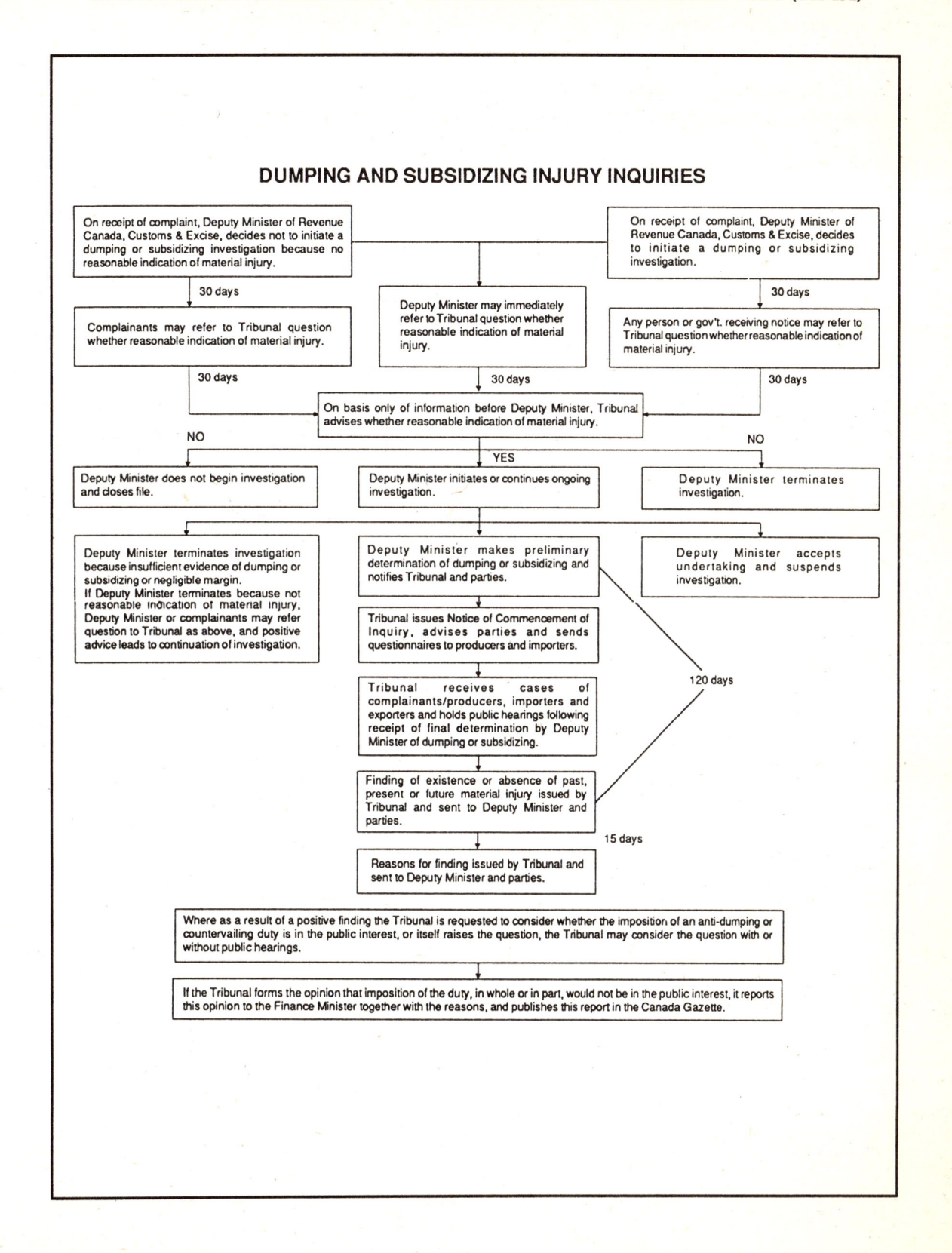

DUMPING AND SUBSIDIZING INJURY INQUIRIES

On receipt of complaint, Deputy Minister of Revenue Canada, Customs & Excise, decides not to initiate a dumping or subsidizing investigation because no reasonable indication of material injury.

↓ 30 days

Complainants may refer to Tribunal question whether reasonable indication of material injury.

↓ 30 days

Deputy Minister may immediately refer to Tribunal question whether reasonable indication of material injury.

↓ 30 days

On receipt of complaint, Deputy Minister of Revenue Canada, Customs & Excise, decides to initiate a dumping or subsidizing investigation.

↓ 30 days

Any person or gov't. receiving notice may refer to Tribunal question whether reasonable indication of material injury.

↓ 30 days

On basis only of information before Deputy Minister, Tribunal advises whether reasonable indication of material injury.

NO — Deputy Minister does not begin investigation and closes file.

YES — Deputy Minister initiates or continues ongoing investigation.

NO — Deputy Minister terminates investigation.

Deputy Minister terminates investigation because insufficient evidence of dumping or subsidizing or negligible margin.
If Deputy Minister terminates because not reasonable indication of material injury, Deputy Minister or complainants may refer question to Tribunal as above, and positive advice leads to continuation of investigation.

Deputy Minister makes preliminary determination of dumping or subsidizing and notifies Tribunal and parties.

Tribunal issues Notice of Commencement of Inquiry, advises parties and sends questionnaires to producers and importers.

Tribunal receives cases of complainants/producers, importers and exporters and holds public hearings following receipt of final determination by Deputy Minister of dumping or subsidizing.

Finding of existence or absence of past, present or future material injury issued by Tribunal and sent to Deputy Minister and parties.

Deputy Minister accepts undertaking and suspends investigation.

120 days

↓ 15 days

Reasons for finding issued by Tribunal and sent to Deputy Minister and parties.

Where as a result of a positive finding the Tribunal is requested to consider whether the imposition of an anti-dumping or countervailing duty is in the public interest, or itself raises the question, the Tribunal may consider the question with or without public hearings.

If the Tribunal forms the opinion that imposition of the duty, in whole or in part, would not be in the public interest, it reports this opinion to the Finance Minister together with the reasons, and publishes this report in the Canada Gazette.

FIGURE #5
MARKING REQUIREMENTS
(As specified in the Customs regulations, D11-3-1)

The following goods are required to be marked with their country of origin whether they are imported from a NAFTA country or a non-NAFTA country:

1. Goods for Personal and Household Use
   (1) Bakeware and cookware made of aluminum
   (2) Bakeware and cookware made of cast iron
   (3) Bath mats, towels and wash cloths, knitted or woven
   (4) Batteries, dry cell
   (5) Blankets
   (6) Brushes, including toothbrushes and handles therefor
   (7) Candles
   (8) Cards, the following: credit and identification, made of any material having a diameter or side exceeding ½ inch in width and imported in sheet form or otherwise
   (9) Chrome plated ware and utensils for use in serving food and beverages
   (10) Cigar and cigarette lighters, except lighters for incorporation into motor vehicles
   (11) Clocks and movements, except clocks and movements for use as original equipment by motor vehicle manufacturers
   (12) Containers, thermostatic, the following: carafes, flasks, jars, jugs and vacuum bottles, and refills or inserts therefor
   (13) Cutlery, chrome plated or stainless steel
   (14) Dishes and ornaments made of china earthenware, ironstone, porcelain, semi-porcelain, stoneware or white granite
   (15) Electronic equipment, the following: phonographs, radio receiving sets, radio-phonograph sets, radio-phonograph-television sets, record players, tape recorders, television receiving sets
   (16) Ironing board covers and pads
   (17) Kitchenware made of metal or plastic, coated, lithographed, painted or otherwise, the following: bread boxes, cake humidors, canisters, foil and paper dispensers, range sets, serving ovens and step-on waste cans
   (18) Knives, the following: jack, pen and pocket; scissors and shears

FIGURE #5 — Continued

- (19) Lawn mowers (powered)
- (20) Matches in books, boxes or folders
- (21) Pencils
- (22) Pens, the following: ball point and fountain, and nib penholders
- (23) Pillowslips and sheets made of cotton
- (24) Razor blades (safety type)
- (25) Thermometers
- (26) Tiles, glazed, unglazed and ceramic mosaic, the following: hearth, floor and wall
- (27) Umbrellas
- (28) Utensils, kitchen type, chrome plated or stainless steel
- (29) Watch bracelets (expansion type)

2. Hardware
- (1) Caps, made of metal, lithographed or printed, for containers, the following: lug, screw and vacuum
- (2) Copper tubing
- (3) Drapery 1-beam rails, made of aluminum, brass, steel or other metal or plastic and component parts thereof
- (4) Electrical measuring devices for panel mounting designed to indicate alternating or direct current microamperes, milliamperes or amperes, millivolts, volts or kilovolts and such other variables as pressure, resistance and temperature that may be translated into alternating or direct current or voltage
- (5) Glass in panes or sheets, the following: common or colourless window, laminated, plate and sheet
- (6) Goods made of porcelain for electrical use
- (7) Files and rasps
- (8) Sink strainers (basket type)
- (9) Tubes electronic
- (10) Twines, the following: baler and binder
- (11) Wire insect screening
- (12) Iron or steel pipes and tubes

3. Novelties and Sporting Goods
- (1) Articles in the style of Indian handicrafts
- (2) Athletic gloves and mitts, including baseball and hockey gloves and mitts
- (3) Bicycles

FIGURE #5 — Continued

(4) Decorations, novelties and ornaments

(5) Enamelled emblems and silver plated or sterling silver bracelets, brooches, pins and spoons, all designed as souvenirs of Canada, its provinces, territories, cities, towns or other geographical locations

(6) Gift wrappings, the following: bindings, braids, ribbons, tapes, ties and trimmings, made chiefly or wholly of textile fibres

(7) Toys, games and athletic and sporting goods

4. Paper Products

(1) Boxes and cartons, empty folding or set-up, made of paper, paper board, plain or corrugated fibre or fibre board, for use as shipping containers

(2) Paper matter and products, lithographed or printed

5. Wearing Apparel

(1) Boots, shoes and slippers

(2) Brassieres, corselettes, garter belts, girdles and lacing corsets

(3) Fabrics, braided or woven, containing rubber yarns, not exceeding 12 inches in width; boot and shoe laces

(4) Gloves made partially or wholly of leather

(5) Hair pieces, the following: wigs, half wigs, switches, postiches, pony tails, toupees and other types of hair pieces designed to be worn on the head of a person

(6) Handbags and purses, except handbags and purses made of beads, metal mesh or similar material

(7) Hats, including berets, bonnets, caps and hats, hoods and shapes made of fur felt, wool felt and wool-and-fur felt

(8) Knitted garments

(9) Raincoats and rainwear made of plastic

(10) Wearing apparel made wholly or substantially of natural or synthetic textile fibres

6. Containers — Only applicable to goods imported from NAFTA countries

(1) Outermost usual containers of goods that are referred to in items 10, 11, 12, 13, or 18 of Schedule II which is contained in Appendix C of this Memorandum

(2) Containers in which empty usual containers are imported

(3) Usual containers that are imported filled, unless the goods they contain are marked in accordance with the Marking of Imported Goods Regulations

9
IMPORT DOCUMENTS FOR YOUR GOODS

This chapter provides general descriptions and examples of the most commonly used import forms and documents.

While Canada Customs and the importing community are working toward a "paperless" system of processing imported goods, they are still some distance from their goal as the following discussion of import documentation certainly demonstrates.

There's at least one document required for every step in the importing process and often more than one to accommodate changes or problems as they occur. In fact, the total number of documents or forms printed by Canada Customs alone, to accommodate the importing process, currently amounts to more than 50.

Many of these are used infrequently by the small importer — if you're just starting your business, it's unlikely that you'll have need of the less-used forms provided in the "D" series Customs regulations. So we are limiting the following discussion accordingly. Some of this information is repeated from chapter 2, when we discussed documentation in relation to paying for your goods, and will appear again in chapters 11 and 12 on accounting to Customs and duty relief. The material is important enough to bear repeating.

a. THE IMPORTING PROCESS

Were we to depict a simple importation on a flow chart, it would look something like Figure #6.

As Figure #6 indicates, you need three types of documents to complete an importation:

(a) an invoice or other acceptable supporting document from your supplier,

(b) a cargo control document indicating how your goods were transported to Canada, and

(c) other forms, permits, or certificates as required by law for admission of the goods.

We've made reference to a few other documents, in the event you decide to return your goods to your supplier or wish to apply for a refund, based on the type and purpose of the goods you've imported.

Now let's take a look at these various forms.

1. The commercial invoice

The importing process is initiated when you place an order with your supplier who then provides you with a commercial invoice, or when you sign and return a pro forma invoice to him or her. These documents, as you may recall from the discussion in chapter 2, contain the same information: your name and address, the name and address of your supplier, and a full description of the goods, payment, and shipping terms, etc. A pro forma invoice, however, is a quotation and is also used sometimes to identify the value of goods for Customs purposes only, as in the case of an item being exported temporarily for warranty repair (it's usually clearly stamped "pro forma").

Today these documents are often exchanged by fax and serve as your reference in determining duties and taxes payable. If you do not have a commercial invoice, you must complete a Canada Customs invoice, as described under section 4. below or a pro forma invoice for low-value shipments (less than $1 200). A typical commercial invoice usually looks something like the one shown in Sample #9.

2. Request for Business Number

If you haven't already done so, you will want to apply for a business number as soon as you've placed your order. The Business Number (BN) is a new numbering system which makes it easier for businesses to contact government and adhere to government requirements concerning corporate income tax, import/export, payroll deductions, and GST. It replaces the multiple numbers (including the importer number) businesses used to be assigned under these accounts, giving them instead a unique registration number which stays the same no matter how many or what types of accounts a particular business acquires. The number itself has 15 digits and consists of two parts: the registration number and the account identifier.

BN was piloted across Canada in 1994 as the "Single Business Registration Number" and received very favorable comment from most participants. As the program evolves, it's expected to offer, among other things, options tailored to business size and type.

Businesses that register for the BN obtain "one-stop" business services from Revenue Canada, including integrated new-business registration, the streamlined addition of accounts, consolidated account information, and integrated account inquiries. Only if it changes its legal basis — becoming incorporated, for example, after having been a sole proprietorship — is a business required to register for a new BN (see Sample #10 and Sample #11).

3. The Cargo Control Document

The cargo control document may take several forms. It is the air waybill, for example, that an airline issues to your supplier or his or her shipping agent once your goods have been accepted for transport. It is also Canada Customs form A-8A, entitled Customs Cargo Control Document and completed by any transport company shipping goods by truck over the border (or by the customs broker for the importer). And it is also form E-14, the form you receive from Canada Customs when you import goods by parcel post. Whatever shape it assumes, a cargo control document serves generally as a notice of arrival (see Sample #12).

You (or your broker) may also complete a corollary document, Canada Customs form A-10 at this time. Form A-10, entitled Customs Cargo Control Abstract, is required when a single, consolidated shipment is to be broken up into smaller, in-bond shipments. For example, suppose five Danish food exporters share a container as an economical means of shipping goods to Canada. The five shipments arrive as one, and the Vancouver-based customs broker for the group receives a cargo control document from the shipping company for the whole container. He or she completes a form A-10 for each small shipment — five A-10 forms altogether — and these replace or cancel out the original cargo control document on Canada Customs' records. Each of the five separate shipments can then be dealt with accordingly (see Sample #13).

FIGURE #6
THE TYPICAL IMPORTING PROCESS

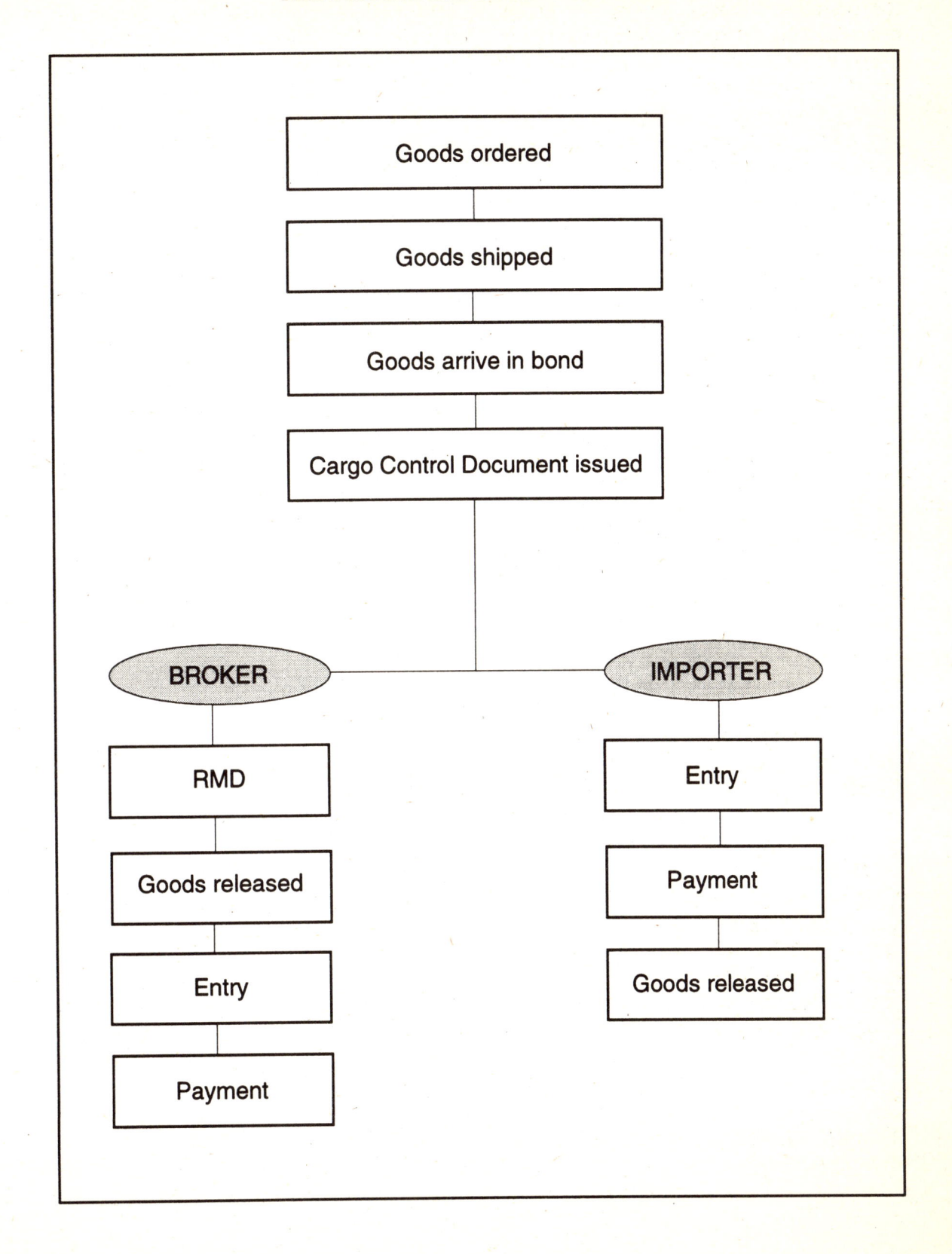

```
                    Goods ordered
                          |
                    Goods shipped
                          |
                  Goods arrive in bond
                          |
              Cargo Control Document issued
                          |
              ┌───────────┴───────────┐
          BROKER                   IMPORTER
            |                          |
           RMD                       Entry
            |                          |
       Goods released               Payment
            |                          |
          Entry                  Goods released
            |
         Payment
```

89

SAMPLE #9
TYPICAL COMMERCIAL INVOICE

Worldwide Trading Company
11233 Lamplighter Square
New York, New York 53394
Tel (718) 995-2339
Fax (718) 995-2340

Sold to: GFM Trading Company   Ship to: Same
555 West Hastings Street
Vancouver, BC
V6B 4N5

Invoice No. 55698	Invoice Date 95.07.28	Terms: Net 30 Days
Customer Order No. 88421	Reference 864A	Carrier: Kingsway PPD

PART NUMBER	QTY ORD	QTY SHPT	DESCRIPTION	UNIT PRICE	EXTENSION
775986	20	10	Model 220 Bicycles	205.00	2050.00
775887	05	05	Model 220SX Bicycles	225.00	2250.00
799633	25	25	Model XXT Bicycle Framesets	110.00	2750.00
					7050.00 USD

Note: 10 - 220's backordered

All past due invoices are subject to a monthly finance fee of 1 1/4%.

SAMPLE #10
REQUEST FOR A BUSINESS NUMBER
(form RC1-E)

Revenue Canada / Revenu Canada

REQUEST FOR A BUSINESS NUMBER (BN)

RC1(E) Rev. 94

Complete this form if you have a new business and you need to apply for a Business Number (BN). If you are a sole proprietor with more than one business, your BN will apply to all your businesses. **Note: All businesses have to complete Parts A and F. All corporations have to provide a copy of the certificate of incorporation/amalgamation.** Please check the box(es) for the types of BN accounts that you need.

- ☐ GST account (complete Part B)
- ☐ Payroll (source) deductions account (complete Part C)
- ☐ Import/export account (complete Part D)
- ☐ Corporate income tax account (complete Part E)

For more information, see the pamphlet titled *The Business Number and Your Revenue Canada Accounts*.

Part A

A1 Identification of business (For a corporation, enter the name and address of the head office.)

Name (For individuals or partnerships, also enter first and last names in A2 below.)

Operating, trade, or partnership name (if different from name): If you have more than one business or if your business operates under more than one name, enter the name(s) here. If you need more space, attach a list.

Business address

Postal/zip code

Mailing address (if different from business address)

c/o

Address

Postal/zip code

Name and address of business's financial institution

Contact person (If you choose to name a contact for your account, please see page 8 of our pamphlet for information.)

First name — Last name

Language: ☐ English ☐ French

Title — Telephone number ( ) — Fax number ( )

A2 Legal status (Check the box(es) that apply to you and enter the information requested. If you need more space, please attach a list.)

- ☐ **Individual (sole proprietor)** In the space below, enter the name (if not provided above), address, and social insurance number of the owner.
- ☐ **Partnership** In the space below, enter the name, address, and social insurance number of each partner.
- ☐ **Corporation** In the space below, enter the name, address, and social insurance number of each corporation director.
- ☐ **Other** (specify) _____ In the space below, enter the name, address, and social insurance number of each officer.

☐ Individual ☐ Partner ☐ Director ☐ Officer

First name — Last name — Social insurance number — Telephone number ( )

Home address — Postal/zip code

☐ Partner ☐ Director ☐ Officer

First name — Last name — Social insurance number — Telephone number ( )

Home address — Postal/zip code

☐ Partner ☐ Director ☐ Officer

First name — Last name — Social insurance number — Telephone number ( )

Home address — Postal/zip code

A3 Major business activity

Describe your major business activity: _____

Specify up to three main products that you mine, manufacture, or sell, or services you provide or contract. Also, please estimate the percentage of revenue that each product or service represents.

_____ %
_____ %
_____ %

A4 Requestor information (Complete this area if you are registering for a BN on behalf of a client. If you want an agent to register on your behalf, please see page 9 of our pamphlet for more information.)

Your name (please print) — Your company's name (please print)

Year — Month — Day

Ce formulaire existe aussi en français

SAMPLE #10 — Continued

A5 GST decision (See the pamphlet *The Business Number and Your Revenue Canada Accounts* to clarify the terms we use below.)

Do you plan to sell or provide goods and/or services in Canada? Yes ☐ No ☐
Note: If you **export**, you may be deemed to be selling or providing goods and/or services in Canada. Please see page 10 of our pamphlet for details.
If *yes*, answer the questions that follow. Page 10 of our pamphlet defines "GST-taxable sales."
If *no*, you cannot register for the GST. **Skip** to Part C and complete the rest of the form where applicable.

Will your annual **worldwide** GST-taxable sales (including those of any associates) be more than $30,000? Yes ☐ No ☐
Are you a non-resident who solicits orders in Canada for goods to be sent by mail or courier, and whose worldwide GST-taxable sales will be more than $30,000? Yes ☐ No ☐
If *yes* to either of the above, you **must** register for the GST. See page 10 of our pamphlet to find out when you should register. To register, go to Part B, "GST account information," below. If *no*, read on.

Do you operate a taxi or limousine service? Yes ☐ No ☐
Are you a non-resident who charges admission directly to audiences at activities or events in Canada? Yes ☐ No ☐
If *yes* to either of the above, you **must** register for the GST, even if your worldwide GST-taxable sales will be $30,000 or less. Go to Part B, "GST account information," below.
If *no*, read on.

Are all the goods and/or services you sell or provide exempt from the GST? Yes ☐ No ☐
If *yes*, you **cannot** register for the GST. Page 10 of our pamphlet discusses exempt goods and services.
If *no*, read on.

Do you wish to register voluntarily? Yes ☐ No ☐
If *yes*, go to Part B, "GST account information", below. There are obligations that you must meet if you register voluntarily. Page 11 of our pamphlet discusses voluntary registration. If *no*, complete the rest of the form where applicable.

Part B
GST account information — Complete sections B1 to B4 if you need a BN GST account. See pages 12 to 14 of our pamphlet titled *The Business Number and Your Revenue Canada Accounts* for more information.

B1 GST account identification (Check box ☐ if same as in A1 on page 1, or add information below.)

Mailing address for GST purposes
c/o
Address
Operating or trade name (Enter name to which we should address correspondence.)
Postal/zip code

Contact person (If you choose to name a contact for your account, please see page 8 of our pamphlet for information.)
First name
Last name
Language ☐ English ☐ French
Title
Telephone number ( )
Fax number ( )

B2 Filing information

Enter the fiscal year-end date of the business (see page 12 of our pamphlet). ☐☐ Month ☐☐ Day
Estimate your annual GST-taxable sales **in Canada** (including those of any associates in Canada). Please check the box that applies:
☐ $30,000 or less;
☐ more than $30,000 but not more than $200,000;
☐ more than $200,000 but not more than $500,000;
☐ more than $500,000 but not more than $1,000,000;
☐ more than $1,000,000 but not more than $6,000,000; or
☐ more than $6,000,000.
Enter the effective date of registration for GST purposes (see page 13 of our pamphlet). ☐☐ Year ☐☐ Month ☐☐ Day

B3 Type of operation

01 ☐ Government, municipality
02 ☐ Registered charity (please provide your registration no.)
03 ☐ Qualifying non-profit organization
04 ☐ Listed financial institution
05 ☐ University, school board, hospital
06 ☐ Joint venture operator (not a partnership)
07 ☐ Non-resident who charges admission directly to spectators or attendees
08 ☐ Non-resident who carries on commercial activities in Canada
09 ☐ Taxi or limousine operator
99 ☐ None of the above

B4 Province or territory (Check the boxes below to indicate the provinces or territories in which you carry out commercial activities or maintain a permanent establishment.)

	Commercial activity	Permanent establishment		Commercial activity	Permanent establishment		Commercial activity	Permanent establishment		Commercial activity	Permanent establishment
Alberta	☐	☐	New Brunswick	☐	☐	Nova Scotia	☐	☐	Quebec	☐	☐
British Columbia	☐	☐	Newfoundland	☐	☐	Ontario	☐	☐	Saskatchewan	☐	☐
Manitoba	☐	☐	Northwest Territories	☐	☐	Prince Edward Island	☐	☐	Yukon Territory	☐	☐

SAMPLE #10 — Continued

Part C
Payroll (source) deductions account information - Complete C1 and C2 if you need a BN payroll (source) deductions account. See pages 14 to 15 of our pamphlet titled *The Business Number and Your Revenue Canada Accounts* for more information.

C1 Payroll (source) deductions account identification (Check box ☐ if same as in A1 on page 1, or add information below.)

Account name (If you want to use a separate name for your BN payroll (source) deductions account, enter that name here.)

Address

Postal/zip code

Mailing address for payroll (source) deductions
- c/o
- Address
- Postal/zip code

Contact person (If you choose to name a contact for your account, please see page 8 of our pamphlet for information.)
First name   Last name

Title   Telephone number ( )   Fax number ( )

Language ☐ English ☐ French

C2 General information (Please complete this area so that we can send you the information you need.)

a) Type of deduction
  ☐ Payroll ☐ Registered retirement savings plan
  ☐ Registered retirement income fund ☐ Other (specify) _____

b) How often will you pay your employees or payees? Please check the pay period(s) that apply.
  ☐ Daily ☐ Weekly ☐ Bi-weekly ☐ Semi-monthly
  ☐ Monthly ☐ Annually ☐ Other (specify) _____

c) Will you use your own computer program for payroll purposes? ☐ No ☐ Yes   If yes, do you need our payroll formulas? ☐ No ☐ Yes

d) Do you use a payroll service bureau? ☐ No ☐ Yes   If yes, which one? (enter name) _____

e) Do you want to receive a copy of the Payroll Deductions Tables program diskette? ☐ No ☐ Yes

f) When will you make the first payment to your employees or payees? ☐☐ Year ☐☐ Month ☐☐ Day

g) What is the maximum number of employees you expect to have working for you at any time in the next 12 months? _____

h) Duration of business operation ☐ Year round ☐ Seasonal
  If seasonal, please check month(s) of operation. | J | F | M | A | M | J | J | A | S | O | N | D |

i) If the business is a corporation, is the corporation a subsidiary or an affiliate of a foreign corporation? ☐ No ☐ Yes   If yes, enter country. _____

j) Are you a franchisee? ☐ No ☐ Yes   If yes, enter the name and country of the franchisor. _____

SAMPLE #10 — Continued

Part D
Import/export account information - Complete D1 and D2 if you need a BN import/export account for Customs accounting purposes. See page 15 of our pamphlet titled *The Business Number and Your Revenue Canada Accounts* for more information.

D1 Import/export account identification (Check box ☐ if same as in Area 1 on page 1, or add information below.)

Import/export account name (if different than name on page 1)

Address

Postal/zip code

Mailing address (if different from above)
c/o
Address

Postal/zip code

Contact person (If you choose to name a contact for your account, please see page 8 of our pamphlet for information.)
First name   Last name   Language
                                     ☐ English ☐ French
Title   Telephone number Fax number
                   (   )   (   )

D2 Import/export information

Type of account   ☐ Importer   ☐ Exporter   ☐ Both
If exporter, enter the type of goods you are exporting:

_____

_____

_____

If exporter, enter the estimated annual value of goods you are exporting: $ _____

Part E
Corporate income tax account information - Complete E1 if you need a BN corporate income tax account. See page 16 of our pamphlet titled *The Business Number and Your Revenue Canada Accounts* for more information.

E1 Corporate income tax account identification (Check box ☐ if same as in A1 on page 1, or add information below.)

Mailing address (if different from business address provided in Part A)
c/o
Address

Postal/zip code

Contact person (If you choose to name a contact for your account, please see page 8 of our pamphlet for information.)
First name   Last name   Language
                                     ☐ English ☐ French
Title   Telephone number Fax number
                   (   )   (   )

Part F
Certification – All businesses have to complete this area.

As an authorized person, I, _____, certify that the information given on this form and in any document attached is, to the best of my knowledge, correct and complete.

_____   _____   Year Month Day
Signature of authorized person   Position or office

94

SAMPLE #11
REQUEST TO CONVERT TO THE BUSINESS NUMBER
(form RC6-E)

Revenue Canada / Revenu Canada

REQUEST TO CONVERT TO THE BUSINESS NUMBER

RC6 (E) Rev. 94

- Use this form to convert to the Business Number (BN), your corporate income tax, import/export, payroll deductions, and goods and services tax (GST) account numbers. Account numbers for GST accounts administered by the ministère du Revenu du Québec will not be modified.
- If you need more details about converting, please read the pamphlet called *Converting to the Business Number*.
- You can convert by mail, fax or telephone. (see below)
- If a payroll service bureau, customs broker, or tax professional handles your accounts, check with them before you convert to the BN.
- You can use your own form as long as it gives all the information we request on this form.
- Please print when you complete this form. The information you provide is kept confidential.

1. Identification

Business Type — **Check the box that applies** — **Name – Please underline your last name. (attach a list if you need more space)**

- Sole proprietor — ☐ First and last names
- Partner — ☐ First and last names of partners
- Corporation — ☐ Name which is on your incorporation papers
- Other — ☐ (Charities, non-profit organizations, associations) Show your organization's name

Other names: please list all names (e.g., operating, registered name, trade name) by which your business is known.

2. Contact person

We will send confirmation of BN conversion, as well as subsequent BN general information, to the contact person you name. The contacts you have already identified for each of your accounts will remain the same.

First name — Last name — Language of communication: English ☐ French ☐

Mailing address

City/municipality — Province/territory/state, country — Postal/zip code

Telephone ( ) — It is important that we are able to call you if we have questions about your conversion request. Please be sure to give us your telephone number.

3. Account numbers to be converted (You have to convert all your accounts at the same time)

GST registration number (including GST numbers administered by the Ministère du Revenu du Québec) ....

Corporate income tax account number ....

*Payroll deductions account number(s) (exclude payroll deductions accounts prefixed by NR) ....

*Import/export account number(s) ....

Note: Attach a list if you need more space.

I would like to start using my BN on: Year   Month   Day

Residents of Canada
- **Mail** this form or your own form to us in the postage paid return envelope provided.
- **Fax** us this form at 1-800-959-8280 anytime.
- **For English service, call** us toll free at 1-800-959-8297 (in Canada) during business hours in your local area.
- **For French service, call** us toll free at 1-800-959-8299 (in Canada) during business hours in your local area.

Non-residents of Canada
- **Mail** this form or your own form to us in the envelope provided.
- **Fax** us this form at (613) 941-0101 anytime.
- **For English service, call** us at (613) 941-0100 from 8:15 a.m. to 5 p.m. (Eastern time).
- **For French service, call** us at (613) 941-0110 from 8:15 a.m. to 5 p.m. (Eastern time).

About two weeks after we receive your completed form, we will send you confirmation of your new BN, a list of your converted accounts, and the date you can start using your BN. Please keep a copy of this form in case we have to contact you.

Printed in Canada

SAMPLE #12
CUSTOMS CARGO CONTROL DOCUMENT
(form A-8A)

```
Revenue Canada          Revenu Canada
Customs, Excise and     Accise, Douanes et Impôt      Acquittal No. / N° de l'acquittement
Taxation
IN BOND        CUSTOMS CARGO CONTROL DOCUMENT
EN DOUANE      DOCUMENT DE CONTRÔLE DU FRET DES DOUANES

U.S. Port of Exit / Bureau de sortie des É.-U.   In Transit / En transit
Blaine, WA

Manifest from / Manifeste de    To / A
Pacific Highway B.C.   Pacific Highway B.C.    Carrier Code              Cargo Control No.
                                               Code du transporteur      N° de contrôle du fret
Consignee Name and Address / Nom et adresse du destinataire
Lucky Bean African Imports                     21TN                      9241949

Shipper Name and Address / Nom et adresse de l'expéditeur
P.R. Exports
1234 Federal Way                               Previous Cargo Control No. / N° de contrôle du fret antérieur
Seattle, Washington

No. of pkgs.   Description and Marks    Weight   Rate    Advances   Prepaid      Collect
Nombre de colis Désignation et marques  Poids    Taux    Avances    Port payé    Port dû

2 CTNS         Pencils                  132 KG


Foreign Point of Lading / Port de chargement étranger   Location of Goods / Emplacement des marchandises

Name of Carrier / Nom du transporteur                   Vehicle Identification / Identification du véhicule
S.A.M. Motor Express  Seattle, WA
A 8A (93/03)

                    MAIL COPY / EXEMPLAIRE DE LA POSTE
```

4. The Canada Customs invoice

If you do not have a commercial invoice from your supplier, you must provide a pro forma or a Canada Customs invoice in support of your entry. At one time you were required to submit this document along with your entry, regardless of what other documentation you had. Today, however, a commercial invoice or a pro forma invoice serves the same purpose and is acceptable in virtually any form (typed, handwritten, by fax, computer prepared), so long as it contains the same information, including the following:

(a) Buyer and seller of the goods

(b) Shipping date

(c) Country of origin of the goods

(d) Transportation mode and place of direct shipment to Canada

(e) Country of transhipment — any country through which the goods may have been shipped, in addition to the country of origin (if applicable)

(f) A full description of the goods, including quantity

(g) Price paid or payable

(h) Currency of settlement

If the total value of your goods is less than C $1 200, or they qualify for tax and duty-free entry, information requirements are less stringent. In such an instance, you need only provide a commercial invoice or a pro forma that contains the following information:

(a) Buyer and seller of the goods

(b) Price paid or payable

(c) A full description of the goods, including quantity

You have already had a look at a commercial invoice, above. As you can see from Sample #14, the Canada Customs invoice, with 25 different spaces or "fields" to complete, is almost identical. In general, it is a more formal document than its substitutes.

5. Other forms

You may require other forms, including a Certificate of Origin (form A), a Certificate of Origin for imports from a NAFTA country (form B-232E), and an Application for Permit (Ext-1466), depending on the nature of your goods.

(a) Certificate of Origin (form A)

Form A applies to goods produced in countries entitled to the General Preferential Tariff (GPT), the Least Developed Developing Country Tariff (LDDC), and the Commonwealth Caribbean Countries Tariff (CARIBCAN). Your supplier obtains a form A certificate from a certifying body in his or her country, as named in the list of Authorized Certifying Authorities contained in Schedule II of the tariff. You must provide it to Customs at the time of the release of your goods, along with a copy of a bill of lading indicating Canada as the final destination of the goods. (Under certain circumstances, the good may be transhipped through other countries.)

(b) Certificate of Origin (B-232E)

Form B-232E applies to goods produced in the NAFTA countries and eligible for the United States Tariff (UST), the Mexico Tariff (MT), or the Mexico-United States Tariff (MUST). The certificate can be completed by either the exporter or the producer (actual manufacturer) of your goods. It does not have to be the original (a fax copy is acceptable), nor does it require the signature of a certifying body. Nor do you have to present it for release of your goods. You must, however, have a properly completed copy of the certificate in your possession and be able to produce it for Customs officials on request.

Throughout this book we refer to this particular Certificate of Origin as form B-232E. This is only the number assigned to it by Canada Customs. Customs authorities in the other two NAFTA countries doubtless have the same form with a different number, for use by their own people. In other words, the "B-232E" reference is not uniformly applicable across all three NAFTA countries, and no one will know what you're talking about if you refer to the number in correspondence with American or Mexican suppliers.

(c) Application for Permit (Ext-1466)

You or your customs broker complete an Application for Permit (Ext-1466) when you are importing goods that are subject to a quota. Quotas — precise limits on the number or volume of goods that can be imported annually — are established by the federal government as a means of protecting Canada's domestic industries. The Canadian clothing industry, for example, is protected by quotas. If you're planning to import T-shirts or some other article of apparel, you must apply to Ottawa before you can obtain your permit. Quotas exist on many other types of goods as well, of course, including some kinds of foods. (See Appendix 1 for information on contacting the appropriate government office.)

The permit process may begin when you first place your order with an exporter in another country. That exporter — let's say he or she is based in Hong Kong — goes to his or her own government offices to look up the quota and determine how many items can still be exported to Canada in the current year. (In this case, for the sake of accurate recordkeeping, Hong Kong and not Canada is responsible for maintaining quota records.) If the quota has been reached, your exporter cannot send your

SAMPLE #13
CUSTOMS CARGO CONTROL ABSTRACT
(form A-10)

98

SAMPLE #14
CANADA CUSTOMS INVOICE

JBE — Canada Customs Invoice

Page 1 of 1 Pages

1 Vendor All American Exporting Company 123 Main Street Glendora, CA 91740-5330	**2 Date of Direct Shipment to Canada** Jul-28-1995 **3 Other References i.e. Purchase Order No.** PO# 2121
4 Consignee Great Canadian Importing Company C/O Acme Storage 345 South Street Vancouver, BC V7H 3X3	**5 Purchaser's Name & Address if other than Consignee** Great Canadian Importing Company 678 Broadway Vancouver, BC V6C 2S6 **6 Country of Transhipment** N/A **7 Country of Origin** U.S.A.
8 Transportation Mode and Place of Direct Shipment to Canada Sam's Transport Company Glendora, CA	**9 Conditions of Sale and Terms of Payment** Sale - Net 30 days **10 Currency of Settlement** U.S. Dollars

11 No. of Pkgs.	12 Description	13 Quantity	14 Unit Price	15 Total
24 cartons	Kroehler Model 789 Guest Chairs - Oak Kroehler Model 567 Executive Desks	12 12	200.00 2,500.00	2,400.00 30,000.00

16 If any of fields 1 to 17 are included on an attached invoice, place an "X" in the box Invoice No. _____ [ ]	17 Total Weight Net 4800# Gross 5000#	18 Invoice Total $32,400.00

19 Exporter's Name & Address if other than Vendor	20 Originator Name & Address S.A. Miller, Controller All American Importing Company 123 Main Street Glendora, CA 91740-5330 Tel (714) 924-7788 Fax (714) 924-7789
21 Department Ruling (if applicable)	**22 If fields 23 to 25 are not applicable, place an "X" in the box [X]**

23 If included in field 17 indicate amount	24 If not included in field 17 indicate amount	25 Place an "X" if applicable
a) Transportation charges, expenses and insurance from the place of direct shipment to Canada $ _____ b) Costs for construction, erection and assembly incurred after importation to Canada $ _____ c) Export Packing $ _____	a) Transportation charges, expenses and insurance to the place of direct shipment to Canada $ _____ b) Amounts for commissions other than buying commissions $ _____ c) Export Packing $ _____	a) Royalty payments or subsequent proceeds are payable by the purchaser [ ] b) The purchaser has supplied goods or services for use in the production of these goods [ ]

J.B. Ellis & Co. Ltd.
Customs Brokers
Customs Consultants
Freight Forwarders

P.O. Box 12100
Suite 2730 Harbour Centre
555 West Hastings Street
Vancouver, B.C., Canada V6B 4N5

Tel: (604) 684-1254
Fax: (604) 684-3342

"For Service from Coast to Coast Across Canada"

99

order. If not, he or she obtains an export licence and forwards a copy to you.

You or your broker then complete form Ext-1466 and submit it to the relevant office in Ottawa (along with a cheque covering the current fee for a permit) where it is reviewed and approved, and a permit then issued. If your broker is doing the work for you, the permit may be issued on the same day at the regional Customs office, via Customs' computerized system. If you are submitting the application yourself, by mail, expect the process to take longer. You can, of course, request that the permit be returned to you by courier; just include your instructions with your form. Sample #15 shows an Application for Permit (form Ext-1466) and Sample #16 shows a typical import permit.

6. Canada Customs Coding form (B-3)

Form B-3 is perhaps the most fundamental of all the documents we've discussed so far. It is the basic consumption entry form for all imported goods destined for commercial use in Canada, regardless of value, and the form you attach all your other documentation to. If you are importing your goods yourself, you must complete a B-3 and submit it to Canada Customs, along with all other required documentation, before your shipment is released to you. Your broker, on the other hand, normally completes the same form after the shipment has been released, as a result of Customs' RMD or "Release on Minimal Documentation" program. (RMD and details on how to complete a B-3 are discussed in chapter 11.)

7. An Adjustment Request

If you have overpaid duties and taxes for your goods, or not paid enough, you (or your customs broker) must complete an Adjustment Request (form B-2) as the first step in getting your money back or paying the shortfall. (More information and an example of a B-2 form are provided in chapter 12 as Sample #24.)

8. Application for Duty Remission

For remission of duty in the case of some types of machines and equipment, you (or your broker) must complete an Application for Duty Remission under the Machinery Remission program (form K-122). You can apply for remission of duty on most machines, equipment and production and replacement parts that are "of a class or kind not available from production in Canada," and are not listed as such in Customs Memoranda D8-5-1 or D8-5-2. (With a remission you avoid paying duty.)

The Machinery Remission program was developed several years ago by the federal government to permit Canadian industry to import machinery from abroad when it's not produced in Canada. As a novice importer, you would be well advised to seek advice from a customs broker or consultant if you believe you are eligible for this program. More details on it are contained in chapter 12 on duty relief along with an example of the relevant form.

9. The Drawback Claim

You (or your customs broker) complete a Drawback Claim, form K-32, for drawback of duty paid on goods that qualify under the Customs' Drawback program (see Sample #26 in chapter 12). The subject of drawbacks, like remissions, is unlikely to interest or involve the beginning importer unless you are a manufacturer. We include it here to provide a more complete list of typical import documents and also to mention one application of the K-32 that you may need to know something about, even as a beginner (with a drawback you are reimbursed for duty paid).

As you'll discover on reading the detailed discussion of drawbacks in chapter 12, drawbacks on duty are made when a shipment is imported into Canada, then further processed or exported in exactly

SAMPLE #15
APPLICATION FOR PERMIT
(form Ext-1466)

Department of Foreign Affairs and International Trade / Ministère des Affaires étrangères et du Commerce international

APPLICATION FOR PERMIT / DEMANDE DE LICENCE

DO NOT USE SHADED AREAS
NE PAS UTILISER LES ZONES OMBRAGÉES

- Permit Type / Type de licence: ☐ Import ☐ Export
- Transaction No. / N° de transaction
- Date
- Permit No. / Licence n°
- Company File No. / N° de dossier de la société
- Canadian Resident / Résident du Canada: ☐ Yes/Oui ☐ No/Non
- Application I.D. / I.D. de Demande
- Officer Identification / Identification de l'agent
- Name of Importer-Exporter / Nom de l'importateur-exportateur
- Name and Address of Applicant / Nom et adresse du requérant
- Send Permit to / Envoyer licence à: ☐ Company / Société ☐ Applicant / Requérant
- Name and address of Supplier / Consignee / Nom et adresse du fournisseur / destinataire
- Language / Langue: ☐ English / Anglais ☐ French / Français
- Country of Origin — finished product / Pays d'origine — produit fini
- Imported From / Pays d'importation
- Submitting Outpost / Soumis par
- Exported To / Exporté au
- Country of Origin — raw material / Pays d'origine — matière première FIB/FIB YRN/FIL. FAB/TISS
- Effective Date / Date en vigueur D/J M Y/A
- NAFTA Processing / Traitement ALENA
  - TPL - Tariff Preference Level / Niveau de Préférence Tarifaire
  - SS - Short Supply / Disponibilité Limitée
  - DM - De Minimis / De Minimis
  - DB - 50% Debit / 50% Débit
- Expiry Date / Date d'échéance D/J M Y/A
- Canadian Port of Entry / Clearance / Port de sortie / d'entrée canadien
- Date of Shipment / Date d'envoi D/J M Y/A
- Date of Entry - Exit / Date d'entré/sortie D/J M Y/A
- Documentation Attached / Documentation ci-jointe: ☐ Yes/Oui ☐ No/Non
- Permit to be / Licence devra être: ☐ Mailed / Postée ☐ Held for pick-up / Retenue pour collecte ☐ By courier collect / Par messagerie collecte ☐ Other (specify) / Autre (préciser)
- Manually Issued / Délivrée à la main ☐

Agree't No. / N° d'acc.	Commodity Code / Code de Produit	Description	Permit Quantity / Quantité de lic.	Unit / Unité	Value ($ Can) / Valeur ($ Can)	Doc Quantity / Quantité Doc

- Permit to be Issued at / Licence sera livrée
- Document No. / N° de documentation
- Document Date / Date de la documentation D/J M Y/A

OTHER TERMS AND CONDITIONS / AUTRES STIPULATIONS ET CONDITIONS

Canada

EXT 1466 (93/11)

SAMPLE #16
PERMIT
(form Ext-1054)

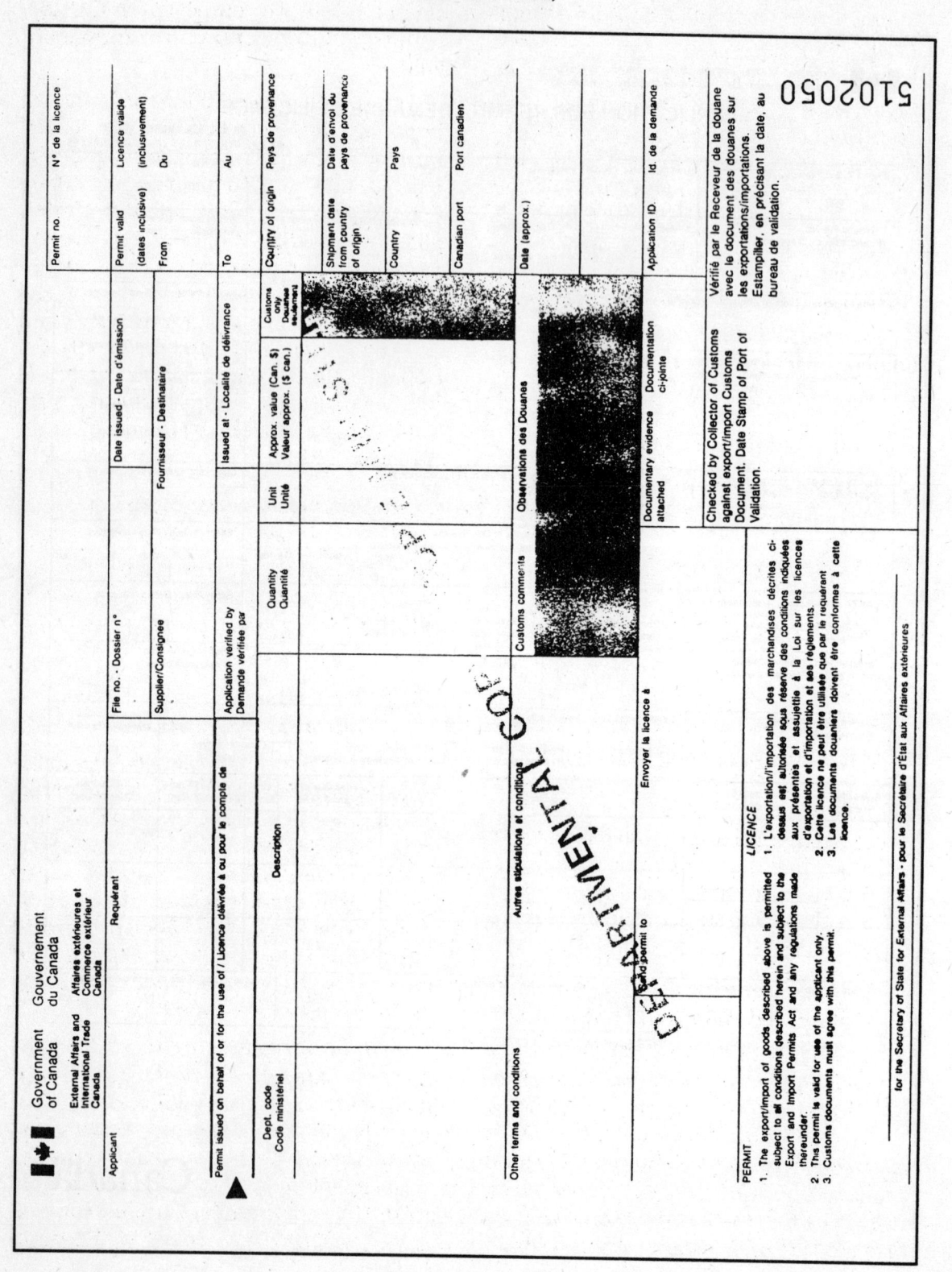

the same condition. A shipment you ordered and imported in error, for example, would qualify, as would the surplus of a shipment you've decided to return to your foreign supplier.

Under such circumstances, you would export your goods, completing an E-15 Certificate of Identification of Goods Exported or Destroyed, and having it verified by a Customs officer. Then you would file a K-32, using the E-15 or other proof of export as your supporting document. Drawback claims may be filed up to four years after the goods have been entered.

Note: the "E" contained in the reference number of several forms refers to the fact that the form is in English. The French version of the forms is also available under the same reference number, but with an "F."

b. RETURNING PRODUCTS TO AN AMERICAN SUPPLIER

For those of you who are planning to import goods from the United States, there are three forms you should be familiar with in case you decide to return a shipment. These are less used, of course, than the import documentation just reviewed, but there may be a time when you are dissatisfied with a shipment and wish to get your money back — including any duty you paid out when you first imported the goods. An important point to remember in the case of all documentation for U.S. exports for whatever reason: Always quote the HS classification number of the items being exported.

1. Declaration for Free Entry of Returned American Products

Provided the goods are of U.S. origin, you (or your customs broker) complete a Declaration for Free Entry of Returned American Products (form 3311), usually available from any Canadian customs broker or your nearest U.S. Customs office. This document, as you can see from Sample #17, is self-explanatory and simple to complete. It serves to advise American authorities that your shipment of U.S. goods is being returned in exactly the same condition as it was on receipt in Canada, without improvements or any increase in value.

This whole subject brings to mind an important difference between the American and Canadian approach to importation, a difference sometimes missed by even major companies. In the United States, every time foreign goods are exported and then re-imported, they are subject to import duties. In Canada, on the other hand, once you have paid duties and taxes on foreign goods, you can export and re-import them without further charges as "duty and taxes previously paid," provided they have not been advanced in condition or value.

2. Commercial or pro forma invoice

You must complete a commercial invoice or pro forma invoice (by hand, if necessary), just as you would for goods you were selling to an American purchaser in an ordinary sales transaction.

3. Certificate of Destruction/Exportation

You next complete a Certificate of Destruction/Exportation (form E-15) for Customs' examination and certification (see Sample #18). The E-15 Certificate has several applications. It is used, for example, when you're returning goods that are not as ordered, when goods have been ordered in error, or if items are being exported for repair. It's also used if goods are being destroyed instead of exported.

As its name suggests, it confirms that the goods in question are no longer in your possession and, once validated by Customs, becomes the main supporting document for any claim you make on a B-2 Adjustment Request for a refund of duty paid. The phrase "under Customs supervision" contained in a number of "D" series

Memoranda means simply that a form E-15 must be completed and certified by a Canada Customs officer who, in so doing, is verifying the export or destruction.

In cases where an E-15 is not available, Customs will usually accept other forms of proof of export, such as a signed bill of lading and/or a copy of the foreign consumption entry for the returned product.

RECOMMENDED READING

Canada. Revenue Canada. *The Business Number and Your Revenue Canada Accounts: January 1995.* [Ottawa]: Government of Canada, 1994.

Canada. Revenue Canada, Customs, Excise and Taxation. *D17 Memoranda on Accounting and Release Procedures.* [Ottawa]: Government of Canada.

Lindsay, Thomas. *An Outline of Customs in Canada.* Calgary: Erin Publications, 1991.

SAMPLE #17
DECLARATION FOR FREE ENTRY OF RETURNED AMERICAN PRODUCTS
(form 3311)

DEPARTMENT OF THE TREASURY
UNITED STATES CUSTOMS SERVICE

Form Approved
OMB No. 1515-0043

DECLARATION FOR FREE ENTRY OF RETURNED AMERICAN PRODUCTS

19 CFR 10.1, 10.5, 10.6, 10.67, 12.41, 123.4, 143.23, 145.35, 162.1c

1. PORT & DISTRICT
2. DATE
3. ENTRY NO. & DATE
4. NAME OF MANUFACTURER
5. CITY AND STATE OF MANUFACTURE
6. REASON FOR RETURN
7. U.S. DRAWBACK PREVIOUSLY ☐ CLAIMED ☐ NOT CLAIMED
8. PREVIOUSLY IMPORTED UNDER TSUSA 864.05? ☐ YES ☐ NO
9. MARKS, NUMBERS, AND DESCRIPTION OF ARTICLES RETURNED
10. VALUE*

*If the value of the article is $10,000 or more and the articles are not clearly marked with the name and address of U.S. manufacturer, please attach copies of any documentation or other evidence that you have that will support or substantiate your claim for duty free status as American Goods Returned.

11. I declare that the information given above is true and correct to the best of my knowledge and belief; that the articles described above are the growth, production, and manufacture of the United States and are returned without having been advanced in value or improved in condition by any process of manufacture or other means; that no drawback bounty, or allowance has been paid or admitted thereon, or on any part thereof; and that if any notice(s) of exportation of articles with benefit of drawback ☐ was ☐ were filed upon exportation of the merchandise from the United States, such notice(s) ☐ has ☐ have been abandoned.

12. NAME OF DECLARANT
13. TITLE OF DECLARANT
14. NAME OF CORPORATION OR PARTNERSHIP (If any)
15. SIGNATURE (See note)

NOTE: If the owner or ultimate consignee is a corporation, this form must be signed by the president, vice president, secretary, or treasurer of the corporation, or by any employee or agent of the corporation who holds a power of attorney and a certificate by the corporation that such employee or agent has or will have knowledge of the pertinent facts.

Notice required by Paperwork Reduction Act of 1980: This information is needed to ensure that importers/exporters are complying with U.S. customs laws, to allow us to compute and collect the right amount of money, to enforce other agency requirements, and to collect accurate statistical information on imports. Your response is mandatory.

Customs Form 3311 (112084)

*U.S GPO 1988-0-542-156/61101

SAMPLE #18
CERTIFICATE OF DESTRUCTION/EXPORTATION
(form E-15)

10
DETERMINING THE LANDED COST OF YOUR GOODS

This chapter provides a step-by-step approach to determining exactly how much your imports will cost you. A summary of everything discussed so far, it serves as a quick refresher before we carry on with the last few chapters.

Landed goods are those that have arrived at the final destination and been processed and released to you. The landed cost of goods is the total of all the costs associated with their shipment and importation.

a. WHAT DO LANDED COSTS INCLUDE?

Landed costs include everything. All the obvious costs, including the purchase price of the goods and shipping charges, contribute to the landed cost. But so do some that aren't so obvious:

- (a) Any long distance phone calls you make or faxes you send from time of order to receipt of shipment
- (b) The bank fees for obtaining an international money order or a letter of credit
- (c) Cargo insurance
- (d) Your customs broker's fee
- (e) Cartage charges for dropping off your goods at your home or warehouse
- (f) Any other miscellaneous charges

Only after these are all accounted for can you price your goods realistically for the Canadian market.

This chapter repeats the steps in the importing process discussed previously, but this time focuses on expenses and makes special reference to the minor expenses we all tend to forget. Each category following identifies a general cost and is broken down into subsections where appropriate.

You may decide to exclude certain costs and place them in the category of office expenses, to be calculated separately at year end. It doesn't really matter how you account for them — they all must be paid out of the dollars you make selling your goods. The advantage to adding up costs on a per-shipment basis, at least to begin with, is that you have a better notion of the cost of your total operation and a figure to compare later shipments to, as you increase your understanding and expertise.

b. PURCHASE PRICE

The purchase price refers to the price you pay for your goods and their packaging — from the factory where they were made (ex factory) or from the point of direct shipment to Canada (ex Hong Kong, for example). This is the figure that appears on your supplier's invoice and is the same one used by Canada Customs to verify duty and taxes payable before the goods are released to you. Any additional charges your supplier wishes to make (for serving as your agent, for example, in a purchase) should be listed separately on the invoice. This is an important point: Customs should know the full price for your goods. Try to ensure that all charges are included on your commercial invoice, then satisfy yourself of their dutiable status and confirm this with your customs broker prior to presentation of your entry. If you are doing your entry yourself, you may wish to confirm the dutiable status of some charges with Customs.

When you are making a final accounting of your costs, remember to include any costs related to contacting your supplier when you place your order and afterwards. Most exporters, even in third-world countries, have a telephone and fax machine (or access to them). Faxes are cheaper than telephoning and provide you with a written record of your communication. Yet charges can still mount up, particularly if you are dealing with someone who is inexperienced or not a native English speaker or whose country has an unreliable telephone system, as in the case of Swaziland or Poland.

It may even be worth making a trip to the export country to ensure that your supply and shipping arrangements are well organized, as discussed in chapter 1. We're not suggesting that you add the cost of an international air ticket onto your landed-cost list, but bear in mind that a portion of your travel, faxes, and telephone calls should always be included in any calculation you make to determine the final price of your goods.

c. FINDER'S FEE AND FOREIGN COMMISSION FEE

If you rely on someone to locate goods for you in the export country, or negotiate with a supplier's agent to obtain your goods, expect to pay a finder's fee or a foreign commission fee. The amount will vary, depending on the services you've requested: three percent to someone for attending an auction and bidding on an article on your behalf; five percent to someone else for locating a particularly good piece of machinery; a fixed fee to friends or relatives who purchase goods for you. This same approach is not unusual in Canada and is a full-time business for some companies abroad. Commissions are discussed in Memorandum D13-4-12 of the "D" series Customs regulations.

d. PACKING AND SHIPPING CHARGES

If you arrange to have your goods packed separately, you will have to pay a fee for this service and may well pay duty on the packing materials themselves. It could be worth the extra cost, however. Suppliers who are inexperienced in exporting sometimes have little idea of how to pack for international transport.

Experienced suppliers often have shipping agents (also called freight forwarders). Shipping agents complete all the necessary documentation, including insurance, and make the shipping arrangements, as per your instructions to the supplier. Then the supplier pays for the service and passes the charges on to you. You can also opt to employ your own shipping agent in the export country, if business looks promising, and be billed directly for the service.

In addition to the main air or ocean freight charge, you could find yourself paying the following:

(a) *Inland freight*, the charge for transporting your goods from the factory to the dock or airport. As already discussed in chapter 6 on valuation, all shipping charges within the country where they're produced are dutiable until your goods arrive at the point of direct shipment to Canada.

(b) *A dockside storage charge* for your goods if they arrive at the port of shipment ahead of the ship they're to be transported on. In Asia, this is called "godown" and may be dutiable, depending on the point of direct shipment for the goods, as discussed in chapter 6. This type of charge is rarely made against air shipments.

(c) *Wharfage charges*, in the case of ocean shipments. These charges vary according to the policies and practices of the port of shipment and are also referred to as cargo, loading, or stowing charges. You pay the same charge again at the port of destination.

(d) *Lighterage charges*, named after a lighter or barge, again in the case of ocean shipments. These apply if your goods are transported by lighter to the ship before being loaded. This happens if the port is overcrowded or too shallow to accommodate a cargo vessel, as is often the case with third-world ports.

(e) *An export tax on your goods*, particularly if they're raw materials. This tax is usually assessed against you as the purchaser of the goods and can be exorbitant, far exceeding the original cost of the merchandise. Such a tax provides third-world countries with an excellent means of obtaining foreign currency, and they exploit it.

(f) *Miscellaneous shipping charges* once your goods reach their port of destination or the airport terminal. In the case of ocean freight, these may take several forms, such as a special sorting charge, a shrink-wrapping charge, or a heavy lift charge. If the goods have been shipped by air, you may be obliged to pay an airport tax before they're released to you and storage charges if there is a delay in their removal beyond the three to five working days most airlines allow for pick up.

(g) *Cartage charges* once your goods have been released. Of course, you may opt to do your own cartage, but it's an expense nonetheless — even if it amounts to little more than the rental of a van for a few hours or a few dollars for gas. Be sure to include it on your list.

e. DUTY AND TAXES

We have already discussed how duty is calculated on your goods and the taxes you can expect to be charged by Canada Customs (see chapters 4, 6, and 7). These are among your major expenses — like purchase price and shipping costs — and must be included in any landed-cost list. If you are fortunate enough to import your products duty free because they're original works of art, for example, or are favored under a particular trade agreement with the exporting country, remember that you must still pay GST on them (which you can recover in most cases) and may also be required to pay excise tax.

Canada Customs will charge you for special services, such as the after-hours clearance of goods. This happens more often than one might think. Consider, for example, the company that's had an equipment failure and needs a new part from abroad to maintain its production schedule. Or the wholesaler planning to attend a giftware show with products scheduled to arrive within hours of the show's opening on a Sunday. In both cases, the companies or their customs brokers must pay for a Customs officer to release the item at a charge of two hours minimum, plus the cost of transporting the officer to the airport or dock if required.

f. BANK CHARGES

Depending on the payment arrangements you've made with your supplier, bank charges can vary from the cost of an international bank draft in Canadian funds (approximately $8) to the fee for processing a letter of credit ($100 or more). Conducting business in Canadian funds is the cheapest approach, but it may not be acceptable to the supplier. American dollars are more acceptable, particularly in third-world countries, and it may be to your advantage eventually to establish an American dollar account both for convenience and as a means of keeping conversion costs to a minimum.

As mentioned in the discussion of letters of credit in chapter 2, your bank may insist that you insure your goods as a further means of protecting its investment in you.

Whatever the total bank charges, add them to your list. Also include the cost of sending the payment to your supplier. This can be considerable, if you opt to wire the money, or minimal, if you send it by ordinary or registered mail.

g. CUSTOMS BROKER'S FEES

A customs broker charges a basic entry fee, usually referred to as a brokerage fee, for the preparation of an entry. Then, depending on the type and extent of services you request, he or she may charge an ancillary fee and make other charges. It's important to sit down with the broker first and discuss exactly what you want as these costs can mount up and make a considerable difference to the final landed cost of your products. A broker will pay your airport handling fee for you when your goods are released, for example, but charge a processing fee for the service. The broker will also pay your duty, for which, depending on your payment pattern, he or she may charge a disbursement fee; or arrange to have your goods delivered, for another small fee. Brokerage services can be as complete or as basic as you want.

h. CALCULATING YOUR LANDED COSTS

Turn now to Worksheet #4 to help you calculate your landed costs. If you've already completed a shipment, try to fill in as much of the form as possible. You'll see that, in addition to helping you establish a pricing structure, the form might serve as a secondary record of each shipment, giving you at a glance, a summary of all shipment details.

RECOMMENDED READING

Canada. Revenue Canada, Customs, Excise and Taxation. *D17 Memoranda on Accounting and Release Procedures*. [Ottawa]: Government of Canada.

WORKSHEET #4
CALCULATING YOUR LANDED COSTS

Shipment of: _____

_____

Supplier: _____

_____

_____

Shipped by: _____

Date ordered: _____

   sent: _____

   received: _____

Payment method: _____

1. Purchase price, foreign currency $ _____

   Canadian dollars   _____

2. Finder's fee/foreign commission fee   _____

3. Packing/shipping charges:

      export packing   _____

      inland freight   _____

      ocean freight   _____

      air freight   _____

      related costs, ocean freight:

        dockside storage   _____

        wharfage charges, departure   _____

        wharfage charges, destination   _____

        lighterage   _____

      other costs, ocean or air:

        export tax   _____

        shipping agent   _____

        airport tax   _____

WORKSHEET #4 — Continued

    cartage after release:
        commercial   _____
        self   _____

4. Insurance   _____

5. Canada Customs charges:
    duty
    excise tax
    GST
    special service   _____

6. Bank charges:
    draft
    letter of credit
    to send payment   _____

7. Customs broker:
    basic entry
    other   _____

8. Miscellaneous:
    telephone
    fax
    other   _____

TOTAL $_____

11
RELEASE AND ACCOUNTING TO CUSTOMS

This chapter provides a discussion of the forms to complete and procedures to follow once your goods have arrived in Canada and are being held, prior to release by Canada Customs.

As we have already remarked several times, the computer has had a considerable impact on importing over the past ten years and continues to revolutionize Canada Customs' method of operations. Only customs brokers and large-scale importers have really been able to take advantage of these new developments, however. Those of us who don't employ a broker or an in-house import clearance technician are still obliged to process our shipments manually.

a. HOW IT'S DONE BY A CUSTOMS BROKER

Just to demonstrate how much things have changed for customs brokers, let's look briefly at how the average broker handles a routine shipment today.

The process consists of two phases: getting the shipment released and accounting for it. As soon as a shipment arrives at its destination, the carrier submits a cargo control document to Customs. This prompts Customs to open a file on its computer system. At the same time, a copy of the document goes to the customs broker, who assembles the Customs or commercial invoices, permits, Certificate of Origin, and any other supporting documentation and presents this "RMD" package to Customs with bar-code labels affixed. The bar code consists of two parts: the brokerage company's account/security number and the

SAMPLE #19
BAR CODE

13540-000366228 / J.B. ELLIS & CO.

Brokerage company's account/security number

Shipment's transaction number

transaction number of the specific shipment being entered. An example of a bar code is shown in Sample #19.

Customs makes a determination to release the goods immediately or examine them. This depends, to a large extent, on where the shipment is from and who the foreign vendor is. A shipment from any country with a reputation for drug trafficking, for example, will almost certainly be detained for examination, delaying its release for a day or two.

Customs releases most shipments immediately. This process is referred to as RMD or "Release on Minimal Documentation"; and to qualify for it, a broker must first post sufficient security with Customs' headquarters in Ottawa. Again, the brokerage's security number forms the first part of the code, confirming that it has posted security. Any importer capable of putting up the required sum with Customs may qualify for RMD, but most starting businesses find the cost too prohibitive.

As soon as the shipment is released, the broker has five working days to organize all related documents — in effect, completing and closing Canada Customs' file on the transaction. This is the accounting phase of the importing process and, if the broker fails to meet the deadline, he or she is fined $100 per transaction missed.

As of April 1993, Customs has instituted a new accounting system for low-value shipments (LVS), generally defined as shipments worth less than C $1 200. Called the LVS system, it authorizes customs brokers and certain commercial importers to account for LVSs by the 24th day of the month following the month of their release, instead of the five days mentioned above. This allows Customs to "batch" all low-value shipments and handle them once monthly, instead of processing them on a per-transaction basis.

These procedures have been devised largely to accommodate an industry that has long complained of the hindrance to trade and commerce resulting from manual processing of import transactions. In accordance with current Customs' policies, it assumes that the professional importing community voluntarily abides by Customs regulations without being controlled at every step. As mentioned elsewhere, because of the continued growth of importing over the past several years, Customs has been obliged to take this approach and, to date, it seems to be working effectively.

The next phase of automation in the importing process will be electronic release. This will replace the paper RMD procedures for most shipments. Electronic release is expected to be implemented in December 1995.

b. IMPORTERS DOING THEIR OWN PROCESSING

The main difference between the individual importer and the customs broker is that the individual has to do his or her accounting before getting the goods unless, as mentioned above, he or she can post a bond with Canada Customs beforehand to cover the cost of import duties and taxes on any shipments released but not accounted for.

Assuming that the bond alternative is not available, the individual must obtain a copy of the cargo control document, gather supporting documentation such as a commercial invoice import permit and Certificate of Origin as required, and then complete a form B-3 entry.

c. THE B-3 ENTRY FORM

The B-3 is the standard consumption entry used in the importing process. Take a look at the B-3 shown in Sample #20. You'll notice that every blank space or "field" on the form has been assigned a number in the upper left-hand corner to assist you in ordering your information. Note also that the body of the form contains five classification blocks, each consisting of three lines numbered fields #21 to #42, and separated from each other by their color. These are provided in case your shipment contains more than one commodity.

Appearances can be deceiving; this form is not as easy to complete as it may first appear. Study each field carefully as you examine the form and consult other chapters for more information on some of the requirements. Whatever you do, don't wait until you're in front of a Customs officer with your cargo control document in hand to start filling it in.

Field #1 is the space for your name and address and the business number (importer number) you obtained after applying for it from Customs as discussed in chapters 1 and 9. If you are an active importing firm, you may use your nine-digit taxation employer number here.

Field #2 is completed by Canada Customs if you haven't arranged beforehand to post a bond or security deposit and are not eligible for the RMD program.

Field #3 is for the type of B-3. Write "C" here to show that this document is a final accounting for the release of your goods after you've paid duties and taxes.(The same B-3 form may be used for several purposes, each identified by the letter or number provided in this field.)

Field #4 is for the Customs office number. Write the number of the Customs office releasing your goods. (See Appendix 6 for a full list of office numbers.)

Field #5 is where you write your GST number. (Don't include the preceding alphabetic characters.)

Field #6 is for the payment code; leave this space blank.

Field #7 is for mode of transport number. Write the number for the transport mode for your goods. The codes are as follows:

(a) Rail: 6
(b) Air: 1
(c) Marine: 9
(d) Highway: 2
(e) Mail: 3

Field #8 is for number of the port of unlading. Write the three-digit number of the Customs office releasing your goods. (See Appendix 6 for Customs office numbers.)

Field #9 is for the total value for duty (VFD). Insert this figure once you've filled in Field #36.

Field #10 is for the subheader number. Write "1" if you're using only one entry form, and number any additional forms sequentially. New subheaders are used on additional pages when any part of Fields #11 to #19 is changed.

Field #11 is where you note the vendor's name and address as shown on his or her invoice to you. If your goods are from the United States you must give the vendor's state code (see Appendix 7) and zip code as well.

Field #12 is for the name of the country of origin. Fill in the code of the country where the goods were finished to their present state. (If they're American made, use the state code; otherwise consult Appendix 7 for the appropriate country code.)

Field #13 is for code of the place of export. If your goods are from the United States, fill in the appropriate state code or U.S. foreign trade zone (see Appendix 8). If they're from any other country, fill in the country code.

Field #14 is for the tariff treatment code. Fill in the code for the tariff treatment under which your goods have been imported, as follows:

(a) British Preferential Tariff: code 1
(b) Most Favoured Nation Tariff: code 2
(c) General Tariff: code 3
(d) Australian Trade Agreement: code 4
(e) New Zealand Trade Agreement: code 5

SAMPLE #20
CANADA CUSTOMS CODING FORM
(form B-3)

CANADA CUSTOMS CODING FORM — PROTECTED (WHEN COMPLETED)

IMPORTER NAME AND ADDRESS — NO. CAEJ12345

GFM TRADING COMPANY
555 WEST HASTINGS STREET
VANCOUVER, BC, CANADA
V6B 4N5

13540-000814151   J.B. Ellis & Co. Ltd.

TYPE	OFFICE NO	GST REGISTRATION NO.	PAYMT CODE	MODE TRANS	PORT OF UNLADING	TOTAL VFD
AB	813	101980837		2	813	11132

SUB HDR NO. 1 — VENDOR NAME

UNITED STATES CAN CO
4186 PARK ROAD
BENICIA, CA UNITED STATES
94510

COUNTRY OF ORIGIN	PLACE OF EXPORT	TARIFF TREATMENT	US PORT OF EXIT
UCA	UCA	10	3004

DIRECT SHIPMENT DATE	CRCY. CODE	TIME LIMIT	FREIGHT
07 14	USD		111

RELEASE DATE: 17 JUL 1995

LOCATION OF GOODS: PACIFIC HIGHWAY

CUSTOMER ORDER NO.: 373713   File# 829588   EXCHANGE RATE: 1.359000

LINE	DESCRIPTION	WEIGHT	PREVIOUS TRANSACTION NO.	SPECIAL AUTHORITY
1	METAL PAINT CANS LESS THAN 50 LITRE C	6199		

CLASSIFICATION NO.	TARIFF CODE	QUANTITY	U/M	VFD CODE	SIMA CODE	RATE OF DUTY	E.T. RATE	RATE OF GST	VALUE FOR CURRENCY CONVERSION
7310.29.99.10		14112.000	NMB	14		3.0		7.0	6,654.80

VALUE FOR DUTY	CUSTOMS DUTIES	SIMA ASSESSMENT	EXCISE TAX	VALUE FOR TAX	GST
9,043.87	271.32			9,315.19	652.06

2	CAN LIDS & PLUGS	1038		
8309.90.00.91			14		3.0		7.0	1,114.84
1,515.07	45.45			1,560.52	109.24

3	PALLETS IN SHUTTLE - AUTHORITY P1006	392		
9814.00.00.10			19		0		51	421.36
572.63	.00			572.63	.00

DECLARATION

I G.F. Mullett (PLEASE PRINT NAME)
of J.B. Ellis + Co. Ltd. (IMPORTER - AGENT)

DECLARE THE PARTICULARS OF THIS DOCUMENT TO BE TRUE AND ACCURATE AND COMPLETE.

DATE: July 18/95   SIGNATURE

CARGO CONTROL NO.: 2ITN-13292319022
CARRIER CODE AT IMPORTATION: 2ITN

DUTIES	316.77
SIMA	.00
EXCISE	.00
GST	761.30
TOTAL	1,078.07

(f) CARIBCAN Countries Trade Agreement: code 7

(g) Least Developed Developing Nations Tariff: code 8

(h) General Preferential Tariff: code 9

(i) United States Tariff: code 10

(j) Mexico Tariff: code 11

(k) Mexico-United States Tariff: code 12

Field #15 is relevant for American goods only, valued at more than C $2 500. Identify the U.S. port of exit — that is, the closest port to the point where your goods were transported into Canada (by whatever means they were shipped). See Appendix 9 for a list of U.S. Customs ports.

Field #16 is the space for the direct shipment date. Fill in the date noted on your Customs or commercial invoice, but only if the currency used in the transaction is not Canadian; otherwise, leave it blank.

Field #17 is for the currency code. Fill in the international data code by referring to the currency codes listed in Appendix 7. The code identifies the currency shown in Field #36.

Field #18 should be completed only if there is an applicable time limit on receiving your goods (applies to temporary imports, such as the 1/60 imports discussed in section **d. 2.**, below).

Field #19 is where you record the shipment charges from the point of direct shipment to you in Canada. In the case of U.S. imports, this need only be completed if your goods are worth more than C $2 500.

Field #20 is for the release date; leave this field blank.

Field #21 is where you number each line in sequence for each tariff classification number (Field #27) assigned.

Field #22 is the description. Show all references to "D" memorandum numbers here — your import permit number, for example, and value and customs ruling numbers, if applicable.

Field #23 is for the previous transaction number and should be left blank.

Field #24 is for the previous transaction line; leave this blank.

Field #25 is for the special authority. Fill in this field with your authority number if you have authority to import goods under special conditions. "Special conditions" are a 1/60 authorization, an order-in-council that authorizes remission of duty, or a tariff customs ruling.

Field #26 is where you specify the correct HS classification number for each commodity in the shipment: each commodity on a separate line, each line numbered in sequence, as described in Field #21 above.

Field #27 is where you note the tariff code if the conditions specified in the concessionary code description apply to your goods and/or circumstances, as indicated in Schedule II of the tariff.

Field #28 is where you note the quantity of goods you're importing in the unit of measure required under the tariff; leave it blank if no unit of measure is applicable.

Field #29 is where you note the unit of measure code used as required in the tariff (see Appendix 10 for codes).

Field #30 is where you should indicate the weight of your shipment to the nearest kilogram on the first line provided for each transaction. (If your goods are from the United States, complete this section only if they're worth more than C $2 500.)

Field #31 is for the Value for Duty (VFD) code. Choose two single-digit codes here: the first to represent whether or not the purchaser and vendor are related, in the case of a sale (code 1 if they are not related and code 2 if they are); the second to indicate what valuation method has been used to establish the value of your goods, as follows:

(a) Price paid or payable without adjustments: code 3

(b) Price paid or payable with adjustments: code 4

(c) Transaction value of identical goods: code 5

(d) Transaction value of similar goods: code 6

(e) Deductive value of imported goods: code 7

(f) Computed value: code 8

(g) Residual method of valuation: code 9

(See sections 48 to 53 of the Customs Act.)

Field #32 is for the SIMA code, used for SIMA assessments, if applicable. The first digit is the special assessment type:

(a) Antidumping: 1

(b) Countervail: 2

(c) Provisional: 3

(d) Surtax: 4

The second digit is the payment mode:

(a) Cash: 1

(b) Bond: 2

(See chapter 8 for more on SIMA.)

Field #33 is where you indicate the rate of duty applicable to your goods according to the tariff. Where both specific and percentage (ad valorem) duty rates apply, show the percentage rate on the first detail line and the specific rate of duty on the next line.

Field #34 is where you show the rate of excise tax (or an exemption code). Leave it blank if excise tax does not apply.

Field #35 is to show the current rate of GST (7% at time of writing).

Field #36 is where you specify the value for currency conversion. This is the invoice value of the goods adjusted to the point where you apply the exchange rate to arrive at the value for duty.

Field #37 is where you specify the value for duty by multiplying the value for currency conversion by the exchange rate. Show the value in Canadian dollars to the cent.

Field #38 is for Customs duty. Specify the amount of duty payable in dollars and cents.

Field #39 is where you fill in the amount of SIMA assessment, if applicable.

Field #40 is where you specify the amount of excise tax you must pay, if applicable.

Field #41 is where you determine the value for tax by adding Fields #37, #38, #39, and #40 together.

Field #42 is where you specify the amount of GST payable in dollars and cents.

Field #43 should be left blank unless you've made a deposit with Customs.

Field #44 is for the warehouse number and should be left blank unless you're entering your goods into a bonded warehouse.

Field #45 is for the cargo control number. Check the upper right corner of your cargo control document for the cargo control number (use the E-14-2 postal reference number, including its alphabetic prefix, in the case of postal shipments).

Field #46 is for Customs duties. Add all the Field #38 lines together to get the Customs duties payable.

Field #47 is for the SIMA assessment. Add all the Field #39 lines together to get the total assessment.

Field #48 is where you add all the Field #40 lines together to get the total excise tax amounts.

Field #49 is where you add all the Field #42 lines together to get the total GST amounts.

Field #50 is where you add all the totals together to get the total duties and taxes you owe the government.

Finally, fill in the name of your company and date and sign your declaration.

d. OTHER ENTRY FORMS

Depending on the purpose for which the goods in question are being imported, different forms may be required. These are discussed below.

1. E-29-B form for temporary imports

A company may import a machine in order to repair it for a foreign customer, in which case it would complete an E-29-B entry form for temporary import. So would an American manufacturer bringing samples of his or her products to a five-day trade show in Toronto.

Because neither company plans to leave the goods permanently in Canada, they may well assume (correctly) that they don't have to pay duties and taxes on them. But the onus is on them to demonstrate that their goods qualify for this status, and they must then see that a bond (or security deposit) is posted with Customs equal to the duties and taxes payable on the goods. Companies that initiate this kind of transaction may be residents or nonresidents of Canada.

There are different regulations in the "D" series Memoranda for each type of temporary import. In the case of sales representative's samples, for example, a reading of the pertinent regulations under D8-1-2 will reveal that the sales rep may be required to provide Canada Customs with an itinerary before being permitted to enter the country. Under the regulations on repairs, another set of requirements applies. We've excerpted a page of the schedule (sections 3 and 5) from Memorandum D8-1-1 to give you an idea of the variety of goods that qualify (see Sample #21).

As in the case of a B-3 entry, the completion of an E-29-B entry form prompts Canada Customs to open a file on the transaction. This file remains open until the temporary imports are exported under supervision, at which time the security deposit is also returned to the company that imported the goods. As long as the goods are in Canada for the purpose indicated on the entry and within the time frame allotted, the importer is not required to pay duty or taxes on them.

2. Another kind of temporary import

The so-called "rental" entries, the $\frac{1}{60}$ and $\frac{1}{120}$ entries must be completed when a company imports goods temporarily, usually for a maximum period of 12 months. Often the goods are equipment, as described under Customs regulations ("D" series, Memorandum D4-5). But they can be other types of items as well: formula cars for racing, for example, or motion picture film. Depending on the nature of the item, the importer must provide certain information to Canada Customs in the application, also as outlined in the regulations.

During the time the goods are in Canada, the importer pays a proportionate amount of duty and taxes on them, on a monthly basis. This figure is determined by establishing the value for duty of the goods, then dividing it by 60 and calculating the duty and taxes on this smaller amount. The importer pays this final figure, a minimum of $25, while the goods are in Canada for a period of up to 12 months. Exactly how much is paid is up to the importer; he or she advises Customs how long he or she will need the goods (for 4 months, for example) and pays the duty and taxes owing for that period. If the importer has to extend this time, he or she merely advises Customs and again files an entry and pays duty and taxes for the extended period. The importer cannot extend beyond 12 months however. At that point he or she must return the goods to a bonded facility or export them under Customs' supervision and begin the application process all over again (or pay the balance of the duties and taxes owing).

The $\frac{1}{120}$ entry is calculated in the same way, but applies to ships and vessels, goods of considerable value, and is therefore determined on a 120 basis.

SAMPLE #21
PAGE FROM CUSTOMS REGULATIONS ON TEMPORARY IMPORTS

	SCHEDULE (sections 3 and 5)			ANNEXE (articles 3 et 5)	
Item	Column I	Column II Class	Article	Colonne I	Colonne II Catérogie
	Goods			**Marchandises**	
15.	Machines and other equipment to be used as temporary replacements for units previously accounted for and undergoing repairs.	2	15.	Machines et autres appareils devant remplacer temporairement ceux qui ont déjà été déclarés en détail et qui subissent des réparations.	2
16.	Articles to be repaired, overhauled or adjusted.	1	16.	Articles devant être réparés, remis en état ou ajustés.	1
17.	Articles to be tested and specialized test equipment permanently attached to or installed on those articles.	1	17.	Articles devant être mis à l'essai et équipement d'essai spécialisé fixé ou installé en permanence sur un article à mettre à l'essai.	1
18.	Specially designed goods imported by an organization referred to in any of Codes 1750 to 1756 of Schedule II to the Act for the maintenance, checking, gauging or repair of scientific equipment in use at or by those organizations.	1	18.	Outils spécialement conçus qu'importe une institution visée aux codes 1750 à 1756 de l'annexe II de la Loi, pour l'entretien, la vérification, le calibrage ou la réparation du matériel scientifique utilisé dans les locaux de ces institutions ou par celles-ci.	1
19.	Specialized test equipment imported by the non-resident manufacturer of an article to be tested in Canada, for use in testing that article.	2	19.	Équipement d'essai spécialisé importé par un fabricant non résident d'un article devant être mis à l'essai au Canada, pour servir à la mise à l'essai de cet article.	2
20.	Equipment, not available from Canadian sources, for use in the testing, evaluating or repair of articles.	2	20.	Matériel qui ne peut être obtenu de sources d'approvisionnement canadiennes et devant servir à la mise à l'essai, à l'évaluation ou à la réparation d'articles.	2
21.	Equipment, not available from Canadian production, for use in the testing of microwave systems or of radiopath routing or for similar use.	2	21.	Matériel qui ne peut être obtenu d'une source de production canadienne et devant servir à effectuer des essais sur les systèmes à hyperfréquences ou sur les systèmes d'acheminement d'ondes radiophoniques ou à des fins semblables.	2
22.	Trucks, equipment and mobile accommodation facilities, not available from Canadian sources, when imported by non-residents for their use in the harvesting of crops.	2	22.	Camions, équipement et installations d'hébergement mobiles, qui ne peuvent être obtenus de sources d'approvisionnement canadiennes, lorsqu'ils sont importés par des non-résidents pour servir à la récolte.	2
23.	Herring pumps, not available from Canadian sources, for use in the unloading of herring during the herring fishing season.	2	23.	Pompes à harengs qui ne peuvent être obtenues de sources d'approvisionnement canadiennes et, devant servir à décharger le hareng au cours de la saison de pêche au hareng.	2
24.	Equipment, not available from Canadian sources, that has been permanently mounted on motor vehicles, for use in exploratory or discovery work in connection with oil or natural gas wells or for the development, maintenance, testing, depletion or production of those wells.	2	24.	Matériel qui ne peut être obtenu de sources d'approvisionnement canadiennes qui a été installé en permanence sur un véhicule automobile et devant servir aux travaux d'exploration ou de découverte des puits de pétrole ou de gaz naturel, ou à la mise en valeur, à l'entretien, à la mise à l'essai, à l'épuisement ou à la production de ces puits.	2
25.	Equipment for use in the conduct of pollution or hygienic surveys in the interest of health or safety.	2	25.	Matériel devant servir aux études sur la pollution et l'hygiène au profit de la santé et de la sécurité.	2
26.	Safety equipment, not available from Canadian sources, for repair or maintenance purposes.	2	26.	Matériel de sécurité qui ne peut être obtenu de sources d'approvisionnement canadiennes et devant servir à la réparation ou à l'entretien.	2

Both the 1/60 and the 1/120 entries are completed on a B-3 entry form and are considered simply a type of B-3. Once a temporary admission entry has been accepted, it becomes an "open file" at Canada Customs and is not closed until the goods are either exported under Customs' supervision, or duty and taxes are paid in full.

Duty and taxes paid out by the importer during the time the goods are in Canada are not refundable. However, should the importer decide to keep the items permanently, the amount paid to date is applied to the total duty and taxes bill.

This type of entry is used by Canadian residents who wish to avoid paying duty and taxes on an expensive item, but still want access to the item in Canada. Take a contractor, for example, retained to lay pipeline across the Straits of Georgia. The company wants to rent a particular type of vessel specifically designed to perform this highly specialized work for the estimated ten-month duration of the contract. No comparable vessel is available in Canada, so the contractor brings the vessel into the country on a 1/120 entry for ten months. He completes the project in eight months, however, and is then in a position to file a refund claim for the two-month balance of duties and taxes already paid.

3. Warehouse and ex warehouse entries

Where an importer wants to import high-volume and/or high-value dutiable goods, but doesn't want to pay duty and taxes on them until they're sold, he or she may store them in a bonded facility. Such facilities are of two types: a public bond area, owned and operated by a storage company, and a private bond area (such as part of the storage yard you've already established for your goods), adequately secured and approved by Customs. A bond area can be as straightforward as the space defined by a line of paint on the pavement of a large, secured storage yard, such as a foreign car company might establish in one of its large lots.

In the case of a private bond area, you must obtain a surety bond (s/b) for the area from a bonding company designated by Customs. A bond covers only the cost of duty and taxes on the secured goods. (Customs specifies the amount of the bond.) It is not insurance and cannot be used to reimburse you for shortage, shrinkage, or damage to the goods. In fact, if you have shortages (for whatever reason) in your bonded area, you, as the bond area operator, are responsible for paying the duty and taxes on the missing items. Customs charges you a nominal fee to have a private bond area and may visit the premises at any time, usually during working hours, to make a routine check of your inventory.

Bonded warehouses are less popular today than they were several years ago when companies carried larger inventories. They are still used to store liquor imports, however, until duty and taxes on the product are paid by the provincial Liquor Control Board or Commission.

A bonded area need not be a concrete-floored warehouse. If you are an importer of leisure craft, for example, it can be a portion of a dock, secured and approved by Customs. You cannot demonstrate your product outside the bond area, however, until all duty and taxes have been paid on it. This requirement is not a problem for importers of moderately priced craft, but can be a real headache for anyone selling one-of-a-kind luxury motor vessels.

When your goods are going into bond, you must complete a B-3 in a Type 10 format. Once the entry has been accepted, you can make arrangements to have your goods transported by a bonded carrier to your warehouse. Such a carrier is one bonded under Canada Customs' requirements, for the purpose of hauling bonded goods.

To take goods out of bond, you must complete another B-3, this time a Type 13, and pay all duty and taxes owing on the items you intend to remove before you move them. Note that you pay duty and taxes at the current rates, not at the rates in place at the time the goods went into bond.

e. WHEN YOUR ENTRY IS INCORRECT

Commodity specialists at Canada Customs routinely review all entries. If an error is detected in the course of such a review, the importer is sent a Detailed Adjustment Statement or DAS, form B-2-1. A DAS shows where adjustments have been made and why, then indicates under what section of the Customs Act you may file an appeal against the decision. It also gives you a deadline for paying any shortfall and advises when interest charges will start being made against the unpaid amount. If you decide to file an appeal, you must pay out the shortfall before proceeding.

Importers who detect a shortfall themselves in duty and taxes paid can submit an amending entry (a B-3, Type 3). Canada Customs will review this entry and send the importer a DAS, confirming the adjustment.

Occasionally Customs determines that someone has overpaid duty and taxes. When this happens it sends out a DAS indicating the change, followed by a refund cheque. As a new importer you should remember that the department is not really in the business of returning money, and you cannot look to them for an automatic refund if you've overpaid.

f. GOODS IMPORTED BY MAIL

In the case of small items, importing by mail may be the easiest and most economical means of shipment — it is often the shipment of choice for imports from the United States. Customs' procedures once the goods arrive are determined by the value of the shipment:

(a) If it's worth less than C $1 200, it is treated much like a non-commercial import. Customs completes a Customs Postal Import form (E-14), itemizing the tariff classification of the goods, rate of duty and taxes, value for duty, the duty and taxes payable, and a handling fee (in effect, a broker's fee). (See Sample #22.) Then it attaches the form to the goods and forwards them to Canada Post for collection of monies owing and delivery.

(b) If it's worth more than C $1 200, Customs sends you a notice to let you know of its arrival and holds the shipment until it receives a properly completed B-3, and all duty and taxes against the shipment are paid. Then it releases the shipment to Canada Post for delivery. (There is no handling fee for commercial processing because you're doing the processing yourself.)

All mail is subject to Customs' inspection and may be opened if it weighs 30 grams or more. Items that weigh less can be opened only with the consent of the recipient or the sender.

In the case of non-commercial imports, the onus is on the exporter to declare the true value of any goods he or she is sending. Any attempt to misrepresent their value could result in processing delays or enforcement action against the goods. Some goods are exempt from duty and taxes, including:

(a) Gifts worth less than $60

(b) Goods for which the value for duty does not exceed $20, as provided under Schedule VII of the Excise Tax Act, not including alcoholic beverages, cigars, cigarettes, manufactured tobacco, and books, periodicals, or magazines

Recipients of non-commercial imports who disagree with the duty and taxes assessed by Customs, or wish to return the goods to their foreign supplier, must complete a Requesting Refund of Duties and Taxes, form B-2G (see Sample #23).

g. GOODS IMPORTED BY COURIER

In recent years, importing by courier, especially in the case of low-value shipments, has become increasingly popular with importers. Customs' procedures for couriered shipments are similar to those for shipments imported by mail. How they're handled depends largely on their value and whether or not your courier participates in the LVS system, described earlier in this chapter.

Where a shipment is worth less than C$1 200, it can be released almost immediately if your courier has a written undertaking with you to deliver the goods after release and you have posted security with Customs. Under LVS, you account for all low-value shipments by the 24th of each month and pay any duties by month's end.

Where a shipment is worth more than C$1 200, your courier advises you of its arrival and you pay all duties owing before it is released. If you have RMD privileges, as also described in this chapter, your goods can be released and delivered by your courier almost immediately

RECOMMENDED READING

Canada. Revenue Canada, Customs, Excise and Taxation. *D17 Memoranda on Accounting and Release Procedures.* [Ottawa]: Government of Canada.

Canada. Revenue Canada, Customs, Excise and Taxation. *A Guide to Importing Commercial Goods: April 1995.* [Ottawa]: Government of Canada, 1995.

Canada. Revenue Canada, Customs and Excise. *Importations by Mail.* [Ottawa]: Government of Canada, 1992.

Canada. Revenue Canada, Customs and Excise. *Importing Commercial Goods into Canada.* [Ottawa]: Government of Canada, 1994.

SAMPLE #22
CUSTOMS POSTAL IMPORT FORM
(form E-14)

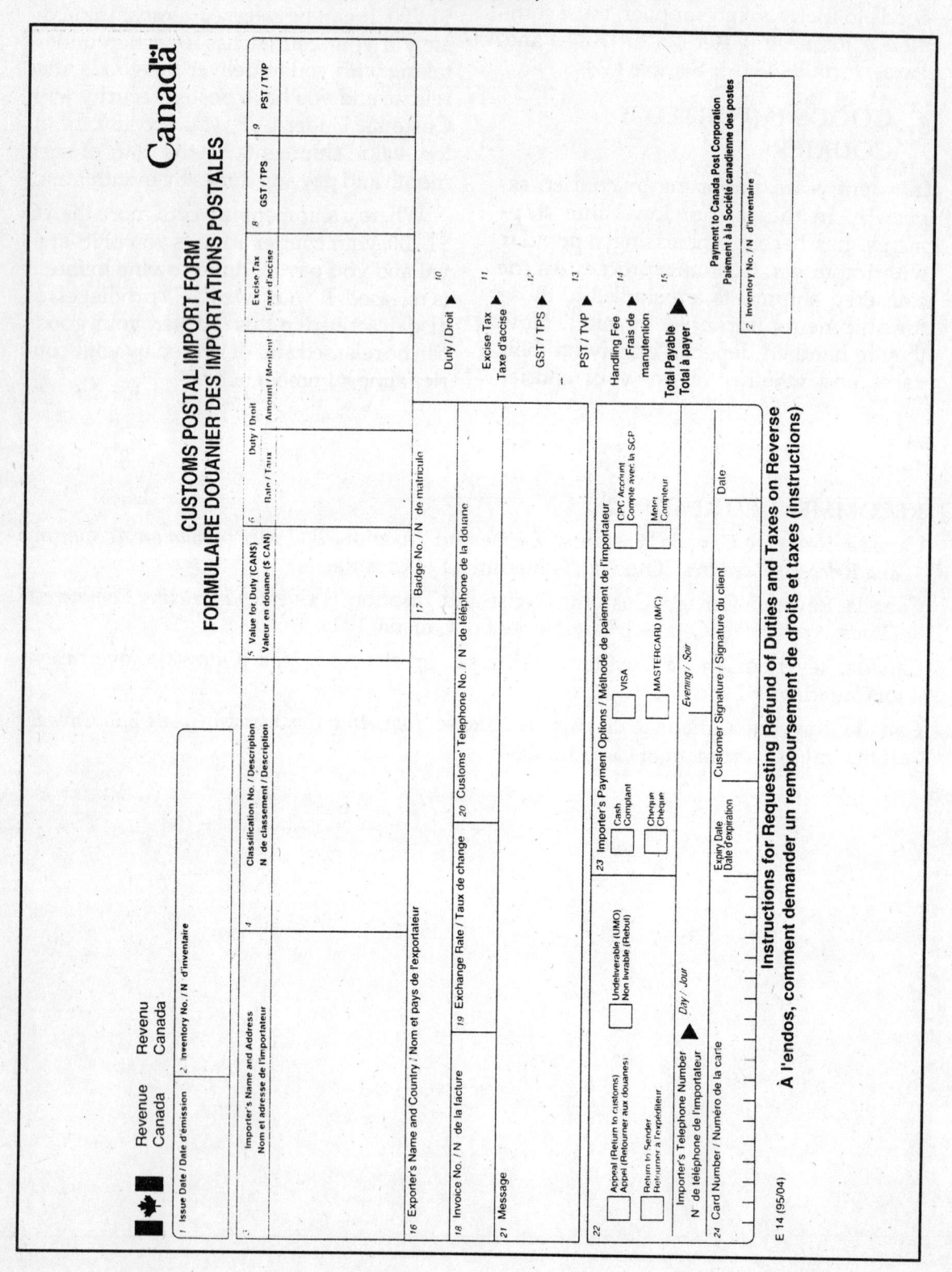

SAMPLE #23
REQUESTING REFUND OF DUTIES AND TAXES
(form B-2G)

12
DUTY RELIEF

This chapter provides information on when and for what reasons you can apply for a drawback or a refund of the duty you've paid on your goods. Some of this information will be of more interest to importers who incorporate their imports into a manufacturing process or sell to manufacturers who do. Because of its complexity, readers are advised to check the recommended reading list at the end of the chapter for more references.

As is obvious from federal assistance programs to would-be exporters, the Canadian government supports the development and expansion of domestic industry both to stimulate growth in international trade and to protect Canadian manufacturers from foreign competition. By comparison, there are few incentives for importers and, again, their primary purpose is to protect and expand domestic manufacturing.

Two such incentives exist in the form of duty relief: drawbacks and machinery remissions. Drawbacks are available for importers who use their imports in the production of goods usually destined for the export market. Machinery remissions are available for companies obliged to import foreign machinery and equipment when comparable machinery is not available from production in Canada. You can apply for a refund for other reasons as well — if the goods you've received are faulty, for example, or a clerical error has been made in the calculation of duty owing. This last group constitutes the most common type of refund claim processed by Customs.

a. IF YOUR GOODS ARE FAULTY — AND OTHER PROBLEMS

Goods do not always arrive in one piece and may be faulty or other than what you ordered. These are just a few of the reasons why you might file a refund claim for part or all of the duty you paid out before they were released to you. You may also file, as specified under the Customs Act, when —

(a) goods are damaged or destroyed, or deteriorate in transit;

(b) goods are of an inferior quality to the type for which duty has been paid;

(c) you pay duty on more goods than are contained in the shipment;

(d) duty is paid in error or is overpaid;

(e) the tariff classification or value for duty of your goods is changed;

(f) you seek refund of a deposit placed with Customs;

(g) goods are replacement parts or equipment provided free or at a reduced rate by your foreign supplier when the items they're replacing were exported under Customs' supervision; or

(h) goods are diverted for a special use.

Depending on the reason for your claim, you are required to complete a specified form, provide certain documents, and meet certain time limits — all clearly defined in Customs regulations.

The required form — form B-2, Adjustment Request — is the same for most types of refund claims. It looks much like a B-3 form and contains many of the same fields (see Sample #24). In fact, you can use the B-3 instructions above to complete most of the document.

One of the most important fields is the "justification for request" at the bottom of the form. This is normally filled in with a single word or a short phrase and the section of the Customs Act under which a refund may be requested as in the case, for example, of "Redetermination under section 61(a)." Fields #18 through #36 are repeated in the form so that you can show both how your goods were described in the original B-3 entry and how they should have been described.

Usually you submit three copies of a B-2 to Customs and receive one back, date stamped to verify that you've met the appropriate deadline. Customs must start paying you interest on the duty being refunded 90 days after you make your submission. You can file for a GST refund on a separate GST rebate form (B-2-R), but only if your business is not GST registered, or you are a non-resident and do not carry on business in Canada. You should otherwise deduct your GST payment from your periodic GST returns. (See chapter 7 for more information on tax refunds.)

Let's look now at a few types of refund requests. Since applicants for refunds must adhere strictly to time limits and documentation requirements, we include this information, where applicable, at the end of each description:

1. Refunds on damaged or deteriorated goods

When your shipment has been destroyed or damaged, or has deteriorated in transit, you must file two Customs forms: the B-2 and the K-11 (Certificate for Damaged Goods). Customs inspects the shipment as soon as it receives your K-11; you must file the K-11 within 90 days from date of entry in the case of nonperishable shipments, three days in the case of perishable ones. Then you have two years (minus the K-11 filing time) to submit a B-2, using the certificate as your supporting document.

2. Refunds on shortshipped, lost, and pilfered goods

If your supplier makes an error in your shipment, you can file a B-2 form within 90 days of the date of release, along with a corrected invoice, a letter (preferably from your supplier) explaining what happened, and any other document that might help clarify the circumstances surrounding the error.

Goods lost through pilferage or during shipment are still subject to full duties and taxes, unless you can demonstrate that they disappeared before they arrived in Canada. In that case, the cargo control document should reflect the shortage. If it doesn't, you submit an Exception Report from the carrier along with a B-2 form, all within 90 days of the shipment's release.

3. Refunds on defective or inferior goods

When your goods are not of the quality you ordered and paid duty on, your first step is to notify Customs in writing of the quality of the shipment — within three days in the case of perishables, 90 days otherwise. Then you have several options. You can return the goods to your supplier or have them destroyed under Customs' supervision; in either case you get a full refund of the duty paid. You can also renegotiate with your supplier to pay a reduced price for the goods, but you cannot then apply for a refund. You should ensure that you're compensated for the loss of duties and taxes already paid in any negotiation you undertake.

Documentation accompanying your B-2 refund request should include —

(a) a credit note from your supplier,

(b) a signed bill of lading,

SAMPLE #24
ADJUSTMENT REQUEST
(form B-2)

(c) a form E-15 (Certificate of Identification) as proof of export if you send the goods back,

(d) a letter from you explaining why the goods are inferior, and

(e) a copy of your original purchase order.

Minus the notification time for this type of refund request, you have two years after the shipment's date of entry to apply for a refund.

4. Refunds when clerical errors are made

When you make an error which is evident on the face of your original B-3 entry, not including errors in tariff classification or valuation, you can request a refund without any supporting documentation. The time limit for submission is two years from the shipment's date of entry. These kinds of errors are also called "obvious errors."

5. Refunds on parts and equipment replaced

When you receive parts or equipment from your supplier to replace items that cannot be repaired, you are liable to pay duty on them, as with any other import. But if your supplier provides these items free or at a reduced price, and the original items were exported under Customs' supervision, you can submit a B-2 refund request for part or all of the duty paid on them. The request must be accompanied by a form E-15 (Certificate of Repair), the export bill of lading for the old parts or equipment, and a letter from you explaining why the repair could not be made and giving a full description of what has transpired to date. The time limit for this type of request is two years from the date of entry of the replacement items.

6. Refunds on duties overpaid as a result of an error or change in tariff classification

We've already discussed the B-2-1, Detailed Adjustment Statement (DAS) issued by Customs commodity specialists when they change the tariff classification of an item (see chapter 11). Here we are referring to an error made in classification when you are accounting for your goods. To obtain a refund of the duty you've overpaid, you submit a form B-2, Adjustment Request, within a year of the date of entry of your goods and provide extensive supporting documentation, including detailed information on the goods (and even samples), and copies of rulings on identical or similar items.

7. Refunds as a result of errors in valuation

To obtain a refund for any excess duty you pay as a result, for example, of your supplier completing a commercial or Customs' invoice incorrectly, you complete a B-2 within a year of the goods being entered and provide a corrected invoice along with a credit note and a letter from your supplier, explaining the mistake.

8. Refunds when goods are diverted for a special use after importation

Let's say, for example, that you've bought some equipment that qualifies as duty free if it's used in the mining industry. You pay full duty on it, but then sell it to a mining company, authorized by the nature of its work, to apply for a refund of the duty. To obtain the refund yourself, you complete a B-2 and submit it within two years of date of entry, along with copies of the invoice you sent the mining company and its purchase order.

Of course, diversions can work in the opposite direction, too. If you've been able to import goods duty free because of their proposed end use, and divert them to another use which takes them out of the duty-free category, you must pay all duty and taxes owing — plus interest, starting 90 days after the goods have been diverted.

b. MACHINERY REMISSION PROGRAM

As mentioned elsewhere in this book, it is a priority of the federal government to foster the growth of domestic industry by providing incentives. One such incentive is the Machinery Remission program, which was established in 1968 when the rates of duty on imported machinery were relatively high.

The purpose of the program is to encourage greater efficiency in Canadian manufacturing operations by providing producers with duty-free access to equipment and parts not available from producers in Canada. At the same time, the program protects Canadian machinery manufacturers by denying remission applications for machinery and equipment that is available from Canadian producers.

The Tariff Simplification Task Force, recently formed by the federal finance department (see chapter 4, section i., Schedule II Codes), is considering the possibility of eliminating the Machinery Remission program as one way of making the tariff easier to understand. This could be done by declaring duty-free those items otherwise eligible for remission under the program. No final decision has yet been made by the Task Force.

The parameters of the program are defined in Customs Memorandum D8-5-1, (D8-5-2 for U.S. Tariff) which contains three schedules:

(a) *Schedule I*, which lists machinery and equipment in two columns by tariff classification: the first itemizing goods that are not produced in Canada and are eligible for remission; the second, goods that are produced here and are thus subject to duty if imported.

(b) *Schedule II*, which lists parts that have to be replaced on a regular basis, all ineligible for remission.

(c) *Schedule III*, which lists repair and replacement parts for machinery and equipment. These may or may not be eligible for remission, depending on whether the machines they're meant for are themselves eligible.

All the products in the Schedules are listed by tariff classification, so if you want to determine whether a particular machine is eligible for remission, you must first establish its HS Tariff classification. If after going through the classification procedures you are still uncertain of the correct HS Tariff item, you may want to write to Customs for a customs ruling (see chapter 4).

If the machine is not listed in the Schedules, and specifically column I of Schedule I, turn to the Annex (Schedule II) of the tariff. The Annex, also called the "Consolidation of Concessionary Provisions," lists all those items that qualify for a reduction in duty and taxes because of their end use or special use (in a particular industry, for example).

If your machine is listed in the Schedules or the Annex as being available from production in Canada, but you feel the product you want to import is not reasonably equivalent to those available, you may decide to file a form K-122, Application for Duty Remission (see Sample #25). "Reasonably equivalent" is judged according to characteristics such as capacity, volume, output, and range.

When making your submission, include all supporting documentation such as letters from Canadian manufacturers confirming that they are unable to produce the machine; literature on the machine describing its capabilities; an explanation of how the consumer or end-user will benefit. Applications for used machines are treated the same as for new products.

Your application is date stamped by Customs and goes to regional authorities first for review, then to the Machinery and

SAMPLE #25
APPLICATION FOR DUTY REMISSION UNDER THE MACHINERY PROGRAM
(form K-122)

SAMPLE #25 — Continued

**APPLICATION FOR DUTY REMISSION
UNDER THE MACHINERY PROGRAM**

A. TWO WAYS TO OBTAIN DUTY REMISSION

1. Duty remission under the Machinery Program may be obtained by two methods:

   (a) by completing this application form

   or

   (b) by reference to a schedule of machinery and equipment included in Appendix A of Customs Memorandum D8-5-1 which pre-authorizes duty remission.

2. Customs Memorandum D8-5-1 describes remission procedures and lists pre-authorized duty remitted machinery and equipment. Copies of the D8-5-1 may be purchased from:

   Department of Supply and Services Canada
   Canadian Government Publishing Centre
   Hull, Quebec
   K1A 0S9
   (819) 997-2560

   Information on machinery and equipment listed in Memorandum D8-5-1 may also be obtained at any Customs Office.

B. INSTRUCTIONS FOR COMPLETING APPLICATION

1. This application must be completed in full, i.e., Part I following immediately after this instruction and Part II on the last page.

2. Separate application forms must be submitted for:

   (a) complete machines

   Each distinct type of machinery, equipment, system or production unit must be described on separate application forms. Accessories, attachments, tools and control equipment must be identified on the application.

   (b) production parts

   Production parts which are to be used in the manufacture of machines or equipment may be eligible for remission of duty. To qualify for remission, the parts must not be available from production in Canada. Applications for production parts must be so indicated in **Part I**.

   (c) replacement parts

   Approved applications automatically provide for remission of duty on replacement parts unless otherwise stated. If the application is requesting remission of duty on replacement parts only, (i.e., for machinery imported under remisssion but for which the replacement parts provision has expired) it must be so indicated on **Part I**.

3. **Applicants must indicate on Part I whether or not they will be the end-users of the machinery.**

4. Applicants should allow 90 days for the processing of an application. **NOTE: No additions will be considered to approved applications.**

5. Please note that it is not necessary to employ an agent in order to submit an application. However, if an agent is employed, applications will be returned to the designated agent identified on the form after consideration by the Machinery and Equipment Advisory Board.

6. To avoid unnecessary payment and subsequent refund of duty on not available machinery, it is to the applicant's advantage to submit an application in advance of the date of importation. In this regard, if there is any uncertainty about the existence of Canadian manufacturers capable of producing a particular piece of machinery or equipment, the Machinery and Equipment Advisory Board will be pleased to provide assistance in identifying Canadian manufacturers prior to the submission of an application.

7. Further information regarding conditions under which duty remission may be considered can be obtained from:

   The Machinery and Equipment Advisory Board
   Connaught Building
   MacKenzie Avenue
   Ottawa, Ontario
   K1A 0L5
   (613) 954-7100

C. INFORMATION REGARDING TARIFF CLASSIFICATION

Applicants wishing to review or discuss tariff classifications pertaining to individual applications should direct questions to: Manager, Tariff Programs and Appraisal Unit, Revenue Canada, Customs and Excise, Regional Office closest to their areas.

NOTE: Following receipt of your application. Customs officials will provide a preliminary tariff classification for the goods described. In order to qualify for consideration under the Machinery Program, goods must be classifiable under qualifying Machinery Program tariff items. It must be emphasized, however, that this tariff classification is preliminary to importation of the goods and does not constitute a ruling under the *Customs Act* nor does it protect the time limit under this Act. Tariff classification will ultimately be determined at the time the goods are entered into Canada.

D. ADDRESS FOR SUBMITTING APPLICATIONS

Mail completed application to: Department of National Revenue, Customs and Excise, P.O. Box 15,000, in the nearest city designated below:

   Halifax, N.S. B3J 3G4
   Quebec, Quebec G1K 7R9
   Montreal, Quebec H3C 3P3
   Ottawa, Ontario K1G 3Z2
   Toronto, Ontario M5W 1R9
   Hamilton, Ontario L8N 3R5
   London, Ontario N6A 4Z8
   Windsor, Ontario N9A 6P8
   Winnipeg, Manitoba R3C 3A4
   Regina, Saskatchewan S4P 3J6
   Calgary, Alberta T2P 2M7
   Vancouver, B.C. V6B 4H2

Equipment Advisory Board in Ottawa for final consideration (approval is by a specific order-in-council). If it's refused, the application is returned to you along with a letter of explanation. You can appeal the decision to the review board if you feel you have adequate grounds. Applications are usually approved for a limited time — three years in the case of machines and ten years for parts.

Normally you would make your submission well in advance of the shipment of the machine to Canada. But if it arrives before you have a decision from the board, or you decide to file your application after the machine has been entered, you can still apply for a refund of the duty you paid — usually to a maximum of two years retroactively. As in the case of most of the refunds already discussed, you submit a B-2 form with a copy of your approved application.

c. CUSTOMS' DRAWBACK PROGRAM

Customs' drawbacks represent another way to recover duty on imported goods. To qualify for a drawback, goods must have been used in one of several ways, or not used at all (as in the case of surplus stock). Again, the "D" Series regulations contain full details of this program, introduced some years ago to improve Canada's manufacturing capacity by making manufacturers more competitive both domestically and in foreign markets.

Two basic types of drawbacks are available from the federal government: export and home consumption. Export drawbacks represent the refund of duty on goods that are exported or incorporated into Canadian-made goods for export — as in the case of rose bushes imported from California, packaged and labelled in Canada, then exported again to American distributors. Home consumption drawbacks are the return of duty on a limited number of goods or materials imported for a specific purpose — as in the case of steel used in the manufacture of cutlery or files.

There are several types of drawbacks within these two general categories. For most of them, you must complete the same form — a K-32 Drawback Claims (see Sample #26). If you have not actually imported the goods yourself, your application must also be accompanied by a K-32-A, a Drawback Certificate of Importation, Sale, or Transfer (see Sample #27). This certificate comes from the original importer and transfers the right to claim a drawback of the duty from him to you. You usually must demonstrate proof of export as well and can use a form E-15 (Certificate of Identification) for this purpose (or a copy of a signed bill of lading or a copy of the U.S. import entry).

Where you have imported goods and then sold them to an exporter, the exporter may complete a K-32-B, a Drawback Certificate of Sale for Exportation, transferring the right to claim a drawback to you (see Sample #28).

In the case of most drawback claims, you are subject to a four-year deadline between the time the goods or materials are imported and the date they're exported again. Section 82(1) of the Customs Act describes the kinds of export drawbacks as discussed in the following sections.

1. Imported goods that are later exported

This applies to goods that are imported into Canada and then exported in the same condition. Consider, for example, the retailer who wants to return surplus stock to his or her supplier for credit. For this type of application, you need proof of export, as discussed above, plus a K-32 form.

2. Imported goods or materials used in or incorporated into goods manufactured or produced in Canada and then exported

The rose bush example cited earlier falls into this category. Again, you require a

SAMPLE #26
DRAWBACK CLAIMS
(form K-32)

SAMPLE #27
CERTIFICATE OF IMPORTATION, SALE OR TRANSFER
(form K-32-A)

SAMPLE #28
DRAWBACK CERTIFICATE OF SALE FOR EXPORTATION
(form K-32-B)

copy of the export bill of lading and a copy of the sales invoice to your foreign customer as well as a K-32 and an E-15 (or other documents).

3. Imported goods or materials used or consumed in the manufacture of Canadian-made exports

This may occur in the case of a furniture manufacturer who imports veneer, particle board, and metal fixtures from another country, then sells the finished product abroad. Here the manufacturer must keep very detailed records of exactly what has been used in which products destined for what market. This information is included in the drawback application, along with an export bill of lading, copies of sales invoices, and the form E-15 (or other documents) mentioned earlier.

As an alternative to this type of drawback, the federal government permits manufacturers to apply for a remission of duty, thus avoiding the payment of duty altogether. This type of remission, called an Inward Processing Remission Order, operates along the lines of the Machinery Remission program. The manufacturer makes an application for remission before the goods or materials arrive and posts a security deposit with Customs equal to the duty and taxes he or she would otherwise be paying. It is not for one-time situations; to qualify, a manufacturer must have a history of having participated in this program for some time or a signed contract with a foreign purchaser in place. Full details are provided in Memorandum D7-3-1 of the regulations.

4. When the same quantity of domestic or imported materials is used in the manufacture of goods for export

This particular category relates to 82(1)(e) of the Customs Act and is generally referred to as the "equivalent clause." It is best explained by an example. Let's say that a manufacturer produces goods for both the domestic and the foreign market. Sometimes the materials are imported and sometimes they are bought in Canada. Under ordinary circumstances, the manufacturer cannot obtain a drawback on goods produced for the domestic market, even though he or she may have used imported materials. But if the manufacturer happens to be exporting products made from domestic materials that are exactly the same as those imported for another production run, he or she can apply for a drawback on those foreign materials used earlier. In other words, as long as the domestic materials are equivalent to the materials imported, the manufacturer can obtain a drawback on the imports, even though they were not used specifically to produce goods for export.

5. Goods deemed exported

Under section 82(2) of the Customs Act, imported goods are "deemed exported" when they are supplied to duty-free shops, vessels, and international airlines, or are sold to the provincial or federal government for export. This particular provision, at least in the case of vessels and airlines, attracts foreign purchasers to Canada for a wide range of supplies. The regulations (Memorandum D7-3-3) specify exactly what types of goods apply.

6. Imported goods or materials used in the manufacture of goods for domestic consumption

Earlier, we cited the example of steel used in the production of cutlery or files. In fact, there are more than two dozen types of goods or materials that qualify for this type of drawback, as listed in Memorandum D7-2 of the regulations. The criteria for application and the actual amount of the drawback vary, depending on the product. The same goods are also listed in the Annex of the tariff (the Consolidation of Concessionary Provisions), also mentioned above.

The regulations governing remissions and drawbacks are complex, and you would be well advised to contact a customs broker if you intend to make application for either of these programs. Indeed, if you are both an importer and a manufacturer, or a large-scale importer who supplies Canadian manufacturers, you probably have someone on staff who scouts government incentives to manufacturers and is already aware of them. New small-scale importers won't be as interested in this subject, but should be — a general understanding of remissions and drawbacks, particularly as they relate to NAFTA, will help you spot potential new products for the import market.

d. DEADLINES, DEADLINES, DEADLINES

As we have mentioned several times, you are subject to many deadlines, depending on the nature of one document or another and your purpose in filing it. Figure #7 provides a reference sheet for time limitations for refunds and drawbacks.

RECOMMENDED READING

Lindsay, Thomas. *An Outline of Customs in Canada*. Calgary: Erin Publications, 1991.

Canada. Revenue Canada, Customs and Excise. *The Customs Drawback Road...to Success and Profit*. [Ottawa]: Government of Canada, 1987.

Canada. Revenue Canada, Customs and Excise. *The New Customs Act in Brief*. [Ottawa]: Government of Canada, 1986.

Canada. Revenue Canada, Customs, Excise and Taxation. *D7 Memoranda on Drawbacks and D8 Memoranda on Remissions and Temporary Importation*. [Ottawa]: Government of Canada.

FIGURE #7
TIME LIMITATIONS FOR REFUNDS AND DRAWBACKS

REFUNDS	TIME LIMITATIONS
To appeal a tariff classification or value for duty	*One year* from date of decison
To contest a decision of a Tariff and Values Administrator	*One year* from date of decision by TVA
To contest a decision of the Deputy Minister	*Ninety days* from the date of decision by the DM
NAFTA Certificates of Origin	*One year* from date of Customs' accounting
Obvious clerical errors	*Two years* from date of Customs'
End-use diversions	*Two years* from date of Customs' accounting
Damaged goods (written notice must be filed with Customs within 90 days of Customs' accounting — three days in the case of perishables)	*Two years* from date of Customs' accounting
Inferior quality (written notice must be filed with Customs within 90 days of Customs' accounting — within three days in the case of perishables)	*Two years* from date of Customs' accounting
Defective, inferior quality or goods not according to order — exported or destroyed under Customs' supervision	*Two years* from date of Customs' accounting

DRAWBACKS	TIME LIMITATIONS
Obsolete or surplus goods destroyed under Customs' supervision	*Five years* from date of Customs' accounting
Goods exported in same condition	*Four years* from date of Customs' accounting
Manufactured goods exported	*Four years* from date of Customs' accounting

13
INVESTIGATIONS AND ENFORCEMENT

This chapter provides information on enforcement provisions under the Customs Act, referring specifically to seizures, adjudications, penalties, and the discretionary powers of Customs officers.

The Customs Act is one of the most powerful pieces of legislation in effect in Canada today. It gives Customs officers wide-ranging powers to search travellers and examine and seize goods in the course of performing their duties. It also defines several types of offences and provides penalties ranging from a demand for unpaid duties and taxes to seizure, fines, summary conviction, and imprisonment.

Importing represents an important source of income for the Canadian government. In 1994 more than $19 billion in duties and taxes were collected by Canada Customs in the course of processing more than 104 million individuals and almost 105 million cars and other conveyances. About 58 200 or 2.8% of these became enforcement actions under the act, involving Customs officials in the activities described in this chapter.

Figure #8 shows the enforcement activities over the last few years.

a. SELF-ASSESSMENT

The act that was in place before the current Customs Act (passed in 1986) was notable for the harshness of its seizure and forfeiture provisions. Under this previous legislation, for example, if a Canadian resident failed to declare goods on first entering Canada, those same goods could be seized at a later date as he or she was returning from abroad on another trip.

Just such an incident occurred, in fact, several years ago when the jewellery of Aleksander Glisic, a naturalized Canadian, was seized by Customs even though he'd brought it to Canada with him when he first emigrated 13 years earlier. In the court case that followed (1984), the presiding judge reluctantly agreed with the Crown on its interpretation of the act.

Perhaps because of the case, the present act prohibits the seizure of goods previously imported into Canada, if the only reason for doing so is that they were not declared at the time of original entry. They must still be in possession of someone entering the country, however, or in the baggage he or she is carrying.

Also under the present act, the onus is on the importer to report on the quantity and value of the goods being imported and to pay any duties and taxes owing. As was discussed earlier, Canada Customs reviews all entries as part of its routine accounting function and may change the tariff classification or value of the goods if it disagrees with the importer. The importer is then alerted of the changes and asked to pay more duty, as required. Thus, the general thrust of the current legislation is more balanced — instead of assuming the guilt of the importer before it's been

FIGURE #8
COMMERCIAL SEIZURES

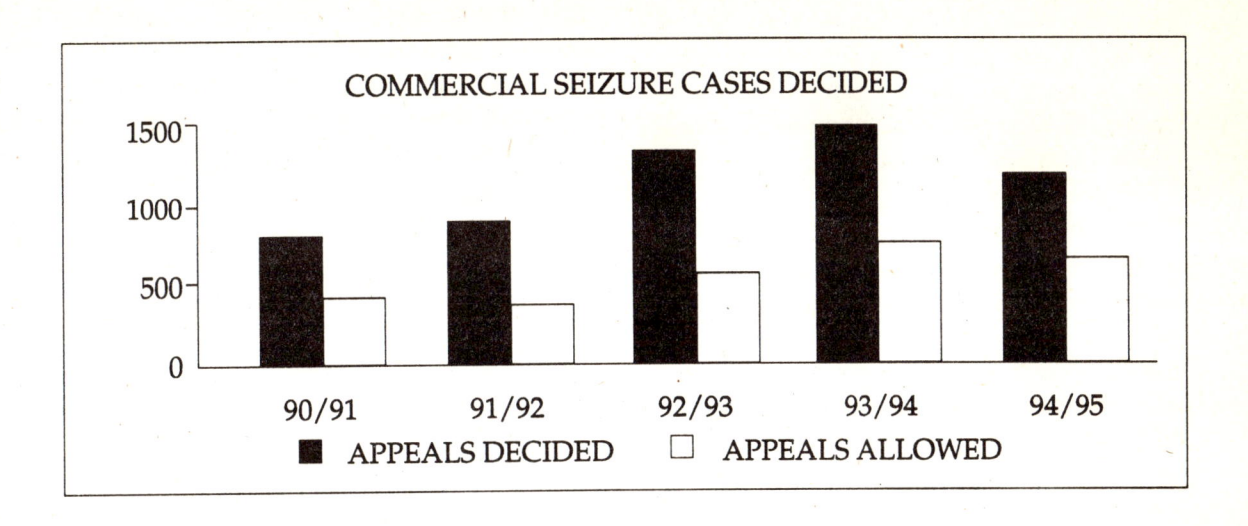

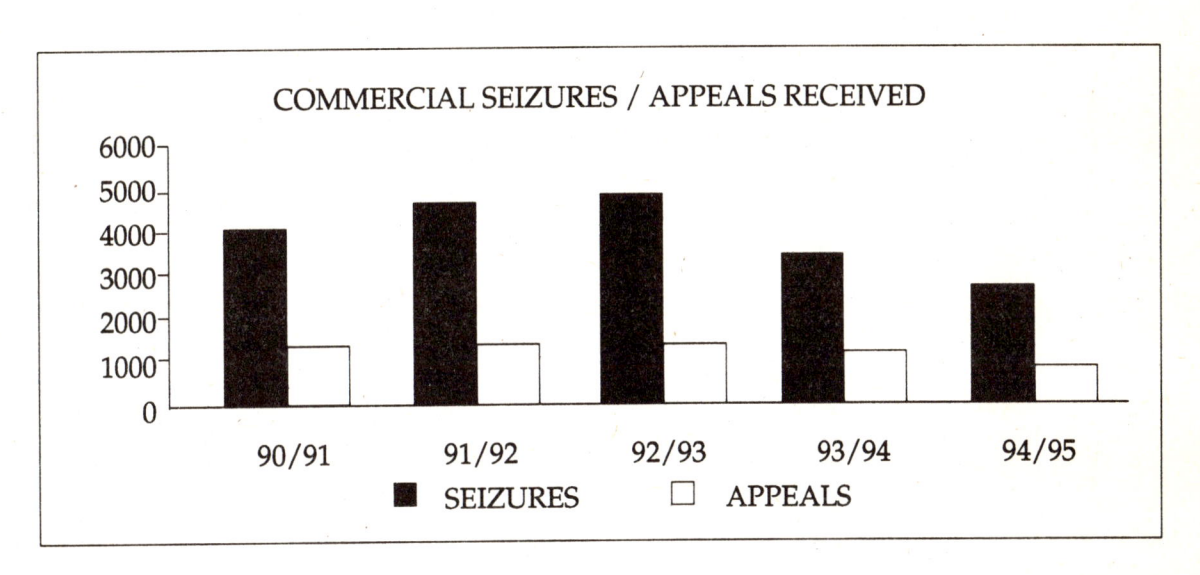

COMMERCIAL SEIZURE CASES DECIDED (bar chart, 90/91–94/95, APPEALS DECIDED vs APPEALS ALLOWED)

COMMERCIAL SEIZURES / APPEALS RECEIVED (bar chart, 90/91–94/95, SEIZURES vs APPEALS)

| | COMMERCIAL APPEALS || COMMERCIAL ||
	DECIDED	ALLOWED	SEIZURES	APPEALS
90/91	807	439	4089	1198
91/92	972	414	5014	1220
92/93	1426	592	5104	1296
93/94	1475	727	3685	1148
94/95	1253	718	2905	891

proven, as the previous act tended to, it assumes his or her honesty.

This approach is taken with casual travellers as well. The onus is on travellers to declare what purchases they have made abroad. It is not the Customs officer's responsibility to ask the right questions, as so many of us like to think.

b. SEIZURES AND FORFEITURES

When an importer contravenes the act, whether the importer is in the importing business or is just visiting the United States for the day, the goods and the conveyance they're being carried in can be seized. This means that the car you're driving if you're stopped at the border with undeclared or prohibited goods is liable for seizure along with the goods themselves.

There are two types of seizures:

(a) In the case of the first type, Customs officials at a port (airport, seaport, or border crossing) actually take possession of the goods and issue a seizure receipt (form K-19S) to the importer (a further form E-368 is used for any statement made by the importer).

(b) Where goods have already been imported and cannot be easily seized, as in the case of building materials that have already been incorporated into a building site, officials make an ascertained forfeiture, completing a Notice of Ascertained Forfeiture (the same form K-19S as above) that details how the goods were entered, how they should have been entered, and the amount to be paid in lieu of seizure. Payment of this amount automatically cancels the notice.

c. RESPONSIBILITIES AND POWERS OF CUSTOMS OFFICERS

The authority given Customs officers is a crucial element in the administration and enforcement of the Customs Act. In general, an officer has the right to search a person who is arriving in or leaving Canada, or who has had access to an area designated for those about to leave (such as a departure lounge), as long as the search is conducted within a reasonable time and only as detailed in section 99 of the act:

> if the officer suspects on reasonable grounds that the person has secreted on or about his person anything in respect of which this Act has been or might be contravened, anything that would afford evidence with respect to a contravention of this Act or any goods the importation or exportation of which is prohibited, controlled, or regulated under this or any other Act of Parliament.

Officers also have the right to examine and take samples of imported goods and goods for export, and to examine any international mail that weighs more than 30 grams — but, again, only if they have reason to believe that the law is being broken.

Finally, under section 111 of the current act, officers may obtain a search warrant from a justice of the peace to search a "building, receptacle, or place" and seize any goods, conveyances, or evidence (such as a company's books) indicating a contravention of the legislation.

d. CUSTOMS' INSPECTION OF IMPORTED GOODS

Primary non-commercial inspection at any Canadian port initially takes the form of verbal and written questioning. Based on the traveller's responses, the primary inspector may then refer the person to a secondary inspector. Secondary inspections usually entail an examination of the traveller's luggage and, based on the inspector's findings, may lead to a more intensive search.

Not surprisingly, an officer's first priority is to detect potentially high-risk goods like drugs, firearms, and banned animal products. But the officer may also want to know where you bought your video camera or laptop computer. On request, Customs will provide a form (form Y-38) to accommodate travellers who plan to use big-ticket Canadian purchases while they're abroad (items that have a serial number to serve as identification). By completing a Y-38 before taking your goods with you, you can save yourself a lot of time and trouble on your return. If your goods do not have a serial number, as in the case of expensive jewellery, have an appraisal made of them before you leave.

Commercial inspections have been complicated in recent years by the evolution of container shipping. Today it is more difficult and expensive to inspect shipments and confirm documentation on them. Where time and workload permit, Customs employs teams of investigators to handle the job and, at some ports, selected containers are actually removed from the dock for inspection purposes. These teams rely on "qualified" leads from several sources to track potential violators.

Under the present legislation, Customs officers may audit an importer's books back as far as six years, although most routine audits are for a two-year period. If they are investigating an alleged contravention of the legislation, they must first obtain a search warrant and are then able to seize records and other material to support their findings. Investigators usually work in teams of two and can spend as little as a day or two or as much as a month at a particular business, depending on the size of the company and what they're looking for. If the audit shows inconsistencies that cannot be explained and corrected to the satisfaction of regional Customs authorities and they penalize the importer, he or she may initiate the adjudication process described below.

Routine audits are by no means a threat to the average importing business. In fact, investigators can help improve a company's functioning by identifying inefficiencies and suggesting government programs it may apply for.

e. THE ADJUDICATION PROCESS

Within 30 days of receiving a Seizure Receipt or a Notice of Ascertained Forfeiture, an importer must register his or her intention to appeal the decision. The importer does this in writing, addressing the correspondence to the seizing Customs office with a carbon copy to the Adjudications Division in Ottawa.

The importer should then start building a case immediately. Within the next few weeks, he or she receives a brief letter from the seizing office, acknowledging receipt of the correspondence within the required time limit and advising that the matter has been forwarded to the Adjudications Division. Then, some weeks later, a formal Notice of Seizure or Ascertained Forfeiture (form K-30) follows, signed on behalf of the deputy minister. A legal-size, white document with blue borders, this Notice gives the importer a final 30 days to file any additional evidence to the minister (in the form of the Adjudications Directorate which reviews all submissions and prepares a recommendation).

The whole process can be conducted by correspondence and amounts to, in effect, a "hearing by mail." Because of workload, however, it may be months before a final decision on an appeal is issued. Importers disputing a seizure should retain a customs consultant or a lawyer with experience in this area before making their submission.

1. Civil penalties

In reviewing a seizure or ascertained forfeiture, the minister decides if the Customs Act or its regulations have been contravened and then determines if any conveyance seized at the same time was used in the contravention.

If no contravention has occurred, the seized goods, the conveyance, and any money (plus interest) or security taken at the time of the action are returned to the importer. If, on the other hand, the minister is satisfied that the law has been violated, he or she can require payment equal to the duty-paid value of the goods or the value of the conveyance before releasing both to the importer.

The minister's decisions take a slightly different form in the case of Notices of Ascertained Forfeiture. Here the minister may return some or all of the money (plus interest) or security paid out by the importer when the action was first taken, or demand that the importer pay more before authorizing the Notice's cancellation.

Importers subject to a seizure or forfeiture are often so embarrassed by the action that they don't contest it, even though there may be mitigating circumstances. They should: the Adjudication Division, on the minister's behalf, is open to reviewing any evidence submitted by the importer before a final decision is made. In its absence, they have no alternative but to impose a more severe penalty.

An importer can file an appeal of the decision in the Federal Court of Canada — Trial Division, but only within 90 days of receiving notification of the decision and only on certain grounds. An importer can challenge the grounds for a seizure, for example, but not the amount of the penalty as determined by the minister. An innocent third party to a seizure action may also file a claim in court within 60 days of the action being taken. (The type of court varies according to the province and is defined under section 138 of the act.)

Figure #9 shows a diagram of the enforcement process.

What happens to goods that are seized? It depends on the Minister's decision, of course. But, where appropriate, they're exported again. Otherwise they're sold at public auction or destroyed. If your African supplier happens to send you elephant hair bracelets, for example, thinking there might be a market for them in Canada, they will be seized and either returned or destroyed by Customs because anything made from elephant is banned in Canada.

2. Criminal penalties

Criminal penalties are applied in the case of more serious offences. Occasionally, importers are subjected to both civil and criminal prosecution.

Offences under the act are described in sections 153 to 159 and include the following:

(a) making false statements

(b) evasion of duties

(c) misdescription of goods in accounting documents

(d) possession of unlawfully imported goods

(e) possession of blank, signed documents

(f) opening and unpacking of goods prior to their release by Customs

(g) smuggling

The most serious of these are punishable by indictment or summary conviction, carrying a maximum fine of $25 000 and/or a maximum prison term of five years. There are other serious repercussions for violators as well — a customs broker who has been convicted of an indictable offence, for example, may have his or her licence revoked. Offenders can be prosecuted up to three years after an offence has occurred.

Of the seven offence sections, the most often applied is section 153 which deals with making false statements verbally or in writing, destroying or altering records, and evading compliance with the act.

FIGURE #9
THE ENFORCEMENT PROCESS

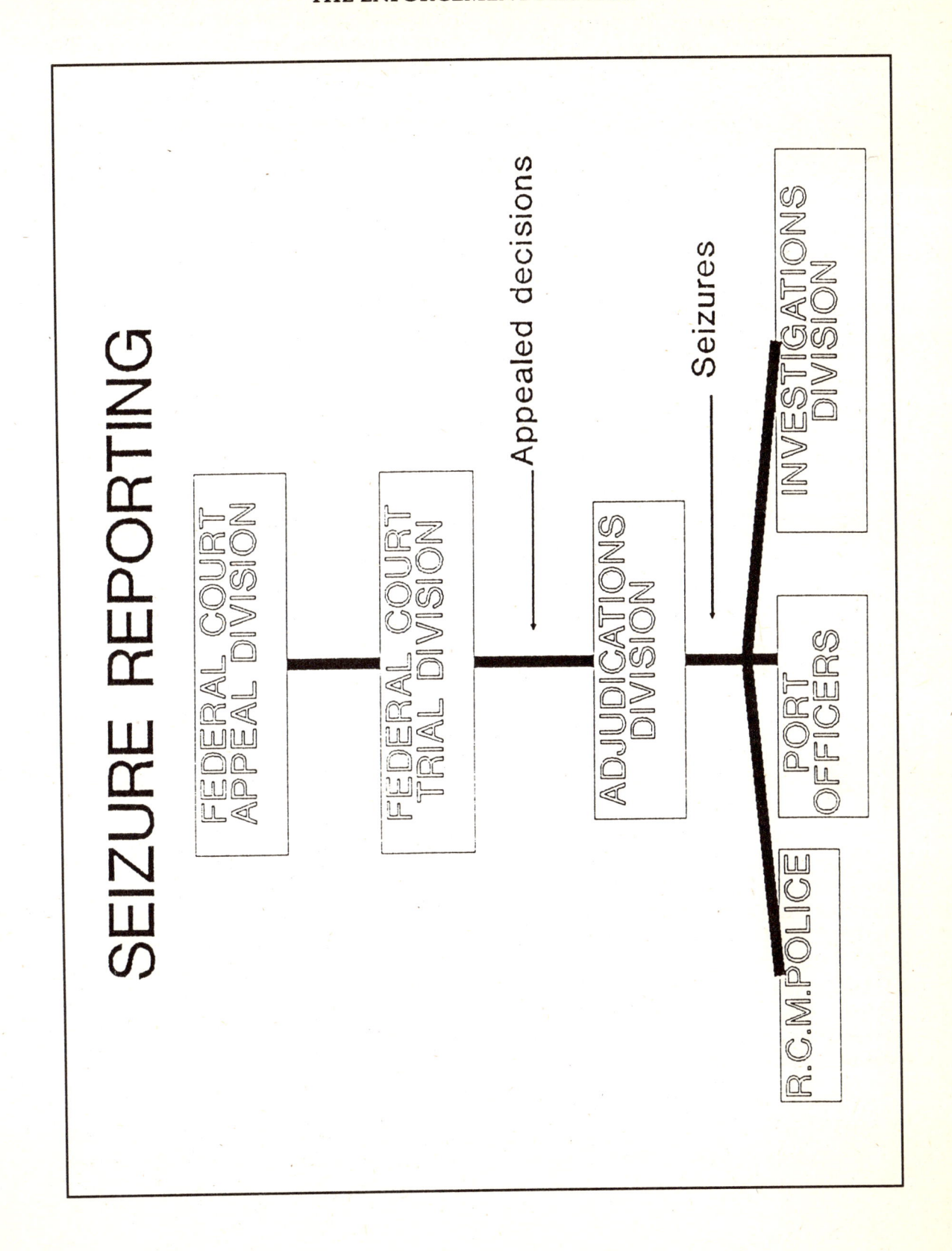

f. CORRECTING ERRORS IN YOUR ENTRIES

You should report any errors you discover in your entries as soon as you become aware of them. Let's say, for example, that you import a raw product which, depending on its end use, is either dutiable or duty free. Most of the time you know exactly how each shipment is going to be used. But occasionally it's put to a use that makes it dutiable when you've already classified it as duty free — it's "diverted," as was discussed in chapter 12. In such a case, you (or your customs broker, on your behalf) should submit a voluntary entry and pay any outstanding duties and taxes. A voluntary entry is a B-3, with a "V" in Field #3 for type of entry.

"Good faith" was not considered a defence under previous legislation and is untested as a defence under the present Customs Act. But common sense dictates that a cooperative, professional approach in all your relations with Customs will only increase your credibility with them.

RECOMMENDED READING

Canada. *The Customs Act*, R.S.C., 1985, c. 1 (2nd Supplement and subsequent amendments).

Canada. Revenue Canada, Customs and Excise. *The New Customs Act in Brief.* [Ottawa]: Government of Canada, 1986.

Dattu, Riyaz. "Customs Seizures: The Legal and Administrative Framework." Paper presented at the County of York Law Association Nutshell Programme, Toronto, February 28, 1989.

14
BUYING A CAR FROM THE UNITED STATES

This chapter provides information on the procedures you follow when you import an automobile from the United States and on the impact of first the FTA and now NAFTA on this type of purchase.

Since the implementation of the FTA in 1989, motor vehicles have become one of the most common purchases made by Canadian consumers over the border. It's not difficult to understand why — the prohibition against used vehicles has been gradually lifted, first under FTA, and now under NAFTA provisions; the duty rate under free trade is also declining; and vehicle prices in the United States are cheaper, even with the fluctuating exchange rate between the two currencies. In fact, many individuals now make a small business of buying good used cars in salt-free areas like the American southwest and bringing them up to Canada, initially to drive as their own and then to sell at a tidy profit.

The importing procedure for this type of product was simplified in April 1995 to allow for the admission of vehicles that do not yet meet Canadian safety and emission standards. As the procedure, described below, now stands, vehicle purchasers pay a fee for the certification of their vehicles once they've been brought into compliance.

a. THE AUTOMOTIVE PRODUCTS TRADE AGREEMENT OR AUTO PACT

In the 1960s, Canada and the United States made an agreement to import specified automobiles, parts, and accessories duty free in return for certain conditions being met. Full details of the conditions, at least for Canadian auto manufacturers, are contained in Customs regulations, Memorandum D10-8-6. The purpose of the agreement, a precursor to the FTA, was to allow manufacturers on both sides of the border to specialize in producing certain types of vehicles for specific markets. This made the industry as a whole more efficient and gave a strong boost to the economy of central Canada where most of the auto manufacturers are based.

Canada has since made similar agreements with other countries, and today it exports Canadian-made parts to certain foreign auto manufacturers, allowing them a partial remission when they import vehicles with these parts back into Canada. As well, foreign manufacturers have established several plants here — again to the benefit of the Canadian economy.

Automobiles, parts, and accessories covered by the Auto Pact are classified under the HS Tariff (chapter 87) and are subject to the same General Interpretive Rules, etc., as any other import. They are also listed in the Consolidation of Concessionary Provisions or Annex (which, as has been mentioned elsewhere, lists all goods qualifying for a reduction in duty because of the particular use they're being put to).

All new foreign vehicles imported into Canada must meet Canadian safety and emission standards, as provided under the recently revised federal Motor Vehicle Safety Act and Regulations. Under the same act, only the manufacturer or his or her agent (not dealers) may import new vehicles — that is, vehicles that haven't previously been sold at the retail level. Used vehicles entered by commercial importers must meet the same requirements as vehicles brought in by individual consumers.

b. REDUCTION OF DUTY RATE UNDER NAFTA

NAFTA provides essentially the same advantages to all American-made imports as the Auto Pact has been doing for new automobiles, parts, and accessories for many years. The big difference for car buyers since the agreement's implementation is that they can now buy used vehicles. (We use the term "vehicle" here as it's applied under the Motor Vehicle Safety Act, in reference to chassis-cabs, motorcycles, multi-purpose passenger vehicles, passenger cars, trucks, snowmobiles and snowmobile cutters, trailers and trailer-converter dollies.)

Used vehicles of other-than-current-year manufacture were prohibited from entry into Canada before 1988. There were a few exceptions to this rule — vehicles 15 years of age or older could be imported, for example, as could gift vehicles and the vehicles of Canadian residents returning from abroad. Also in this category was a vehicle that replaced one damaged beyond repair in an American automobile accident, as long as the purchaser was able to provide a police report to Customs.

Starting in 1989, however, vehicles eight years of age or older were permitted to enter Canada as long as they conformed to all safety and emission requirements. And the next five years saw the age limit on vehicles continue to drop — to six years in 1990, four years in 1991 and two years in 1992 — until it was eliminated altogether on January 1, 1993.

During this same period, the duty rate on imported vehicles declined as well. As you may recall from our discussion of NAFTA in chapter 5, the tariff rate on most American-made imports is being reduced over several different time periods, depending on the particular product. In the case of vehicles, the reduction schedule is over ten years, and is as follows:

(a) Up to 1988: 9.2% duty

(b) As of January 1, 1989: 8.3% duty

(c) 1990: 7.4% duty

(d) 1991: 6.4% duty

(e) 1992: 5.5% duty

(f) 1993: 4.6% duty

(g) 1994: 3.6% duty

(h) 1995: 2.6% duty

(i) 1996: 1.7% duty

(j) 1997: 0.8% duty

(k) 1998: Free

One group of vehicles — those more than 25 years old that conform to all other NAFTA requirements — are already duty free.

Before the FTA, vehicles imported from the United States were subject to the Most Favoured Nation or MFN tariff rate of 9.2%. Today this rate still applies to cars manufactured in a country other than the United States, even though they may have been imported and driven in the United States before being sold to a Canadian importer. Were you to purchase a Mercedes-Benz, a Fiat or any other non-American vehicle in the United States, for example, you must pay duty according to the MFN rate.

c. REQUIREMENTS FOR IMPORTED VEHICLES

To qualify for certification and licensing in Canada, a vehicle — American or foreign built — must have been registered in the

United States and bear the original manufacturer's statement of compliance label (SOC) to U.S. federal motor vehicle safety standards. It must also conform to the Canadian safety and emissions standards of the year in which it was built, as detailed in the Motor Vehicle Safety Act and its regulations. If your car does not conform to Canadian standards, it falls into one of two categories — modifiable or unmodifiable.

In the case of modifiable vehicles, you pay an inspection and certification fee to Transport Canada at the time you enter the vehicle and then have it modified and inspected within 45 days of the entry date. If it is unmodifiable, the vehicle cannot be brought into Canada at all. Unmodifiable vehicles are those that cannot be safely modified to meet Canadian standards. The important point to remember here is that, whether or not your vehicle conforms at the time of entry, you can still bring it into Canada as long as you have all modifications made within 45 days of it entering.

Some types of vehicles are exempted from all certification and licensing requirements, including:

(a) Vehicles manufactured more than 15 years before the date they are imported

(b) Vehicles entering Canada on a temporary basis — being driven by a tourist, for example

(c) Vehicles in transit to another country

(d) Buses built before January 1, 1971

Vehicles built in 1985 and later are unlikely to conform to Canadian standards in several areas, including daytime running lights, bumper standards, seat belt anchorages, tether anchorages, a bilingual maintenance label on airbags, and metric markings on the speedometer. You can have the modifications made by any source qualified to do the work — or even make them yourself — as long as they pass inspection when you take them into a Transport Canada inspection station before the end of your 45-day deadline.

In the course of shopping for a vehicle, you may come across one that was built in Canada, then shipped to an American market. Do not assume that it conforms to Canadian standards simply because it was manufactured here. If it was destined for an American market such as Florida, it may well conform only to Florida standards and lack certain fundamental requirements under Canadian law.

Similarly, don't be drawn into buying a custom or kit car without first ensuring that it can be modified to comply to Canadian standards. By their very nature, these types of vehicles are guaranteed to pose modification problems of one sort or another, eliminating any cost advantage in purchasing them. Some very attractive, foreign-built vehicles also fall into this category, such as those purchased in a third country and then "federalized" (modified to meet American federal safety and emission standards) when they were imported into the United States by returning nationals. These vehicles are prohibited entry into Canada unless they are at least 15 years old.

In response to the increase in consumer purchases of American vehicles, Transport Canada regularly publishes a "List of Vehicles Admissible from the United States," available as part of an information package on vehicle entry procedures. To order the package call the Registrar for Imported Vehicles in Pickering, Ontario, at the following number:
(905) 837-7918 or
1-800-333-0558 (toll-free)

The same office will respond to questions about specific models, if you are already car hunting and want to check the eligibility of a particular vehicle make and year. This is always advisable before you make your purchase.

As well as federal requirements, a U.S. import must meet provincial safety standards before it can be registered and licensed. This means taking your purchase through your province's inspection facilities once all modifications have been approved by Transport Canada. Inspection facilities vary from one province to the next. If you live in B.C., for example, and your vehicle is over nine years old, you must visit your local Air Care facility. Also, unless you live in Alberta or are a settler entering your vehicle as part of your personal effects, you will be required to pay provincial tax on your purchase.

d. THE INSPECTION AND APPROVAL PROCESS

The inspection and registration program was established as a result of amendments made to the federal Motor Vehicle Safety Act, administered by Transport Canada. Among other things, the amendments established a Registrar of Imported Vehicles to coordinate inspection and registration procedures. The registrar position was actually contracted out to private industry and is currently occupied by R.G. Marks of Toronto. Marks, in consort with its agents, Livingston Customs Brokers and The Minacs Group Inc., is responsible for administering the program.

The inspection and registration program itself has four basic steps: border entry, vehicle modification, inspection and certification, and licensing. Each step and the documents needed are described below.

1. Border entry

Commerical importers must import their vehicles through one of 24 designated Revenue Canada Customs stations across Canada. (See Figure #10 for the full list.) As a private importer, you are subject to no such restriction, though you might decide to choose a designated station anyway because processing is easier and you pay less for inspection and certification.

Before you go to the station, make sure you have all the required identification and papers, including the following:

(a) the title,

(b) bill of sale,

(c) your driver's licence,

(d) a manufacturer's statement of compliance (SOC) label, and

(e) proof that the vehicle either hasn't been subject to recalls or has been altered to comply.

The SOC label should be right on the car and is usually located on the left front door or door jam. If you can't find it, you should obtain a letter from the manufacturer confirming that the vehicle complies to U.S. federal motor vehicle safety standards.

At the station, you'll be redirected to the Registrar's agent (either Livingston Customs Brokers or a subcontractor to Livingston). The agent reviews your papers, verifies the title status of the vehicle with U.S. authorities and, based on his or her findings, determines if the vehicle is eligible for importation. The title status check confirms that the vehicle isn't wrecked or stolen.

If the vehicle is eligible, the agent completes a Transport Canada Vehicle Import form 1 (form13-0132) (see Sample #29), filling in your name and address, etc., and noting VIN (Vehicle Identification Number), type, model make, year, and title status. At the same time, you are required to pay $195 in fees for the inspection and certification process (by cheque or credit card). This amount goes up to $245 if you enter through a non-designated Customs station. Non-designated stations, however, also offer you the option of paying the required fees directly to the Registrar by cash or money order.

Once the paperwork is completed, the agent conducts a visual inspection of your

FIGURE #10
PORTS DESIGNATED TO HANDLE MOTOR VEHICLE IMPORTATIONS

British Columbia
- Kingsgate
- Osoyoos
- Pacific Highway
- Huntingdon

Alberta
- Coutts

Saskatchewan
- North Portal

Manitoba
- Emerson

Ontario
- Cornwall
- Fort Erie
- Fort Frances
- Lansdowne
- Niagara Falls (Queenston Bridge)
- Pigeon River
- Prescott
- Sarnia
- Sault Ste. Marie
- Windsor (Ambassador Bridge)
- Windsor Tunnel

Quebec
- Lacolle
- Rock Island
- St. Armand-Philipsburg
- Stanhope

New Brunswick
- Edmunston
- St. Stephen
- Woodstock Road

SAMPLE #29
VEHICLE IMPORT FORM 1
(form 13-0132)

vehicle to verify the VIN, then gives you the Import Form and redirects you to Customs. At Customs you pay any duties and taxes owing and are issued a Customs clearance (section 22K of the Import Form). As of the date on this clearance, you have 45 days to bring the vehicle into compliance.

If your vehicle already complies with Canadian standards, the agent will provide you with an Import Form indicating that it complies and redirect you to Customs. There is no fee for this service.

2. Vehicle modification

The agent will forward a copy of the Import Form to the Registrar and within the next ten days you will receive a package that includes a Modification and Inspection Form outlining the items on your vehicle that must be modified to meet Canadian standards. (If you've opted to pay the Registrar directly by cheque or money order, you won't receive this package until you have made your payment.)

Any qualified outlet can make the modifications, or you can make them yourself. It's not who makes the changes that concerns Transport Canada, only that they meet Canadian standards. You should also check to ensure your vehicle warranty is not affected in the process. Some importers try to have the modifications made in the United States before they enter Canada. But this can be more trouble than it is worth because the work requires an in-depth knowledge of Canadian safety standards.

As we've already mentioned, you have 45 days under federal law in which to complete the work. But be warned: some provinces place tighter time limits on unregistered vehicles, obliging you to have the modifications made sooner. Check with provincial authorities as soon as you have imported your vehicle to establish exactly how much time you have.

3. Inspection and certification

Transport Canada has established more than 200 inspection stations across Canada to accommodate vehicle importers. Once you've made the required modifications to your vehicle and completed the Modification and Inspection Form, you must visit one of these facilities to have the changes inspected and certified. Be sure to take with you any supporting documentation on the parts, materials, and modification work you've had done.

If your vehicle complies, the inspection station faxes your completed Modification and Inspection Form to the Registrar and stamps the Import Form you received at the border. The Registrar then forwards an authorization code to you, to be added to the Import Form, and a compliance label which you should affix immediately to the vehicle. This whole process usually takes about 48 hours. But if you need the certification sooner, you can pay an extra fee to obtain your authorization code immediately.

If your vehicle does not comply, you can carry out further modifications and return for a second inspection, for an additional fee. Vehicles that cannot be brought into compliance must be exported from Canada.

4. Licensing

You must present the Import Form with the authorization code to provincial authorities in order to have your car registered and licensed. As we've already mentioned, under provincial law your vehicle may also have to undergo a further safety inspection before licensing.

e. CALCULATING DUTY AND TAXES

As in the case of any other purchase you make abroad, you must calculate at least three, and possibly four, separate figures to determine what you owe the federal government in duty and taxes —

(a) purchase price in Canadian dollars,

(b) duty,

(c) excise tax, if applicable, and

(d) GST.

Provincial taxes are also payable, but only on the registration of the vehicle in your home province or territory.

Excise tax must be paid on vehicles with air conditioning units, even when the units are not operational. The charge is a flat $100. A so-called luxury tax, it has been imposed to discourage the purchase of vehicles that consume excessive amounts of fuel in their operation. Oversized vehicles — weighing 2 007 kilograms (4 400 pounds) in the case of automobiles or 2 268 kilograms (5 000 pounds) in the case of station wagons or vans — are also liable to excise tax, calculated according to their excess weight, as follows:

(a) first 100 pounds in excess: $30

(b) next 100 pounds in excess: $40

(c) next 200 pounds in excess: $50

(d) each 100 pounds after: $60

f. CAVEAT EMPTOR

When you're shopping for your U.S. vehicle, take particular care to research its history before you actually make your purchase.

It is common for a bank or other lending institution to place a lien against a large chattel, like a van, to secure a loan with a borrower. If you buy a van while the lien is in place, it can be seized if the loan falls into arrears. In such a situation, you lose everything — the vehicle, the money you paid for it, and any additional costs associated with its purchase and repair before you reach the border. Of course, you can sue the seller. But you must initiate court proceedings in the jurisdiction where the sale was made and, if the seller is already in financial trouble, you're not likely to get anything.

All this can be avoided if you check the vehicle's history through the state registration authority, giving yourself a few days to get a response in the event that you need to contact authorities in other states as well. Alternatively, you can opt to deal only with reputable used-car sales outlets, avoiding private sales altogether. Since 1988, several such companies have sprung up along the border and in places like Palm Springs, specifically to accommodate visiting Canadians. For a brokerage fee, some will even custom buy a vehicle for you and assist you in shipping it and organizing the paperwork for importation.

Whether you check into the title status of your purchase or not, Transport Canada does so when you process your vehicle at the border. They're interested mainly in identifying stolen or wrecked vehicles. But their title search should also uncover any outstanding liens. If liens are in place against your vehicle, you cannot import it and, as mentioned earlier, you will lose all the money you have invested in the purchase to date.

Buying a car in the United States is otherwise no different than buying a car at home. All the same admonishments apply: road test it, have it checked by a mechanic, and comparison shop to make sure you have the right vehicle at the best price. Several books have been written on this subject, from the days of Ralph Nader onwards, and if you're an inexperienced purchaser, you might do a little reading before you approach your first car lot. The used-car trade, while well regulated in comparison to a couple of decades ago, is still a competitive, hard-sell industry.

RECOMMENDED READING

Ingram, David. *David Ingram's Border Book.* Surrey, British Columbia: Hancock House, 1992.

Michaels, Rick. *Auto Riches: How to Make Big Profits Importing New and Used Vehicles From the U.S.* Edmonton (P.O. Box 58055, T5L 4Z4): Auto Riches, 1991.

Marks, Ronald G., Registrar. *Your Guide to Importing a Vehicle from the United States into Canada.* Pickering: Registrar of Imported Vehicles, 1995.

Canada. Transport Canada, Vehicle Importation. *List of Vehicles Imported from the U.S.* Ottawa: Government of Canada, 1995. (Available from the Office of the Registrar of Imported Vehicles; updated regularly.)

APPENDIX 1
TRADE ADMINISTRATION SERVICES AND CUSTOMS BORDER SERVICES OFFICES

Atlantic

Ralston Building
1557 Hollis Street
P.O. Box 3080
Stn. Parklane Centre
Halifax, Nova Scotia
B3J 3G6
Tel: (902) 426-2911

Quebec

130 Dalhousie Street
P.O. Box 2267
Quebec, Quebec
G1K 7P6
Tel: (418) 648-4445

400 d'Youville Square
Montreal, Quebec
H2Y 2C2
Tel: (514) 283-9900

Northern Ontario

2265 Laurent Boulevard
Ottawa, Ontario
K1G 4K3
Tel: (613) 993-0534
(613) 998-3326 (after 4:30 p.m. and weekends)

Southern Ontario

1 Front Street W.
2nd Floor
P.O. Box 10
Station A
Toronto, Ontario
M5W 1A3
Tel: (416) 973-8022
(416) 676-3643 (weekends and holidays)

26 Arrowsmith Road
P.O. Box 2989
Hamilton, Ontario
L8N 3V8
Tel: (905) 308-8715 (Hamilton only)
1-800-361-5603 (toll free)

451 Talbot Street
10th Floor
London, Ontario
N6A 4T9
(Trade Administration Services only)
Tel: (519) 645-5834

P.O. Box 2280, Station A
Walkerville Post Office
Windsor, Ontario
N8Y 4R8
Tel: (519) 257-6400

Prairies

Federal Building
269 Main Street
Winnipeg, Manitoba
R3C 1B3
Tel: (204) 983-6004

720 Harry Hays Building
220 - 4th Avenue S.E.
Calgary, Alberta
T2G 4X3
Tel: (403) 292-8750
(403) 292-4660

Pacific

333 Dunsmuir Street
Vancouver, British Columbia
V6B 5R4
Tel: (604) 666-0545

APPENDIX 2
"D" SERIES MEMORANDA

The following list represents the numbering system of the "D" series Memoranda or Customs regulations and includes a full Table of Contents for D13 of the series, on valuation, to demonstrate how complete the regulations are.

The Customs regulations provide the details on how the Customs Act and related legislation are administered. In effect, they give Customs operations its underlying structure. You'll notice that the regulations are divided into 21 sections.

While the numbering system is not as complete as the full Table of Contents for the "D" series, it does give you some idea of where to begin your research if you're looking for information on a particular subject. Most public libraries carry copies of the "D" series, or you can contact your closest Customs office for information on where to find one.

D1 — **General**
D1-1 List of Customs offices
D1-2 Special Services
D1-3 Fee for information and documents
D1-4 Invoice requirements of Canada Customs
D1-6 Authority to act as agent
D1-6 Agents' accounting for imported goods and payment of duties regulations
D1-7 Posting security for transacting bonded operations
D1-8 Licensing of customs brokers
D1-10 Canada-United States Treaty for the Suppression of Smuggling
D1-14 Interim memorandum procedure
D1-15 Customs and Excise directives
D1-16 Disclosure of information pursuant to the Customs Act

D2 — **International Travel**
D2-1 Temporary importation of baggage and conveyances by non-residents
D2-2 Settlers' effects
D2-3 Returning persons exemption regulations
D2-4 Temporary importation of conveyances by residents of Canada
D2-5 Legislative requirements — presentation of persons
D2-6 Residential status of travellers arriving in Canada

D3 —	**Transportation**
D3-1	Regulations respecting the importation, transportation and exportation of goods
D3-2	International air traffic
D3-3	Forwarded and consolidated cargo — Import Movements
D3-4	Highway cargo
D3-5	Vessels in international service
D3-6	Railway rolling stock
D3-7	Cargo containers used in international service
D3-8	Cargo control contraventions
D4 —	**Warehousing, Duty Free Shops, and Ships' Stores**
D4-1	Customs bonded warehouses regulations
D4-2	Ships' stores regulations
D4-3	Duty Free Shop
D5 —	**International Mail**
D5-1	Customs International Mail Processing System
D6 —	**Refunds**
D6-2	Refund of duties and taxes
D7 —	**Drawbacks**
D7-2	Drawbacks — home consumption drawbacks
D7-3	Drawbacks — inward processing
D8 —	**Remissions and Temporary Importation**
D8-1	Temporary importation regulations
D8-2	Canadian goods abroad
D8-3	Advertising material remission order
D8-4	Information pertaining to remission orders
D8-5	Machinery Program
D8-6	Instructions pertaining to conditional remission orders subject to post audit
D8-7	Remissions — post-audit — vessels
D8-8	Remissions — post-audit — vehicles
D8-9	Defense production and development sharing remission order
D8-10	Satellites and satellite subsystems remission order
D8-11	Remissions — post-audit — fabrics, blouses, and shirts

D9 — **Prohibited Importations**
D9-1 Ten entries (including copyrighted books, substitutes for butter, used or secondhand motor vehicles, periodicals, and white phosphorous matches)

D10 — **Tariff Classification; Commodities**
D10-13 Classification of goods
D10-14 Tariff items — Interpretation
D10-15 Tariff codes — Schedule II
D10-16 Tariff codes — by regulation
D10-17 Information requirements

D11 — **General Tariff Information**
D11-2 Selected Tariff Board decisions on Tariff Classification of Goods
D11-3 Marking of imported goods
D11-4 Proof of Origin regulations
D11-6 Determination/re-determination and appraisal/re-appraisal of goods
D11-8 Administrative policy — end-use provisions
D11-10 Interpretation of the Customs and Excise Offshore Application Act

D12 — **Tariff Amendments**
D12-1 Notice of ways and means motion to amend the Customs Tariff
D12-2 Customs Duties reduction or removal order
D12-3 Chemicals and plastics duties reduction or removal order
D12-4 Customs Tariff schedules, amendment orders
D12-5 Customs duties accelerated reduction orders

D13 — **Valuation**
D13-1-1 Valuation for duty regulations
D13-1-2 Direct shipment of goods regulations
D13-2-1 Responsibility of importers and/or authorized agents with respect to valuation
D13-2-3 Exchange rate for calculation of value for duty under the Customs Act
D13-2-4 Valuation of goods imported into Canada that are not in accordance with contract
D13-2-5 Customs valuation: effects and transitional implications of the GST
D13-3-1 Methods of determining value for duty
D13-3-2 Related persons (Customs Act, sections 45 to 53)
D13-3-3 Transportation and associated costs
D13-3-4 Place of direct shipment
D13-3-5 Customs valuation: common delivered/zone prices

D13-3-7 Engineering, development work, etc., undertaken elsewhere than in Canada
D13-3-8 Generally accepted accounting principles
D13-3-9 Package deals
D13-3-10 Goods imported in split shipments
D13-3-11 Valuation of goods imported into Canada to be used in the assembly, construction, or fabrication of a facility or a machine sold on an installed contract basis
D13-3-12 Assists
D13-3-13 Customs valuation: interest charges for deferred payment for imported goods
D13-3-14 Quota payments
D13-4-1 "Transaction Value" method of valuation
D13-4-2 Customs valuation: sold for export to Canada
D13-4-3 Customs valuation: price paid or payable
D13-4-4 Limitations on the use of transaction value
D13-4-5 Transaction Value method for related persons
D13-4-7 Adjustments to the price paid or payable
D13-4-8 Assists
D13-4-9 Royalties and licence fees
D13-4-10 Discounts
D13-4-11 Confirming commissions and credit risk insurance
D13-4-12 Commissions and brokerage
D13-5-1 Application of sections 49 and 50 of Customs Act
D13-7-1 Determination of the price per unit
D13-7-3 Deductions from the price per unit
D13-8-1 "Computed Value" method
D13-9-1 "Residual Basis of Appraisal" method
D13-10-1 Used goods
D13-10-2 Used automobiles, motor vehicles, and pleasure craft
D13-11-1 Goods sold in Canada while entered temporarily for conventions and exhibitions
D13-11-2 Value for duty of certain information-based products
D13-11-3 Value for duty of printed or lithographed paper matter
D13-11-4 Value for duty of promotional material
D13-11-5 Value for duty of export packing

D14 — Special Import Measures Act
D14-1 Special Import Measures Act regulations

D15 —		**Special Import Measures Act: Investigations**
D15-1		Twenty-nine entries, each dealing with a different product
D16 —		**Surtax**
D16-1		Information pertaining to the application, collection and refund of surtax
D17 —		**Accounting and Release Procedures**
D17-1		Accounting for imported goods and payment of duties regulations
D17-2		Coding of Adjustment Request forms
D18 —		**Excise Goods**
D18-1		Importation of stills
D18-2		Imported tobacco products
D19 —		**Acts and Regulations of other Government Departments**
D19-1		Agriculture
D19-2		Atomic Energy
D19-3		Canadian Wheat Board
D19-4		Communications
D19-5		Consumer and Corporate Affairs
D19-6		Energy, Mines, and Resources
D19-7		Environment
D19-8		Fisheries and Oceans
D19-9		Health and Welfare
D19-10		External Affairs
D19-11		National Energy Board
D19-12		Transport
D19-13		General legislation
D20 —		**Exportations**
D20-1		Reporting of exported goods regulations
D21 —		**International Programs**
D21-1		Customs diplomatic privileges
D21-2		Revenue exemptions and privileges granted to the United Nations
D21-3		Commonwealth, NATO, and other Importations
D21-4		Joint Canada–United States projects

APPENDIX 3
OTHER ACTS AND REGULATIONS
ADMINISTERED BY CANADA CUSTOMS

The acts listed below represent most of the legislation administered by Canada Customs on behalf of other departments of the federal government. On the right is the number of the "D" series memorandum that details what aspect of a particular act Customs is responsible for.

Aeronautics Act	D3-1-5
Animal Disease and Protection Act	D19-1-1
Atomic Energy Control Act	D19-2-1
Bretton Woods Agreement Act	D21-2-6
Canada Post Office Act	D5-1-1
Canada Shipping Act	D3-1-5
	D3-5-1
	D3-5-7
Canada Wheat Board Act	D19-3-1
Copyright Act	D9-1-2
Criminal Code	D19-13-2
Cultural Property Export and Import Act	D19-4-1
Currency and Exchange Act	B Memo
Customs Tariff	D19-13-2
Dairy Products Regulations	D19-1-3
Egg and Processed Eggs Regulations	D19-1-4
Explosives Act	D19-6-1
Export and Import Permits Act (Exportations)	D19-10-3
Export and Import Permits Act (Importations)	D19-10-2
Fish Inspection Act	D19-8-1
Fisheries Act	D19-8-2
Food and Drugs Act	D19-9-1
	D19-9-2
Fresh Fruit and Vegetables Regulations	D19-1-7
Game Export Act	D19-13-1
Hazardous Products Act	D19-5-1
Honey Regulations	D19-1-8
Importation of Intoxicating Liquors Act	D3-1-3
Importation of Offensive Weapons Regulations	D19-13-2

International Boundary Commission Act	D19-6-2
Maple Products Regulations	D19-1-8
Meat Inspection Act	D19-1-2
Motor Vehicle Safety Act	D19-12-1
Motor Vehicle Tire Safety Act	D19-12-2
Narcotic Control Act	D19-9-2
National Energy Board Act	D19-11-1
National Transportation Act	D3-5-1
Pacific Shellfish Regulations	D19-8-4
Pest Control Products Act	D19-1-11
Plant Quarantine Act	D19-1-9
Precious Metal Marking Act	D19-5-4
Privileges and Immunities (I.O.) Act	D21-2-1
	D21-2-2
	D21-2-3
	D21-2-4
	D21-2-5
	D21-2-7
Privileges and Immunities Accession Order (U.N.)	D21-2-1
Processed Poultry Regulations	D19-1-2
Processed Products Regulations	D19-1-8
Proof of Origin Regulations	D11-4-2
Radiation Emitting Devices Act	D19-9-1
Radio Act/General Radio Regulations/Radio Interference Regulations	D19-4-2
Seeds Act	D19-1-10
Textile Labelling Act	D19-5-3
Transport Act	D3-7-2
Valuation for Duty Regulations	D13-1-1
Visiting Forces Act	D21-3-1
White Phosphorous Matches Act	D9-1-13

APPENDIX 4
CUSTOMS VALUATION QUESTIONNAIRE

The following list of questions illustrates the type of information and documentation required by Revenue Canada–Customs during a value for duty review:

REQUESTED INFORMATION AND DOCUMENTATION

1. Copies of Customs entries, commercial and Canada Customs invoices, and any other relevant entry documents covering the ten most recent importations of the goods in question. Should these not be representative of your firm's complete line of the products in question, please submit additional documents as appropriate.

2. A description of any restriction on the use or disposition of the imported goods by your firm.

3. A description of any conditions or considerations to which the sale, or the price, is subject.

4. An explanation of the corporate relationship between your firm and the vendor.

5. A description of any arrangement whereby any part of the value of any proceeds of any subsequent resale, use, or disposition of the goods by your firm accrues directly or indirectly to the vendor.

6. Details of any buying, selling, or other commissions and brokerage paid or incurred by your firm and a full description of the functions performed by the recipient of the commission or brokerage fee in respect of the goods under review and all relevant documentation covering such commissions during the period in question.

7. Full details of the packing costs and charges incurred by your firm in respect of the goods under review.

8. Complete details as to the method of freight settlement for the goods in question.

9. Complete details (costs, country of origin, amounts paid) regarding any of the following goods and services supplied directly or indirectly by your firm for use in connection with the production of the imported goods:
   (a) materials, components, parts, and other goods incorporated;
   (b) tools, dies, moulds, and other goods utilized in the production of the imported goods;
   (c) any materials consumed in the production of the imported goods; and
   (d) engineering, developing work, art work, design work, plans, and sketches necessary for the production of the imported goods.

10. Details of any royalties or licence fees that your firm must pay, directly or indirectly, in respect of the goods under review and copies of the relevant agreements between your firm and the receiving party.

11. An explanation of any costs or charges included in the invoiced selling price incurred for the construction, erection, assembly, or maintenance of the goods and/or any technical assistance in respect of the goods after importation.

12. Amounts for any Canadian duties and taxes included in the price paid or payable of the goods under review.

13. Full details regarding any discounts, rebates, or any other decrease in the price extended to your firm by the vendor in respect of the goods under review.

Reproduced with permission from the Canadian Trade Law Reporter formerly published by and copyright CCH Canadian Limited, Don Mills, Ontario.

14. A copy of your firm's most recent annual report and profit and loss statements, as well as those for the two preceding years.

15. The annual dollar and unit volume of imports for the goods in question by your firm for the most recent calendar year as well as an estimate for the current calendar year. If your firm purchases the goods from more than one vendor, please provide this information by vendor as well as in total.

16. A complete list of all other goods which your firm imports from the above vendor.

17. An outline of your firm's channels of distribution and a description of the level of trade of your firm.

REQUESTED INFORMATION AND DOCUMENTATION — RELATED PARTIES

1. Copies of commercial invoices showing a representative sample of sales of the goods in question by the vendor to unrelated customers in the domestic market; or

2. Evidence that the transfer price to your firm allows the vendor to recover all costs plus a profit which is representative of the profit earned overall by the related vendor in the domestic market. In this regard, it would be appropriate to provide the most recent annual report for the related vendor and a breakdown of the transfer price on the various imported subject goods showing the cost of production (material, labor, and overhead), general expenses and profit; or

3. Any other information that demonstrates the absence of influence on the price of the subject goods imported from the related vendor.

ADDITIONAL EXPLANATION FOR RELATED PARTIES

In addition to Customs memorandum D13-4-5, paragraph 3, other considerations for proving a lack of influence may be:

1. Proof of the exporter's sales to unrelated customers to whom they sell directly. Such sales, in order of preference, would be to:

(a) unrelated, arm's length customers in Canada; or

(b) unrelated, arm's length customers in other countries;

The arm's length prices are then compared to the inter-company transfer price. If there is a difference between the prices an attempt should be made to explain these. Costs included in unrelated company sales such as bad debt expense, sales support staff, warranty, trade level, etc., which may not be applicable in the inter-company price, should be considered.

Objective and quantifiable information must be provided to explain a difference in prices. If differences to within a reasonable variance cannot be explained, a method other than transaction value must be used for those goods.

2. Another consideration may be to provide a copy of a ruling the exporter may have received from a foreign customs authority regarding exports to a related company under the transaction value system. The supporting documentation and investigation for the ruling would also have to be provided. It must reflect current conditions and be representative of exports to the Canadian company. Due to varying emphasis of countries on influence due to relationships, such a submission in itself may not be sufficient.

3. The above considerations are not restrictive or conclusive and are examples of the type of information that could establish absence of influence. A company may wish to alter one of the above considerations or attack the problem from a completely different angle in documenting a case to prove an absence of influence.

APPENDIX 5
INDUSTRY ORGANIZATIONS AND GOVERNMENT MINISTRIES

The following list gives you the addresses and telephone numbers of the head offices of organizations and government agencies you can contact for further information and materials on different aspects of importing. You may want to contact these offices and inquire if there is a regional office nearer to you.

a. FEDERAL GOVERNMENT AGENCIES

Agriculture Canada
Sir John Carling Building
930 Carling Avenue
Ottawa, Ontario
K1A OC5
Tel: (613) 759-1000

Canadian International Trade Tribunal
333 Laurier Avenue W.
Ottawa, Ontario
K1A 0G7
Tel: (613) 990-2452
Fax: (613) 990-2439

Industry Canada (amalgamation of Consumer and Corporate Affairs Canada, Communications Canada, and Science and Industry Canada)
235 Queens Street
Ottawa, Ontario
K1A 0H5
Tel: (613) 941-0222

Foreign Affairs and
International Trade Canada
Lester B. Pearson Building
125 Sussex Drive
Ottawa, Ontario
K1A 0G2

General information:
Tel: 1-800-267-8376 (toll-free)
Import permits and controls, including dairy and poultry products:
Tel: (613) 995-8104
Textiles and clothing:
Tel: (613) 996-3711

Federal Business Development Bank
800 Victoria Square
Tour de la Bourse, C.P. 335
Montreal, Quebec
H4Z 1L4
Tel: 1-800-361-2126 (toll free)

Regional offices:
Vancouver (604) 666-7800
Winnipeg (204) 983-7811
Toronto (416) 973-1144
Montreal (514) 283-3657
Halifax (902) 426-7860

Revenue Canada, Customs, Excise and Taxation
NAFTA inquiries: Origin Determination
Connaught Building
555 MacKenzie Avenue
6th Floor
Ottawa, Ontario
K1A 0L5
Tel: 1-800-661-6121 (toll-free)
NAFTA inquiries: U.S. Customs
(in English only)
(202) 927-0066
NAFTA inquiries: Mexico Customs
(in Spanish only)
(525) 211-3545

Statistics Canada
Reference Centre
R.H. Coats Building Lobby
Tunney's Pasture
Ottawa, Ontario
K1A 0T6
Tel: (613) 951-8116

b. PROVINCIAL GOVERNMENT AGENCIES

All provinces have offices on business development, small business, or consumer and commercial relations. The actual titles vary but they perform the same functions and usually provide literature (free or for a nominal charge) on many aspects of business development, including import/export. Check the blue pages of your telephone book for the appropriate office in your region.

c. INDUSTRY AND RELATED BUSINESS ORGANIZATIONS

Canadian Council for International Business (formerly International Chamber of Commerce)
55 Metcalfe Street
Suite 1160
Ottawa, Ontario
K1P 6N4
Tel: (613) 230-5462
Fax: (613) 230-7087
(The Council can provide names and addresses of chambers of commerce all over the world and recommend and forward import-related publications, depending on your particular needs.)

Canadian Importers Association
210 Dundas Street W.
Suite 700
Toronto, Ontario
M5G 2E8
Tel: (416) 595-5333
Fax: (416) 595-8226
(Several publications and many services available to members)

Canadian International Freight Forwarders Association
P.O. Box 929
Streetsville, Ontario
L5M 2C5
Tel: (905) 567-4633
Fax: (905) 542-2716

Canadian Manufacturers' Association
75 International Boulevard
4th Floor
Etobicoke, Ontario
M9W 6L9
Tel: (416) 798-8000
Fax: (416) 798-8050

Canadian Society of Customs Brokers
111 York Street
Ottawa, Ontario
K1N 5T4
Tel: (613) 562-3543
Fax: (613) 562-3548

APPENDIX 6
CUSTOMS OFFICE CODES

000   **NOVA SCOTIA**

001	Amherst
009	Halifax
026	Halifax International Airport
007	Halifax Mail Centre
010	Kentville
011	Liverpool
013	Lunenburg
014	Middleton
015	New Glasgow
019	Port Hawkesbury
020	Shelburne
021	Sydney
022	Truro
025	Yarmouth

100   **PRINCE EDWARD ISLAND**

101	Charlottetown
102	Summerside

200   **NEW BRUNSWICK**

214	Andover
201	Bathurst
225	Campobello
221	Caraquet
215	Centreville
216	Clair
202	Dalhousie
208	Deer Island
213	Edmundston
204	Fredericton
219	Gillespie Portage
217	Grand Falls
224	Grand Manan
206	Moncton
207	Newcastle
209	St. Andrews
205	St. Croix
218	St. Leonard
211	St. Stephen
212	Woodstock

300   **QUEBEC**

318	Abercorn
329	Armstrong
355	Baie-Comeau
376	Beebe
363	Cap Aux Meules
365	Chartierville
301	Chicoutimi
337	Clarenceville
356	Cowansville
371	Daaquam
303	Drummondville
330	Dundee
362	East Hereford
369	East Pinnacle
332	Frelighsburg
304	Gaspé
370	Glen Sutton
305	Granby
333	Hemmingford
366	Hereford Road
334	Highwater
342	Joliette
343	Lachute
372	Lac-Mégantic
351	Lacolle
348	Lévis
359	Marieville
344	Montmagny

MONTREAL

395	Main Long Room
396	International Airport (Dorval)
398	Intermediate Terminal (C.D.L.)
399	International Airport (Mirabel)
367	Morses Line
368	Noyan
331	Pohénégamook
312	Quebec
345	Richmond
313	Rimouski
340	Rivère-du-Loup

314	Rock Island	424	Midland
375	Rock Island, Rte. 143	486	Newmarket
349	Rouyn-Noranda	427	Niagara Falls
328	St-Armand-Philipsburg	428	North Bay
320	St-Hyacinthe	476	Oakville
321	St-Jean	487	Orangeville
346	St-Jérôme	429	Orillia
335	St-Pamphile	430	Oshawa
361	Sept-Iles	431	Ottawa
315	Shawinigan	418	Owen Sound
316	Sherbrooke	469	Pembroke
317	Sorel	470	Perth
354	Stanhope	435	Peterborough
347	Thetford Mines	471	Port Colborne
322	Trois-Rivières	439	Prescott
307	Trout River	436	Rainy River
350	Val D'or	433	Renfrew
323	Valleyfield	445	St. Catharines
327	Victoriaville	446	St. Thomas
308	Woburn	440	Sarnia
		441	Sault Ste. Marie
400	**ONTARIO**	442	Simcoe
494	Arnprior	474	Smith Falls
459	Barrie	465	Sombra
402	Belleville	425	Stratford
460	Bracebridge	444	Sudbury
480	Brampton	437	Thunder Bay
404	Brantford	447	Tillonsburg
405	Brockville	467	Timmins
457	Cambridge		
406	Chatham	**TORONTO**	
407	Cobourg	491	Customs Mail Centre
455	Collingwood	495	Main Long Room
409	Cornwall	496	Interport Sufferance Warehouse (Dixie)
410	Fort Erie	497	International Airport (Pearson)
411	Fort Frances	498	Midcontinent Truck Terminal (Queensway)
412	Goderich		
414	Guelph	499	Sufferance Truck Terminal (K.R.)
483	Halton Hills	449	Trenton
417	Hamilton	450	Wallaceburg
419	Kenora	451	Welland
420	Kingston	**WINDSOR**	
401	Kitchener	452	Detroit/Canada Tunnel
456	Lansdowne	453	Ambassador Bridge
464	Leamington	454	Windsor Main Office
422	Lindsay	492	Woodstock
423	London		

500	**MANITOBA**	709	Chief Mountain
507	Boissevain	719	Climax
521	Cartwright	705	Coutts
511	Churchill	708	Del Bonita
524	Coulter	702	Edmonton
520	Crystal City	703	Lethbridge
502	Emerson	704	Medicine Hat
503	Gretna	710	Red Deer
522	Lena	711	Wild Horse
523	Lyleton		
517	Piney	**800**	**BRITISH COLUMBIA AND YUKON**
509	Snowflake	841	Aldergrove
506	South Junction	892	Beaver Creek
505	Sprague	815	Boundary Bay
516	Tolstoi	838	Campbell River
519	Windy Gates	834	Carson
518	Winkler	816	Cascade
504	Winnipeg	836	Chopaka
510	Winnipeg International Airport	830	Courtenay
		801	Cranbrook
	NORTHWEST TERRITORIES	894	Dawson City
512	Inuvik	839	Dawson Creek
513	Iqaluit	840	Douglas
514	Tuktoyaktuk	829	Flathead
515	Yellowknife	893	Fraser
		817	Huntingdon
600	**SASKATCHEWAN**	814	Kamloops
614	Big Beaver	831	Kelowna
612	Carievale	818	Kingsgate
615	Coronach	827	Kitimat
610	Estevan	835	Midway
718	Monchy	804	Nanaimo
601	Moose Jaw	828	Nelway
716	North Battleford	819	Osoyoos
613	Northgate	842	Pacifc Customs Brokers Highway Sufferance Warehouse
602	North Portal	813	Pacific Highway
616	Oungre	832	Paterson
715	Prince Albert	807	Penticton
604	Regina	891	Pleasant Camp
607	Regway	825	Port Alberni
617	Torquay	826	Powell River
618	West Poplar River	820	Prince George
712	Willow Creek	808	Prince Rupert
700	**ALBERTA**	824	Roosville
706	Aden	822	Rykerts
701	Calgary	837	Sydney
707	Carway		

171

VANCOUVER
- 803 Mail Centre
- 809 Main Long Room
- 806 Marine and Rail
- 810 United Terminals
- 821 Vancouver International Airport
- 823 Vernon
- 811 Victoria
- 833 Waneta
- 890 Whitehorse

900 NEWFOUNDLAND
- 921 Argentia
- 908 Burgeo
- 911 Corner Brook
- 919 Fortune
- 912 Gander
- 913 Goose Bay
- 910 Grand Falls
- 907 Harbour Breton
- 922 Harbour Grace
- 914 St. John's

950 PRECLEARANCE OPERATIONS
- 951 Lahr

APPENDIX 7
LIST OF COUNTRIES, CURRENCY, AND CODES
(including U.S. States)

COUNTRY/U.S. STATE	CODE	CURRENCY	CURRENCY CODE
AFGHANISTAN	AF	Afghani	AFA
ALBANIA	AL	Lek	ALL
ALGERIA	DZ	Algerian Dinar	DZD
AMERICAN SAMOA	AS	US Dollar	USD
ANDORRA	AD	Spanish Peseta	ESP
		French Franc	FRF
		Andorran Peseta	ADP
ANGOLA	AO	Kwanza	AOK
ANGUILLA	AI	East Caribbean Dollar	XCD
ANTARCTICA	AQ	US Dollar	USD
ANTIGUA AND BARBUDA	AG	East Caribbean Dollar	XCD
ARGENTINA	AR	Austral	ARA
ARUBA	AW	Aruban Guilder	AWG
AUSTRALIA	AU	Australian Dollar	AUD
AUSTRIA	AT	Schilling	ATS
BAHAMAS	BS	Bahamian Dollar	BSD
BAHRAIN	BH	Bahraini Dinar	BHD
BANGLADESH	BD	Taka	BDT
BARBADOS	BB	Barbados Dollar	BBD
BELGIUM	BE	Belgian Franc	BEF
BELIZE	BZ	Belize Dollar	BZD
BENIN	BJ	CFA Franc BCEAO	XOF
BERMUDA	BM	Bermudan Dollar	BMD
BHUTAN	BT	Indian Rupee	INR
		Ngultrum	BTN
BOLIVIA	BO	Bolivian Peso	BOP
BOTSWANA	BW	Pula	BWP
BOUVET ISLAND	BV	Norwegian Krone	NOK
BRAZIL	BR	**Brazilian Real**	**BRL**
BRITISH INDIAN OCEAN TERRITORY	IO	US Dollar	USD
BRUNEI DARUSSALAM	BN	Brunei Dollar	BND
BULGARIA	BG	Lev	BGL
BURKINA FASO	BF	CFA Franc BCEAO	XOF
BURUNDI	BI	Burundi Franc	BIF
BYELORUSSIAN SSR	BY	Rouble	SUR
CAMEROON	CM	CFA Franc BEAC	XAF
CANADA	CA	Canadian Dollar	CAD
CAPE VERDE	CV	Cape Verde Escudo	CVE
CAYMAN ISLANDS	KY	Cayman Islands Dollar	KYD
CENTRAL AFRICAN REPUBLIC	CF	CFA Franc BEAC	XAF
CHAD	TD	CFA Franc BEAC	XAF
CHILE	CL	Chilean Peso	CLP
CHINA	CN	Yuan Renminbi	CNY
CHRISTMAS ISLAND	CX	Australian Dollar	AUD
COCOS (KEELING) ISLANDS	CC	Australian Dollar	AUD
COLOMBIA	CO	Colombian Peso	COP
COMOROS	KM	Comoro Franc	KMF
CONGO	CG	CFA Franc BEAC	XAF
COOK ISLANDS	CK	New Zealand Dollar	NZD
COSTA RICA	CR	Costa Rican Colon	CRC
CÔTE D'IVOIRE	CI	CFA Franc BCEAO	XOF
CUBA	CU	Cuban Peso	CUP
CYPRUS	CY	Cyprus Pound	CYP
CZECHOSLOVAKIA	CS	Koruna	CSK
DENMARK	DK	Danish Krone	DKK
DJIBOUTI	DJ	Djibouti Franc	DJF
DOMINICA	DM	East Caribbean Dollar	XCD
DOMINICAN REPUBLIC	DO	Dominican Peso	DOP
EAST TIMOR	TP	Timor Escudo	TPE
		Rupiah	IDR
ECUADOR	EC	Sucre	ECS
EGYPT	EG	Egyptian Pound	EGP
EL SALVADOR	SV	El Salvador Colon	SVC
EQUATORIAL GUINEA	GQ	Ekpwele	GQE
ETHIOPIA	ET	Ethiopian Birr	ETB
FALKLAND ISLANDS (MALVINAS)	FK	Falkland Islands Pound	FKP
FAVROE ISLANDS	FO	Danish Krone	DKK
FIJI	FJ	Fiji Dollar	FJD
FINLAND	FI	Markka	FIM
FRANCE	FR	French Franc	FRF
FRENCH GUIANA	GF	French Franc	FRF
FRENCH POLYNESIA	PF	CFP Franc	XPF
FRENCH SOUTHERN TERRITORIES	TF	French Franc	FRF
GABON	GA	CFA Franc BEAC	XAF
GAMBIA	GM	Dalasi	GMD
GERMANY	DE	Deutsche Mark	DEM
GHANA	GH	Cedi	GHC
GIBRALTAR	GI	Gibraltar Pound	GIP
GREECE	GR	Drachma	GRD
GREENLAND	GL	Danish Krone	DKK
GRENADA	GD	East Caribbean Dollar	XCD
GUADELOUPE	GP	French Franc	FRF
GUAM	GU	US Dollar	USD
GUATEMALA	GT	Quetzal	GTQ
GUINEA	GN	**Franc**	**GNF**
GUINEA-BISSAU	GW	Guinea-Bissau Peso	GWP
GUYANA	GY	Guyana Dollar	GYD
HAITI	HT	Gourde	HTG
		US Dollar	USD
HEARD AND MCDONALD ISLANDS	HM	Australian Dollar	AUD
HONDURAS	HN	Lempira	HNL
HONG KONG	HK	Hong Kong Dollar	HKD
HUNGARY	HU	Forint	HUF
ICELAND	IS	Iceland Krona	ISK
INDIA	IN	Indian Rupee	INR
INDONESIA	ID	Rupiah	IDR
IRAN (ISLAMIC REPUBLIC OF)	IR	Iranian Rial	IRR
IRAQ	IQ	Iraqui Dinar	IQD
IRELAND	IE	Irish Pound	IEP
ISRAEL	IL	Shekel	ILS
ITALY	IT	Italian Lira	ITL
IVORY COAST (refer to Côte d'Ivoire)			
JAMAICA	JM	Jamaican Dollar	JMD
JAPAN	JP	Yen	JPY
JORDAN	JO	Jordanian Dinar	JOD
KAMPUCHEA, DEMOCRATIC	KH	Riel	KHR
KENYA	KE	Kenyan Shilling	KES
KIRIBATI	KI	Australian Dollar	AUD
KOREA, DEMOCRATIC PEOPLE'S REPUBLIC OF	KP	North Korean Won	KPW
KOREA, REPUBLIC OF	KR	Won	KRW
KUWAIT	KW	Kuwaiti Dinar	KWD
LAOS PEOPLE'S DEMOCRATIC REPUBLIC	LA	Kip	LAK
LEBANON	LB	Lebanese Pound	LBP
LESOTHO	LS	Rand	ZAR
		Loti	LSL
LIBERIA	LR	Liberian Dollar	LRD
LIBYAN ARAB JAMAHIRIYA	LY	Libyan Dinar	LYD
LIECHTENSTEIN	LI	Swiss Franc	CHF
LUXEMBOURG	LU	Luxembourg Franc	LUF
MACAU	MO	Pataca	MOP
MADAGASCAR	MG	Malagasy Franc	MGF
MALAWI	MW	Kwacha	MWK
MALAYSIA	MY	Malaysian Ringgit	MYR
MALDIVES	MV	Rufiyaa	MVR
MALI	ML	CFA Franc BCEAO	XOF
MALTA	MT	Maltese Lira	MTL
MARSHALL ISLANDS	MH	US Dollar	USD
MARTINIQUE	MQ	French Franc	FRF
MAURITANIA	MR	Ouguiya	MRO
MAURITIUS	MU	Mauritius Rupee	MUR
MEXICO	MX	Mexican Peso	MXP
MICRONESIA	FM	US Dollar	USD
MONACO	MC	French Franc	FRF
MONGOLIA	MN	Tugrik	MNT
MONTSERRAT	MS	East Caribbean Dollar	XCD

173

COUNTRY/U.S. STATE	CODE	CURRENCY	CURRENCY CODE	COUNTRY/U.S. STATE	CODE	CURRENCY	CURRENCY CODE
MOROCCO	MA	Moroccan Dirham	MAD	UNITED STATES	US	US Dollar	USD
MOZAMBIQUE	MZ	Metical	MZM	■ ALABAMA	UAL		
MYANMAR	MM	Kyat	BUK	■ ALASKA	UAK		
NAMIBIA	NA	**South African Rand**	**ZAR**	■ ARIZONA	UAZ		
		Namibian Dollar	**NAD**	■ ARKANSAS	UAR		
NAURU	NR	Australian Dollar	AUD	■ CALIFORNIA	UCA		
NEPAL	NP	Nepalese Rupee	NPR	■ COLORADO	UCO		
NETHERLANDS	NL	Netherlands Guilder	NLG	■ COLUMBIA (DISTRICT OF)	UDC		
NETHERLANDS ANTILLES	AN	Netherlands Antillian Guilder	ANG	■ CONNECTICUT	UCT		
				■ DELAWARE	UDE		
NEUTRAL ZONE	NT	Kuwaiti Dinar	KWD	■ FLORIDA	UFL		
NEW CALEDONIA	NC	CFP Franc	XPF	■ GEORGIA	UGA		
NEW ZEALAND	NZ	New Zealand Dollar	NZD	■ HAWAII	UHI		
NICARAGUA	NI	**Cordoba Oro**	**NIO**	■ IDAHO	UID		
NIGER	NE	CFA Franc BCEAO	XOF	■ ILLINOIS	UIL		
NIGERIA	NG	Naira	NGN	■ INDIANA	UIN		
NIUE	NU	New Zealand Dollar	NZD	■ IOWA	UIA		
NORFOLK ISLAND	NF	Australian Dollar	AUD	■ KANSAS	UKS		
NORTHERN MARIANA				■ KENTUCKY	UKY		
ISLANDS	MP	US Dollar	USD	■ LOUISIANA	ULA		
NORWAY	NO	Norwegian Krone	NOK	■ MAINE	UME		
OMAN	OM	Rial Omani	OMR	■ MARYLAND	UMD		
PAKISTAN	PK	Pakistan Rupee	PKR	■ MASSACHUSETTS	UMA		
PALAU	PW	US Dollar	USD	■ MICHIGAN	UMI		
PANAMA	PA	Balboa	PAB	■ MINNESOTA	UMN		
		US Dollar	USD	■ MISSISSIPPI	UMS		
PAPUA NEW GUINEA	PG	Kina	PGK	■ MISSOURI	UMO		
PARAGUAY	PY	Guarani	PYG	■ MONTANA	UMT		
PERU	PE	**Nuevo Sol**	**PEN**	■ NEBRASKA	UNE		
		Inti	PEI	■ NEVADA	UNV		
PHILIPPINES	PH	Philippine Peso	PHP	■ NEW HAMPSHIRE	UNH		
PITCAIRN	PN	New Zealand Dollar	NZD	■ NEW JERSEY	UNJ		
POLAND	PL	Zloty	PLZ	■ NEW MEXICO	UNM		
PORTUGAL	PT	Portuguese Escudo	PTE	■ NEW YORK	UNY		
PUERTO RICO	PR	US Dollar	USD	■ NORTH CAROLINA	UNC		
QATAR	QA	Qatari Rial	QAR	■ NORTH DAKOTA	UND		
REUNION	RE	French Franc	FRF	■ OHIO	UOH		
ROMANIA	RO	Leu	ROL	■ OKLAHOMA	UOK		
RWANDA	RW	Rwanda Franc	RWF	■ OREGON	UOR		
ST. HELENA	SH	St. Helena Pound	SHP	■ PENNSYLVANIA	UPA		
ST. KITTS-NEVIS	KN	East Caribbean Dollar	XCD	■ RHODE ISLAND	URI		
SAINT LUCIA	LC	East Caribbean Dollar	XCD	■ SOUTH CAROLINA	USC		
ST. PIERRE AND MIQUELON	PM	French Franc	FRF	■ SOUTH DAKOTA	USD		
ST. VINCENT AND THE				■ TENNESSEE	UTN		
GRENADINES	VC	East Caribbean Dollar	XCD	■ TEXAS	UTX		
SAMOA	WS	Tala	WST	■ UTAH	UUT		
SAN MARINO	SM	Italian Lira	ITL	■ VERMONT	UVT		
SAO TOME AND PRINCIPE	ST	Dobra	STD	■ VIRGINIA	UVA		
SAUDI ARABIA	SA	Saudi Riyal	SAR	■ WASHINGTON (STATE OF)	UWA		
SENEGAL	SN	CFA Franc BCEAO	XOF	■ WEST VIRGINIA	UWV		
SEYCHELLES	SC	Seychelles Rupee	SCR	■ WISCONSIN	UWI		
SIERRA LEONE	SL	Leone	SLL	■ WYOMING	UWY		
SINGAPORE	SG	Singapore Dollar	SGD	UNITED STATES MINOR			
SOLOMON ISLANDS	SB	Solomon Islands Dollar	SBD	OUTLYING ISLANDS	UM	US Dollar	USD
SOMALIA	SO	Somali Shilling	SOS	URUGUAY	UY	Uruguayan Peso	UYP
SOUTH AFRICA	ZA	Rand	ZAR	VANUATU	VU	Vatu	VUV
SPAIN	ES	Spanish Peseta	ESP	VATICAN CITY STATE			
SRI LANKA	LK	Sri Lanka Rupee	LKR	(HOLY SEE)	VA	Italian Lira	ITL
SUDAN	SD	Sudanese Pound	SDP	VENEZUELA	VE	Bolivar	VEB
SURINAM	SR	Surinam Guilder	SRG	VIETNAM	VN	Dong	VND
SVALBARD AND JAN				VIRGIN ISLANDS,			
MAYEN ISLANDS	SJ	Norwegian Krone	NOK	BRITISH	VG	US Dollar	USD
SWAZILAND	SZ	Lilangeni	SZL	VIRGIN ISLANDS, US	VI	US Dollar	USD
SWEDEN	SE	Swedish Krona	SEK	WALLIS AND FUTUNA			
SWITZERLAND	CH	Swiss Franc	CHF	ISLANDS	WF	CFP Franc	XPF
SYRIAN ARAB REPUBLIC	SY	Syrian Pound	SYP	WESTERN SAHARA	EH	Moroccan Dirham	MAD
TAIWAN, PROVINCE OF				YEMEN	YE	Yemeni Rial	YER
CHINA	TW	New Taiwan Dollar	TWD			Yemeni Dinar	YDD
TANZANIA, UNITED				YUGOSLAVIA	YU	New Yugoslavian Dinar	YUD
REPUBLIC OF	TZ	Tanzanian Shilling	TZS	ZAIRE	ZR	Zaire	ZRZ
THAILAND	TH	Baht	THB	ZAMBIA	ZM	Kwacha	ZMK
TOGO	TG	CFA Franc BCEAO	XOF	ZIMBABWE	ZW	Zimbabwe Dollar	ZWD
TOKELAU	TK	New Zealand Dollar	NZD				
TONGA	TO	Pa'anga	TOP				
TRINIDAD AND TOBAGO	TT	Trinidad and Tobago Dollar	TTD				
TUNISIA	TN	Tunisian Dinar	TND				
TURKEY	TR	Turkish Lira	TRL				
TURKS AND CAICOS							
ISLANDS	TC	US Dollar	USD				
TUVALU	TV	Australian Dollar	AUD				
UGANDA	UG	Uganda Shilling	UGS				
UKRAINIAN SSR	UA	Rouble	SUR				
UNION OF SOVIET							
SOCIALIST REPUBLIC	SU	Rouble	SUR				
UNITED ARAB EMIRATES	AE	UAE Dirham	AED				
UNITED KINGDOM	GB	Pound Sterling	GBP				

APPENDIX 8
U.S. FOREIGN TRADE ZONES

Code	Location	Operator
1	New York, NY	S & F Warehouse, Inc.
2	New Orleans, LA	Board of Commissioners of the Port of New Orleans
3	San Francisco, CA	Foreign Trade Services Inc.
3A	San Francisco, CA	Lilli Ann
5	Seattle, WA	Port of Seattle Commission
7	Mayaguez, PR	Puerto Rico Industrial Dev. Co.
7B	Penuelas, PR	Corco
8	Toledo, OH	Toledo-Lucas County Port Authority
8A	Toledo, OH	Jeep Corporation
9	Honolulu, HI	State of Hawaii
9A	Oahu, HI	Hiri, Ewa
9B	Honolulu, HI	Hawaiian Flour Mills
9C	Honolulu, HI	Dole Processed Food Co.
9D	Kahului, HI	Maui Pineapple Co. Ltd.
9E	Oahu, HI	Chevron
12	McAllen, TX	McAllen Trade Zone, Inc.
14	Little Rock, AR	Little Rock Port Authority
14A	Forest City, AR	Sanyo
15	Kansas City, MO	Greater Kansas City FTZ, Inc.
15A	Claycomo, MO	Ford Motor
15B	Kansas City, MO	General Motors
16	Sault Ste. Marie, MI	Economic Development Corp. of Sault Ste. Marie
17	Kansas City, KS	Greater Kansas City FTZ, Inc.
17A	Kansas City, KS	General Motors
18	San Jose, CA	City of San Jose
18A	San Jose, CA	Olympus
18B	Fremont, CA	Nummi, GM & Toyota
19	Omaha, NB	Dock Board of the City of Omaha
20	Suffolk, VA	Virginia Port Authority
20A	Virginia Beach, VA	Stihl
21	Dorchester County, SC	Carolina Trade Zone
21A	Charleston, SC	Porsche
22	Chicago, IL	Illinois International Port District
22A	Chicago, IL	UNR-Leavitt
22B	Chicago, IL	Ford Motor
22C	Du Page County, IL	Power Packaging Inc.
22D	Kane County, IL	Power Packaging Inc.
22E	Du Page County, IL	Power Packaging Inc.
23	Buffalo, NY	County of Erie
23A	Webster, NY	Xerox Corp.
23B	Chautauqua City, NY	Greater Buffalo Press
24	Pittston, PA	Econ Dev Council of N Eastern Penn.
24A	Harrisburg, PA	Olivetti
25	Port Everglades, FL	Port Everglades Port Authority
26	Shenandoah, GA	Georgia Foreign Trade Zone, Inc.
26A	Atlanta, GA	General Motors
26B	La Grange, GA	Goetze Gasket Co.
26C	Hapeville, GA	Ford
27	Boston, MA	Massachusetts Port Authority
27A	Fall River, MA	Sterlingwale
27B	Quincy, MA	General Dynamics
27C	Lawrence, MA	Lawrence Textiles
27D	Farmingham, MA	General Motors
28	New Bedford, MA	City of New Bedford
28A	New Bedford, MA	Codman and Shurtleff
28B	Avon, MA	Codman and Shurtleff
28C	Randolph, MA	Codman and Shurtleff
29	Louisville, KY	Louisville & Jefferson County
29A	Georgetown, KY	Clark Equipment
29B	Louisville, KY	Ford
29C	Jefferson County, KY	General Electric
29D	Jefferson County, KY	IBM
29E	Scott County, KY	Toyota
30	Salt Lake City, UT	Redevelopment Agency of Salt Lake City
31	Granite City, IL	Tri-City Regional Port District
31A	St Louis, MO	Chrysler
32	Miami, FL	Greater Miami Foreign Trade Zone, Inc.
33	Pittsburgh, PA	Regional Industrial Dev. Corp. of Southwestern Pennsylvania
33A	Westmoreland Co., PA	Volkswagen
33B	Allegheny County, PA	Verosol USA, Inc.
34	Niagara County, NY	County of Niagara
35	Philadelphia, PA	The Philadelphia Port Corp.
35A	Landsdale, PA	Ford
36	Galveston, TX	Port of Galveston
37	Orange County, NY	Foreign Trade Dev. Co. of Orange Cty., Inc.
37A	North Tarrytown, NY	General Motors
38	Spartanburg County, SC	Carolina Trade Zone
39	Dallas/Fort Worth, TX	Dallas/Fort Worth Regional Airport Board
39A	Athens, TX	Harvey Industries
40	Cleveland, OH	Cleveland Port Authority
40A	Lorain, OH	Ford
40B	Lordstown, OH	General Motors
41	Milwaukee, WI	Foreign Trade Zone of Wisconsin, Ltd.
41A	Kenosha, WI	American Motors
41B	Manitowoc, WI	Muskegon
41C	Janesville, WI	General Motors
41D	Oak Creek, WI	General Motors
41E	Sturgeon Bay, WI	Bay Shipbuilding Corp.
41F	Milwaukee, WI	Ambrosia Chocolate Co.
42	Orlando, FL	Greater Orlando Aviation Authority
43	Battle Creek, MI	BC/CAL/KAL Inland Port Authority of S. Central Michigan Development Corp.
43A	Springfield & Oshtemo, MI	Clark Equipment
44	Morris County, NJ	N.J. Dept. of Commerce & Economic Dev. Office of Int'l Trade
44B	Hazlet, NJ	Int'l Flavors and Fragrances
44C	Union Beach, NJ	Int'l Flavors and Fragrances
44D	South Brunswick, NJ	Int'l Flavors and Fragrances
45	Portland, OR	Port of Portland
45A	Multnomah Cty, OR	Beall Pipe
46	Cincinnati, OH	Greater Cincinnati FTZ, Inc.
46A	Hamilton City, OH	General Electric
46B	Union City, OH	Honda
46C	Norwood, OH	General Motors
46D	Shelby County, OH	Honda
46E	Cincinnati, OH	U.S. Shoe
47	Campbell County, KY	Greater Cincinnati FTZ, Inc.

Code	Location	Operator
48	Tucson, AZ	Papago-Tucson FTZ Corp.
49	Newark/Elizabeth, NJ	Port Authority of NY and NJ
49A	Edison, NJ	Ford
49B	Linden, NJ	General Motors
50	Long Beach, CA	Board of Harbor Commissioners of the Port of Long Beach
50A	Long Beach, CA	Toyota
50B	San Diego, CA	National Steel and Shipbuilding Co.
51	Duluth, MN	Seaway Port Authority of Duluth
52	Suffolk County, NY	County of Suffolk
53	Rogers County, OK	City of Tulsa-Rogers Cty. Port Authority
53A	Oklahoma City, OK	General Motors
54	Clinton County, NY	Clinton County Area Dev. Corp.
55	Burlington, VT	Greater Burlington Industrial Corp.
55A	St Abanos, VT	Pedigree
56	Oakland, CA	Oakland International Trade Center, Inc.
56A	Benecia, CA	Mazda
57	Mecklenburg County, NC	Piedmont Distribution Center
57A	Mecklenburg County, NC	IBM
58	Bangor, ME	City of Bangor
59	Lincoln, NB	Lincoln Chamber of Commerce
59A	Lincoln, NB	Kawasaki
60	Nogales, AZ	Rivas Realty
61	San Juan, PR	Puerto Rico Commercial Dev. Co.
62	Brownsville, TX	Brownsville Navigation District Port of Brownsville
63	Prince George's County, MD	Prince George's County Government
64	Jacksonville, FL	Jacksonville Port Authority
65	Panama City, FL	Panama City Port Authority
66	Wilmington, NC	N.C. State Port Authority
67	Morehead City, NC	N.C. State Port Authority
68	El Paso, TX	El Paso International Airport
70	Detroit, MI	Greater Detroit Foreign-Trade Zone, Inc.
70A	Romeo, MI	Ford
70B	Detroit, MI	Chrysler
70C	Wayne, MI	Ford
70D	Wixom, MI	Ford
70E	Dearborn, MI	Ford
70F	Ypsilanti, MI	General Motors
70G	Pontiac, MI	General Motors
70H	Sterling Heights, MI	Chrysler
70I	Flat Rock, MI	Mazda Motor Mfg.
70J	Trenton, MI	Chrysler
70K	Detroit/Hantramck, MI	General Motors
70L	Orion Township, MI	General Motors
70M	Lansing, MI	General Motors
71	Windsor Locks, CT	Industrial Development Commission of Windsor Locks
72	Indianapolis, IN	Indianapolis Economic Development Corporation
72A	Kokomo, IN	General Motors
72B	Indianapolis, IN	Eli Lilly & Co.
72C	Lafayette, IN	Eli Lilly & Co.
72D	Clinton, IN	Eli Lilly & Co.
72E	Indianapolis, IN	Chrysler Corp.
72F	Kokomo, IN	Chrysler Corp.
72G	New Castle, IN	Chrysler Corp.
72H	Lafayette, IN	Subaru-Isuzu
73	Baltimore/Washington Int'l Airport, MD	All Cargo Expediting Services, Inc.
74	Baltimore, MD	City of Baltimore
74A	Sparrows Point, MD	Bethlehem Steel Corp.
75	Phoenix, AZ	City of Phoenix
76	Bridgeport, CT	City of Bridgeport
77	Memphis, TN	Mid-South Terminals Company Ltd.
77A	Memphis, TN	Sharp Mfg. Co.
78	Nashville, TN	Metropolitan Nashville-Davidson County Port Authority
78A	Smyrna, TN	Nissan
78B	Lebanon, TN	Toshiba
78C	Hartsville, TN	TVA Hartsville Nuclear Plant
78D	Phipps Bend, TN	TVA Phipps Bend Nuclear Plant
79	Tampa, FL	City of Tampa
80	San Antonio, TX	City of San Antonio
81	Portsmouth, NH	New Hampshire State Port Authority
81A	Portsmouth, NH	Nashua
81B	Colebrook, NH	Manchester Mfg.
82	Mobile, AL	Mobile Airport Authority
82A	Mobile, AL	ADDSCO
83	Huntsville, AL	Huntsville-Madison County Airport
83A	Huntsville, AL	Chrysler
84	Harris County, TX	Port of Houston Authority
85	Everett, WA	Puget Sound Foreign-Trade Zone Association
86	Tacoma, WA	Puget Sound Foreign-Trade Zone Association
86A	Tacoma, WA	Tacoma Boatbuilding
87	Lake Charles, LA	Lake Charles Harbor & Terminal District
87A	Lake Charles, LA	Conoco
88	Great Falls, MT	Economic Growth Council of Great Falls
89	Clark County, NV	Nevada Development Authority
89A	Reno, NV	Porsche
90	Onondaga, NY	County of Onondaga
90A	Cortland County, NY	Smith Corona
90B	Onondaga County, NY	Chrysler
91	Newport, VT	Northeastern Vermont Dev. Assoc.
92	Harrison County, MS	Greater Gulfport/Biloxi Foreign-Trade Zone, Inc.
92A	Escatawpa, MS	Moss Point Marine
93	Raleigh/Durham, NC	Triangle J Council of Governments
94	Laredo, TX	Laredo International Airport
95	Starr County, TX	Starr County Industrial Foundation
96	Eagle Pass, TX	Maverick Co. Dev. Corp.
97	Del Rio, TX	City of Del Rio
98	Birmingham, AL	City of Birmingham
99	Wilmington, DE	State of Delaware
99A	Wilmington, DE	J. Schoeneman
99B	Newark, DE	Chrysler Corp.
99C	Wilmington, DE	General Motors
100	Dayton, OH	Greater Dayton Foreign-Trade Zone, Inc.
101	Clinton County, OH	Airborne FTZ, Inc.
102	St. Louis, MO	St. Louis County Port Authority

Code	Location	Operator
102A	Hazelwood, MO	Ford
102B	Westzville, MO	General Motors
103	Grand Forks, ND	Grand Forks Dev. Foundation
104	Savannah, GA	Savannah Airport Commission
105	Providence and North Kingstown, RI	Rhode Island Port Authority and Economic Dev. Corp.
106	Oklahoma City, OK	The City of Oklahoma City
107	Des Moines, IA	Centennial Warehouse Corp.
107A	Forest City, IA	Winnebago Ind.
108	Valdez, AK	The City of Valdez, Alaska
109	Watertown, NY	The County of Jefferson
109A	Watertown, NY	New York Air Brake Co.
110	Albuquerque, NM	Foreign-Trade Zone of New Mexico
110A	Albuquerque, NM	Summa Medical Corp.
111	JFK Int'l Airport, NY	Port Authority of New York and New Jersey
111A	New York, NY	Jack Young Associates
112	Colorado Springs, CO	Front Range Foreign-Trade Zone, Inc.
113	Ellis County, TX	Trade Zone Operations, Inc.
114	Peoria, IL	Economic Development Council, Inc.
114A	Peoria, IL	Caterpillar Tractor Co.
114B	Belvedere, IL	Chrysler
114C	Peoria, IL	Diamond Star
115	Beaumont, TX	Foreign-Trade Zone of Southeast Texas Inc.
115A	Jefferson Cty, TX	Bethlehem Steel Corp.
116	Port Arthur, TX	Foreign-Trade Zone of Southeast Texas, Inc.
117	Orange, TX	Foreign-Trade Zone of Southeast Texas, Inc.
118	Ogdensburg, NY	Ogdensburg Bridge and Port Authority
119	Minneapolis-St. Paul, MN	Greater Metropolitan FTZ Commission
120	Cowlitz County, WA	Cowlitz Economic Development Council
121	Albany, NY	Capital District Regional Planning Commission
122	Corpus Christi, TX	Port of Corpus Christi Authority
122A	Corpus Christi, TX	Coastal States Petroleum
122B	Corpus Christi, TX	Southwestern Refining
122C	Corpus Christi, TX	Trifinery
122D	Corpus Christi, TX	Baker's Port, Inc.
122E	Corpus Christi, TX	Berry Contracting, Inc.
122F	Corpus Christi, TX	CC Distributing, Inc.
122G	Corpus Christi, TX	Compressors of Texas
122H	Corpus Christi, TX	Hitox
122I	Corpus Christi, TX	Champlin
122J	Nueces County, TX	Valero
122K	Corpus Christi, TX	Reynolds Metals
123	Denver, CO	Aspen Distribution
124	Gramercy, LA	South Louisiana Port Commission
124A	Gramercy, LA	TransAmerican
125	South Bend, IN	Material Trans Action
126	Sparks, NV	Nevada Development Authority
127	West Columbia, SC	Richland-Lexington Airport District
128	Whatcom County, WA	Lummi Indian Business Council
129	Bellingham, WA	Port of Bellingham
130	Blaine, WA	Port of Bellingham
131	Sumas, WA	Port of Bellingham
132	Coos County, OR	International Port of Coos Bay Commission
133	Quad-City, IA/IL	Quad-City Foreign-Trade Zone Inc.
134	Chattanooga, TN	Partners for Economic Progress, Inc.
135	Palm Beach County, FL	Port of Palm Beach District
136	Brevard County, FL	Canaveral Port Authority
137	Washington Dulles Int'l Airport, VA	Washington Dulles Foreign-Trade Zone
138	Franklin County, OH	Rickenbacker Port Authority
139	Sierra Vista, AZ	Sierra Vista Economic Development Foundation Inc.
140	Flint, MI	City of Flint
140A	Flint, MI	General Motors
140B	Midland, MI	Dow Chemical
141	Monroe County, NY	County of Monroe, New York
141A	Rochester, NY	Eastman Kodak
142	Salem, NJ	City of Salem Port Authority
143	West Sacramento, CA	Sacramento-Yolo Port District
144	Brunswick, GA	Brunswick Foreign-Trade Zone, Inc.
145	Shreveport, LA	Caddo-Bossier Parishes Port Commission
146	Lawrence County, IL	Bi-State Authority
146A	Clay County, IL	North American Lighting and Hella Electronics
146B	Clay County, IL	North American Lighting and Hella Electronics
147	Reading, PA	Foreign Trade Zone Corporation of Southwestern Pennsylvania
148	Knoxville, TN	Industrial Development Board of Blount County
149	Freeport, TX	Port of Freeport
150	El Paso, TX	Westport Econ. Dev. Corp.
151	Findlay, OH	Community Dev. Foundation
151A	Findlay and Moraine, OH	Cooper Tire and Rubber Co.
152	Burns Harbor, IN	Indiana Port Commission
152A	Lafayette, IN	Caterpillar
153	San Diego, CA	City of San Diego
154	Baton Rouge, LA	Greater Baton Rouge Port Commission
155	Calhoun/Victoria Counties, TX	Calhoun-Victoria Foreign-Trade Zone, Inc.
155A	Victoria County, TX	Safety Railway
155B	Victoria County, TX	Safety Steel
156	Weslaco, TX	City of Weslaco
156A	Weslaco, TX	McManus
156B	Weslaco, TX	Gulf of Bruyn
156C	Weslaco, TX	Sundor
157	Casper, WY	Natrona County Int'l Airport
158	Vicksburg/Jackson, MS	Vicksburg/Jackson Foreign Trade Zone
159	St. Paul, AK	City of St. Paul
160	Anchorage, AK	Municipality of Anchorage
161	Wichita, KS	Board of Commissioners of Sedgewick
162	New Haven, CT	Greater New Haven Chamber of Commerce
163	Ponce, PR	PR Int'l Disribution Center and Free Zone

APPENDIX 9
U.S. PORT OF EXIT CODES

Port	Code
Aberdeen-Hoquiam, WA	3003
Aguadilla, PR	4901
Airborne Air Park, Wilmington, OH	4181
Akron, OH	4112
Alameda, CA	2813
Albany, NY	1002
Albuquerque, NM	2407
Alburg, VT	0212
Alcan, AK	3104
Alexandria, VA	5402
Alexandria Bay, NY	0708
Algonac, MI	3814
Allentown-Bethlehem-Easton Airport, Lehigh Valley, PA	1181
Alpena, MI	3843
Amarillo, TX	5502
Ambrose, ND	3410
Anacortes, WA	3010
Anchorage, AK	3126
Andrade, CA	2502
Annapolis, MD	1301
Antioch, CA	2828
Antler, ND	3413
Apalachicola, FL	1817
Appomattox River, VA	1404
Ashland, WI	3602
Ashtabula/Conneaut, OH	4122
Ashtabula, OH	4108
Astoria, OR	2901
Atlanta, GA	1704
Austin, TX	5506
Avon, CA	2831
Avondale, LA	2012
Baltimore, MD	1303
Bangor, ME	0102
Bangor, MI	3804
Bar Harbor, ME	0112
Bath, ME	0111
Baton Rouge, LA	2004
Battle Creek, MI	3805
Baudette, MN	3424
Bay City, MI	3804
Bayshore, MI	3843
Baytown, TX	5301
Beaufort-Morehead City, NC	1511

Port	Code
Beaumont, TX	2104
Beecher Falls, VT	0206
Belfast, ME	0132
Belle Chasse, LA	2002
Bellingham, WA	3005
Benicia, CA	2830
Billingsport, NJ	1105
Birmingham, AL	1904
Black River, MI	3802
Blaine, WA	3004
Boca Grande, FL	1807
Boise, ID	2907
Boston, MA	0401
Boundary, WA	3015
Braintree, MA	0401
Brewer, ME	0102
Bridgeport, CT	0410
Bridgewater, ME	0127
Brownsville, TX	2301
Brunswick, GA	1701
Bucksport, ME	0132
Buffalo-Niagara Falls, NY	0901
Burlington, VT	0207
Butte, MT	3305
Calais, ME	0115
Calcite, ME	3818
Calexico, CA	2503
Calumet Harbour, IL	3801
Cambridge, MD	1302
Camden, NJ	1107
Cameron County, TX	2301
Cape Charles City, VA	1406
Cape Vincent, NY	0706
Capitan, CA	2715
Carbury, ND	3421
Carquinez Strait, CA	2830
Carrabelle, FL	1806
Carrollton, MI	3804
Champlain-Rouses Point, NY	0712
Charleston, SC	1601
Charleston, WV	1409
Charlotte, NC	1512
Charlotte Amalie, VI	5101
Chateaugay, NY	0711

Port	Code	Port	Code
Chattanooga, TN	2008	Eagle Point, NJ	1105
Chelsea, MA	0401	East Chicago, IN	3904
Chester, PA	1102	Eastport, ID	3302
Chicago, IL	3901	Eastport, ME	0103
Chicago River, IL	3901	Ecorse, MI	3801
Christiansted, VI	5104	Edgemoor, DE	1103
Cincinnati, OH	4102	El Paso, TX	2402
Claymont, DE	1103	El Segundo, CA	2711
Clayton, NY	0714	Emery World-Wide, Dayton, OH	4195
Cleveland, OH	4101	Empire, OR	2903
Columbia, SC	1604	Erie, PA	4106
Columbus, NM	2406	Escanaba, MI	3808
Columbus, OH	4103	Essexville, MI	3804
Concession, LA	2002	Estero Bay, CA	2719
Conneaut, OH	4109	Eureka, CA	2802
Coos Bay, OR	2903	Evansville, IN	4116
Coral Bay, VI	5103	Everett, MA	0401
Corpus Christi, TX	5312	Everett, WA	3006
Crisfield, MD	1304	Fabens, TX	2404
Crockett, CA	2815	Fairbanks, AK	3111
Cruz Bay, VI	5102	Fairport, OH	4111
Cutler, ME	0103	Fajardo, PR	4904
Dallas-Fort Worth, TX	5501	Fall River, MA	0407
Dalton Cache, AK	3106	Federal Express, Anchorage, AK	3195
Dania, FL	5203	Federal Express, Memphis, TN	2095
Danville, WA	3012	Federal Express, Portland, OR	2991
Davenport, IA	3908	Fernandina Beach, FL	1805
Dayton, OH	4104	Ferry, WA	3013
Delair, NJ	1107	Ferrysburg, MI	3844
Delaware City, DE	1103	Flint, MI	3804
Del Bonita, MT	3322	Fort Covington, NY	0705
Del Rio, TX	2302	Fort Fairfield, ME	0107
Denver, CO	3307	Fort Kent, ME	0110
DePerre, WI	3703	Fort Lauderdale, FL	5203
Derby Line, VT	0209	Fort Pierce, FL	5205
Des Moines, IA	3907	Fort Wayne Airport, IN	4183
Destrehan, LA	2009	Fortuna, ND	3417
Detour, MI	3819	Fort Worth, TX	5501
Detroit, MI	3801	Frederiksted, VI	5105
DHL, Cincinnati, OH	4197	Freeport, TX	5311
DHL, Jamaica, NY	4772	Fresno, CA	2803
DHL, Los Angeles, CA	2770	Friday Harbor, WA	3014
Douglas, AZ	2601	Front Royal, VA	1410
Duluth, MN	3601	Frontier, WA	3020
Dunseith, ND	3422	Galveston, TX	5310
Durham, NC	1503	Gary, IN	3905
Eagle Pass, TX	2303	Georgetown, SC	1602

Port	Code
Gloucester, MA	0404
Gloucester City, NJ	1113
Good Hope, LA	2014
Gramercy, LA	2010
Grand Haven, MI	3816
Grand Portage, MN	3613
Grand Rapids, MI	3806
Grays Harbor, WA	3003
Great Falls, MT	3304
Green Bay, WI	3703
Greenville, MS	2011
Greenville-Spartanburg, SC	1603
Gretna, LA	2002
Groton, CT	0413
Guanica, PR	4905
Guayanilla, PR	4912
Gulfport, MS	1902
Hannah, ND	3408
Hansboro, ND	3415
Harrisburg, PA	1109
Hartford, CT	0411
Harvey, LA	2002
Hector Int'l Airport, Fargo, ND	3481
Herring Bay, AK	3102
Hidalgo, TX	2305
Highgate Springs/Alburg, VT	0212
Hilo, HI	3202
Hollywood, FL	5203
Honolulu, HI	3201
Honolulu Int'l Airport, HI	3205
Hopewell, VA	1408
Hoquiam, WA	3003
Houlton, ME	0106
Houston Airport, TX	5309
Houston, TX	5301
Humacao, PR	4906
Huntington Beach, CA	2709
Huntsville, AL	1910
Huron, OH	4117
Indianapolis, IN	4110
Ingleside Terminal, TX	5312
Inner Harbor Navigational Canal, LA	2002
Int'l Courier Assoc., LA	5270
Int'l Falls-Ranier, MN	3604
Jackman, ME	0104
Jackson Municipal Airport, MS	2081
Jacksonville, FL	1803

Port	Code
James River, VA	1404
John F. Kennedy Int'l Airport, NY	1012
Jonesport, ME	0122
Juneau, AK	3101
Kahului, HI	3203
Kalama, WA	2909
Kansas City, MO	4501
Kenmore Air Harbor, WA	3018
Kenosha, WI	3708
Ketchikan, AK	3102
Key West, FL	5202
Knoxville, TN	2016
Kodiak, AK	3127
Lake Charles, LA	2017
Laredo, TX	2304
Las Vegas, NV	2722
Laurier, WA	3016
Lawrence, MA	0416
Lawrenceburg, IN	4102
Lebanon Airport, NH	0181
Limestone, ME	0118
Linnton, OR	2904
Little Rock, AR	2003
Lockport, IL	3901
Logan Airport, Boston, MA	0417
Long Beach, CA	2709
Longview, WA	2905
Lorain, OH	4121
Los Angeles, CA	2704
Los Angeles Int'l Airport, CA	2720
Louisville, KY	4115
Lubbock, TX	5503
Lubec, ME	0103
Lukeville, AZ	2602
Luling, LA	2009
Lynden, WA	3023
Mackinac Island, MI	3820
Madawaska, ME	0109
Maida, ND	3416
Manistee, MI	3815
Manitowoc, WI	3706
Mantua Creek, NJ	1105
Marcus Hook, PA	1118
Mare Island Strait, CA	2829
Marinette, WI	3702
Marquette, MI	3809
Marrero, LA	2002

Port	Code
Martinez, CA	2820
Marysville, MI	3802
Massena, NY	0704
Mayaguez, PR	4907
Mayberry Slough, CA	2828
Mellville, RI	0503
Memphis, TN	2006
Menominee, MI	3702
Metaline Falls, WA	3025
Miami, FL	5201
Miami Int'l Airport, FL	5206
Michigan City Harbor, IN	3905
Midland Int'l Airport, Midland, TX	5582
Millington, OR	2903
Milwaukee, WI	3701
Minneapolis — St. Paul, MN	3501
Mobile, AL	1901
Moline, IL	3908
Monterey, CA	2805
Morehead City, NC	1511
Morgan, MT	3319
Morgan City, LA	2001
Morristown Airport, Newark, NJ	4681
Morristown, NY	0701
Morro, CA	2719
Munising, MI	3803
Muskegon, MI	3815
Naco, AZ	2603
Nashville, TN	2007
Natrona County Int'l Airport, Casper, WY	3382
Nawiliwili — Port Allen, HI	3204
Neah Bay, WA	3027
Neche, ND	3404
Newark, NJ	1003
New Bedford, MA	0405
New Haven, CT	0412
New London, CT	0413
New Orleans, LA	2002
Newport Bay, CA	2709
Newport, OR	2902
Newport, RI	0501
Newport News, VA	1402
New York, NY	1001
Niagara Falls, NY	0901
Nighthawk, WA	3011
Nippon Courier Hub, Chicago, IL	3991

Port	Code
Nogales, AZ	2604
Noonan, ND	3420
Norfolk, VA	1401
North Bend, OR	2903
Northgate, ND	3406
Norton, VT	0211
Noyes, MN	3402
NYACC, Jamaica, NY	4771
Oak Island, MN	3423
Oakland, CA	2811
Ogden Allied, San Pedro, CA	2771
Ogdensburg, NY	0701
O'Hare Int'l Airport, IL	3906
Oklahoma City, OK	5504
Oleum, CA	2829
Olympia, WA	3026
Omaha, NE	3903
Opheim, MT	3317
Orange, TX	2103
Orlando, FL	1808
Oroville, WA	3019
Oswego, NY	0904
Owensboro, KY	4116
Panama City, FL	1818
Lascagoula, MS	1903
Paulsboro, NJ	1105
Pearl Harbor, HI	3201
Pelican, AK	3124
Pembina, ND	3401
Pensacola, FL	1819
Peoria, IL	3902
Perth Amboy, NJ	1004
Petersburg, AK	3112
Petersburg, VA	1404
Petty Island, NJ	1107
Philadelphia, PA	1101
Philadelphia Int'l Airport, PA	1108
Phoenix, AZ	2605
Piegan, MT	3316
Pigeon Point, DE	1103
Pinecreek, MN	3425
Pittsburg, CA	2828
Pittsburgh, PA	1104
Plymouth, MA	0406
Point Roberts, WA	3017
Point Wells, WA	3001
Ponce, PR	4908

Port	Code
Portal, ND	3403
Port Allen, HI	3204
Port Angeles, WA	3007
Port Aransas, TX	5312
Port Arthur, TX	2101
Port Canaveral, FL	1816
Port Costa, CA	2830
Port Everglades, FL	5203
Porthill, ID	3308
Port Hueneme, CA	2713
Port Huron, MI	3802
Port Inland, MI	3803
Port Isabel, TX	2301
Portland, ME	0101
Portland, OR	2904
Port Lavaca, TX	5313
Port Manatee, FL	1821
Port Neches, TX	2104
Port St. Joe, FL	1820
Port San Luis, CA	2707
Portsmouth, NH	0131
Portsmouth, RI	0503
Portsmouth, VA	1401
Port Sulphur, LA	2005
Port Tampa, FL	1801
Port Townsend, WA	3008
Presidio, TX	2403
Presque Isle, MI	3842
Progresso, TX	2309
Providence, RI	0502
Provincetown, MA	0409
Quad Cities, IL (Iowa, Davenport, Moline, Rock Island)	3908
Quincy, MA	0401
Racine, WI	3708
Ranier, MN	3604
Raymond, MT	3301
Redwood City, CA	2821
Reedville, VA	1407
Reedy Point, DE	1103
Reidsville, NC	1506
Reno, NV	2833
Revere, MA	0401
Richford, VT	0203
Richmond, CA	2812
Richmond-Petersburg, VA	1404
Rickenbacker Airport, Columbus, OH	4182

Port	Code
Rio Grande City, TX	2307
River Rouge, MI	3801
Riverview, MI	3801
Robbinston, ME	0115
Roberts Landing, MI	3814
Rochester, NY	0903
Rock Island, IL	3908
Rockland, ME	0121
Rogers City, MI	3818
Roma, TX	2310
Roosville, MT	3318
Roseau, MN	3426
Rouses Point, NY	0712
Sabine, TX	2102
Sacramento, CA	2816
Sacramento Point, CA	2831
Saginaw-Bay City-Flint, MI	3804
St. Albans, VT	0201
St. Clair, MI	3802
St. John, ND	3405
St. Joseph, MO	4502
St. Louis, MO	4503
St. Paul Airport, Anchorage, AK	3181
St. Paul, MN	3501
St. Petersburg, FL	1814
St. Rose, LA	2013
Salem, MA	0408
Salt Lake City, UT	3303
San Antonio, TX	5507
San Diego, CA	2501
Sand Point, AK	3125
Sandusky, OH	4105
Sandy Point, ME	0132
San Francisco, CA	2809
San Francisco Int'l Airport, CA	2801
San Joaquin River, CA	2828
San Juan, PR	4909
San Juan Int'l Airport, CA	4913
San Luis, AZ	2608
San Luis Obispo, CA	2707
San Pablo Bay, CA	2829
San Pablo, CA	2829
San Ysidro, CA	2504
Santa Teresa Airport, Dona Ana County, NM	2481
Sarles, ND	3409
Sasabe, AZ	2606

Port	Code
UPS, Louisville, KY	4196
UPS, Newark, NJ	4670
Utica, NY	0907
Valdez, AK	3107
Vallejo, CA	2829
Van Buren, ME	0108
Vanceboro, ME	0105
Vancouver, WA	2908
Ventura, CA	2712
Vicksburg, MS	2015
Waddington, NY	0701
Walhalla, ND	3407
Ward Cove, AK	3102
Warroad, MN	3423
Washington, DC	5401
Waukegan Airport, Chicago, IL	3981
Waukegan Harbor, IL	3901
Westhope, ND	3419
West Palm Beach, FL	5204
Westville, NJ	1105
Westwego, LA	2002
Weymouth, MA	0401
Whitetail, MT	3312
Whitlash, MT	3321
Wichita, KS	4504
Wilkes-Barre/Scranton, PA	1106
Wilmington, DE	1103
Wilmington, NC	1501
Winston-Salem, NC	1502
Winterport, ME	0132
Worcester, MA	0403
Wrangell, AK	3105
Wyandotte, MI	3801
York River, VA	1402
Ysleta, TX	2402

APPENDIX 10
UNITS OF MEASURE

UNIT NAME	CODE	UNIT NAME	CODE
LENGTH		**AREA**	
Millimetre	MMT	Square millimetre	MMK
Centimetre	CMT	Square centimetre	CMK
Decimetre	DMT	Square decimetre	DMK
Metre	MTR	Square metre	MTK
Hectometre	HMT	Square kilometre	KMK
Kilometre	KMT	**NUMBER**	
Megametre	MAM	Piece	pce
VOLUME/CAPACITY		Number	NMB
Cubic millimetre	MMQ	Hundred	CEN
Cubic centimetre	CMQ	Thousand	MIL
Cubic decimetre	DMQ	Million	MIO
Cubic metre	MTQ	Dozen	DZN
Thousand cubic metres	TMQ	Score	SCO
Million cubic metres	HMQ	Gross	GRO
Millilitre	MLT	Great gross	GGR
Centilitre	CLT	Number of packs	NAP
Decilitre	DLT	Pair	PAR
Litre	LTR	Dozen pairs	DPR
Hectolitre	HLT	Number of parcels	NPL
Megalitre	MAL	Number of sets	SET
Litre, pure alcohol	LPA	**OTHER**	
Hectolitre, pure alcohol	HPA	Joule	JOU
WEIGHT		Kilojoule	KJO
Metric carat	CTM	Watt-hour	WHR
Milligram	MGM	Kilowatt-hour	KWH
Gram	GRM	Megawatt-hour	MWH
Hectogram	HGM	Gigawatt-hour	GWH
Kilogram	KGM	Watt	WTT
Kilogram of named substance	KNS	Kilowatt	KWT
Kilogram — 90% air dry	KSD	Megawatt	MAW
Deciton	DTN	Kilovolt-ampere	KVA
Metric ton	TNE	Megavolt-ampere	MVA
Kiloton	KTN	Curie	CCI
		Millicurie	MCI

GLOSSARY

AD VALOREM
Latin for "in proportion to the value of goods in question"; a rate determined as a percentage of the value of an item — a duty rate of 6.5%, for example, is ad valorem.

ADVISING BANK
A bank in the country of your supplier that agrees to advise your supplier of the terms and conditions of your letter of credit; your supplier can either accept the letter of credit as is or request changes at this time.

AIR WAYBILL (AWB)
Provided by an airline to a supplier or his or her agent when a shipment is turned over for air transport; not as formal as an ocean bill of lading; generally referred to as a transport document.

ALPHA INDEX
The Canadian Export-Import Alphabetical Index published occasionally by Statistics Canada; provides an alphabetical listing of items and their tariff classification number; last published in January, 1988.

BACK-TO-BACK FINANCING
The practice of buying and selling in the same currency; an importer, for example, might ask his or her Japanese supplier to quote in Canadian dollars; eliminates risk of currency fluctuation.

BILL OF LADING
Represents the contract of carriage between a shipper and a shipping company with full contract details usually printed on the reverse side of the document; originally used for shipments by sea. Today there are several kinds of bills of lading: truck bills of lading, air bills of lading, and rail bills of lading. A bill of lading is more formal than an air waybill.

BN
Business Number; numbering system that assigns a single 15-digit number to businesses for use in meeting government requirements concerning corporate income tax, import/export, payroll deductions, and GST. BN replaces multiple numbers businesses were once assigned under these accounts.

BPT
British Preferential Tariff Treatment; applies to developing countries that are members of the Commonwealth and to Australia and New Zealand (used to include Great Britain until it joined the European Union).

C & F
Cost and Freight (may also appear as CFR [cost, freight]); a quotation from a supplier that includes cost of goods and freight, but not insurance, to the port of destination; often used by companies that import in quantity and have a blanket insurance policy for all their shipping.

C & I
Cost and Insurance; a quotation from a shipper that includes cost of the goods and insurance, but not shipping; used by companies that have a blanket agreement with a shipping company.

CANADIAN INTERNATIONAL TRADE TRIBUNAL
An independent quasi-legal body comprising nine full-time members, appointed by the federal government; handles inquiries and appeals emerging from provisions

under the Special Import Measures Act, the Customs Act, the Excise Tax Act, and NAFTA. The Tribunal is not part of a specific government department or agency. It reports to Parliament through the Minister of Finance.

CADEX

Customs Automated Data Exchange System; electronic system for transmitting entry data from brokers and large-scale importers; implemented in 1988.

CARGO RECEIPT

Issued by the receiving agent when your shipment arrives at its destination acknowledging that the shipment has arrived; not a document of title and not transferable.

C.A.S.E. (Counselling Assistance to Small Enterprise)

Business counselling service provided by the Federal Business Development Bank; counsellors are usually retired entrepreneurs with a record of success in their particular field; any type of business is eligible for the service, so long as it has no more than 200 employees; participants pay a minimal package fee for a series of counselling sessions.

CCD

Cargo Control Document; the document you receive confirming that your shipment has arrived at its destination; takes many forms — can be an air waybill; or Canada Customs form A-8A, completed by transport companies shipping goods by truck over the border; or form E-14, completed by Canada Customs when it receives a shipment by parcel post.

CIF

Cost, Insurance, and Freight; a quotation from a supplier that includes all costs, including the basic cost of the goods, insurance while they're in transit, and transport charges to port of destination; usually followed by a reference to the shipment's port of destination, as in "CIF YVR" — cost, insurance, and freight to Vancouver.

CITES

Convention on International Trade in Endangered Species of Fauna and Flora; an international agreement created to protect certain animal and plant species against overexploitation by international trade; has a membership of more than 110 countries and controls over 48 000 species and subspecies of animals and plants.

CUSTOMS BROKER

A person or company that processes goods through Customs on behalf of private individuals and commercial enterprises; brokerage services include completing entry forms and any other required documentation; on client's behalf, paying all duty and GST owing (may require an advance from the client, depending on credit terms); arranging, on request, for storage or shipment of goods once they're cleared. Brokerage fees are subject to GST, but are not dutiable.

CUSTOMS 2000

A discussion paper and policy document representing a vision of Canada Customs, Excise and Taxation for the year 2000 and describing the strategy for implementing changes over the next decade.

D SERIES MEMORANDA

The departmental memoranda or regulations of the Customs Act; provide details, including the relevant forms, on how all provisions under the act are regulated and enforced; consist of several volumes of material.

DAS

Detailed Adjustment Statement (form B2-1) completed and sent by Customs to the importer when an error is detected in an entry; shows where adjustments have been made to the entry and why, and gives the importer a deadline by which all outstanding duties must be paid.

D/A

Documents against Acceptance; a payment alternative in which the importer arranges to pay his or her supplier with a bill of exchange (draft) through his or her bank. The importer's bank processes all documentation from the supplier's bank, then the importer sells the goods and pays for them on a specific date, as previously agreed between the importer and the supplier, and noted on the bill of exchange; in effect, a form of credit made available to the importer for a set period.

DDP

Delivered Duty Paid; comprehensive quotation from a supplier that includes all costs, even duties and taxes, to the doorstep of the purchaser; favored by non-resident importers who ship in quantity to Canadian purchasers.

D/P

Documents against Payment; a payment alternative in which the supplier's bank provides all required documentation to the importer's bank. If the documents are in good order, the importer pays for the shipment, at his or her convenience; an arrangement that offers almost as much protection to the importer as a letter of credit, without the expense.

DOCUMENTARY CREDIT

Another term for a letter of credit; it has earned this name because all the conditions of a letter of credit may be met through the presentation of documents.

DRAWBACK

A partial or full refund of duties paid on goods put to a certain use, as specified in the Customs regulations (D7 series). The drawback program was developed by the federal government to improve the country's manufacturing capacity. Two types of drawbacks are available to importers — export and home consumption. To apply, importers must complete a form K-32 and provide supporting documentation.

DRAYAGE (CARTAGE) RECEIPT

An interim transport document issued to the supplier by the transport company responsible for carrying goods to their point of shipment — as in the case of a trucking firm taking a shipment to the docks or the airport.

DUMPING

The purchase and importing of goods into Canada at prices lower than what they would sell for in their own domestic market.

ESSENTIAL CHARACTER

Distinguishing qualities or traits of an item, causing it to be described or interpreted in a certain way — as in a vehicle body "having the essential character of" a vehicle. An item's "essential character" determines how it is classified in the HS Tariff.

EXCHANGE RATE

The price of one currency in terms of another.

EXCISE TAX

Tax applied under the provisions of the Excise Tax Act on so-called luxury items including jewellery, precious and semi-precious stones, quality watches and clocks, vehicle air conditioners, cigarettes, gasoline, airplane and diesel fuel.

EXW

Ex Warehouse or Ex Works (also Ex Factory); a quotation from a supplier that represents the cost of goods at their point of origin and nothing else.

FAIR MARKET VALUE SYSTEM

The valuation system applied by Canada Customs before introduction of the transaction value system in 1985; based on the freely offered selling price of an item with the home market at the time and place of direct shipment into Canada, not the price actually paid by the importer.

FAS

Free Alongside Ship; a quotation from a supplier that includes delivery of goods to their point of export and through customs formalities; all other charges, including the cost of loading the goods onto the vessel or airplane, are the responsibility of the importer.

FOB

Free On Board; a quotation from a supplier that includes the cost of the goods plus the cost, including loading charges, of putting them on a vessel or airplane; supplier also completes all customs formalities.

FOREIGN EXCHANGE OPTION

One of several strategies designed to protect and benefit importers from currency fluctuations; an agreement with a bank to buy or sell foreign currency at a specific rate up to a specified date, in return for a premium fee. The option holder is not required to follow through with the purchase or sale of the option when it falls due.

FORWARD RATE CONTRACT

One of several strategies designed to protect and benefit importers from currency fluctuations; a contract with a bank to purchase or sell a specified sum of foreign currency at a specific date or within a specific period of time; may be a "fixed" contract (transacted on a specific date) or an "options" contract (purchaser determines exact transaction date within a specified period).

FREIGHT FORWARDER

A person or company that handles the shipment of goods; responsibilities include arranging shipment details and completing documentation; is also a useful source of information on market trends, insurance, methods of transport, container shipping and warehousing; usually maintains offices or agencies in several countries.

FTA

Canada–United States Free Trade Agreement, implemented on January 1, 1989, and replaced by the North American Free Trade Agreement (NAFTA) in January, 1994.

GATT

General Agreement on Tariffs and Trade; an international agreement created at the end of the World War II and adopted by the leading trading countries at that time.

GIRs

General Interpretive Rules; the nine rules governing the use of the HS Tariff; are of two types: general rules (six) which apply internationally and Canadian rules (three), unique to Canada.

GODOWN

A dockside charge for goods that arrive at the port of shipment ahead of the ship; may be dutiable depending on the point of direct shipment to Canada. This term is commonly used in Asia.

GPT

General Preferential Tariff Treatment; applies to certain developing countries; to qualify, goods must be shipped directly to Canada (with or without transhipment).

GST

Goods and services tax, as provided under the Excise Tax Act; a consumer-paid tax. Businesses that do $30 000 worth of business or more annually must register to collect the GST on behalf of the federal government.

HS TARIFF

Harmonized Commodity Description and Coding system, as provided under the Customs Tariff Act, also called the Harmonized System Tariff; developed by the Customs Co-operation Council in Brussels, Belgium, for use by members of GATT; implemented by Canada in January, 1988.

IMPORTER NUMBER

A permanent number assigned by Canada Customs to commercial importers before they may complete their first commercial entry; initiated in the late 1980s, with some 400 000 registered as of February, 1993; requires completion of form T-124.

INCOTERMS

Rules established by the International Chamber of Commerce to standardize use of international trade terms. INCOTERMS determine the division of cost and risk between buyer and seller, and the obligation each has to the other.

INLAND FREIGHT

Freight charges resulting for the shipment of goods within their country of origin before exportation; may be dutiable, depending on the point of direct shipment to Canada.

LANDED COST

The total of all costs associated with the shipment and importation of goods, including purchase price, shipping charges, insurance, customs broker's fee, cartage charges, bank fees, and associated telephone and fax charges.

LEADS AND LAGS

One of several strategies designed to protect and benefit importers from currency fluctuations; refers to the practice of delaying a foreign currency transaction (lagging) when currency rates are falling and speeding up settlement (leading) when they're on the rise.

LETTER OF CREDIT

A written undertaking for payment to a supplier made by a bank at the request of an importer; also called a conditional undertaking because payment is made only when the conditions of the importer (or applicant), as specified in the letter of credit, have been met by the supplier (or beneficiary).

LIGHTERAGE CHARGES

Charges for transporting goods by lighter (barge) to a vessel; usually incurred if a port is overcrowded or too shallow to accommodate a cargo vessel, as in the case of several third-world ports.

LVS

Low Value System; Canada Customs' accounting system for low value shipments (worth less than $1 200); authorizes customs brokers and some commercial importers to complete accounting for this type of shipment no later than the 24th day of the month following their release, instead of the usual five days permitted for other shipments.

MACHINERY REMISSION PROGRAM

Developed by the federal government to encourage Canadian companies to buy equipment as a means of improving the efficiency of their operations from a foreign supplier providing comparable equipment is not produced in Canada. Under the program, companies pay duty on only the first $500 of a machine's total value; requires completion of form K-122.

MARKING

Refers to the marking regulations under D11-3-1 which require that certain products be stamped with the name of the country of origin before being permitted to enter Canada (in French or English, but not both); a type of non-tariff barrier.

MFN TARIFF TREATMENT

Most Favoured Nations Tariff Treatment; applies to all countries with which Canada has a trading agreement. Other tariff treatments may apply and may have more favorable rates.

MUTATIS MUTANDIS

Latin for "in the comparison of cases"; quoted in the General Interpretive Rules of the HS Tariff (Rule Six of the international rules and Rules One and Three of the Canadian rules).

NAFTA

North American Free Trade Agreement; signed by Canada, the United States, and Mexico in December, 1992, and implemented January 1, 1994. As a result of the agreement, two new columns have been added to the tariff: the Mexico Tariff Treatment (MT) and the Mexico–United States Tariff Treatment (MUST).

NCR

National Customs Ruling; ruling on the tariff classification of an imported product; issued on request to importers and their agents or customs brokers. NCRs apply country wide and may also be referred to in the determination of value and origin of goods.

NEGOTIATING BANK

The bank in the supplier's country that cashes (negotiates) the letter of credit provided by the importer through his or her Canadian bank. Letters of credit are either freely negotiated (can be cashed at any bank) or restricted (can be cashed only at a designated bank).

NON-TARIFF BARRIER

A requirement that goods produced abroad must meet before being imported into Canada; acts as a barrier by obliging importers to pay more for goods by demanding that they meet specific marking regulations, for example, as provided under Customs regulations (in this instance, D11-3-1).

NRI

Non-resident importer; a company that is not resident in Canada but still performs an importing role in Canada.

$1/60$ AND $1/120$ ENTRIES

Also called "rental" entries because they are used when a company wants to import goods temporarily, usually to a maximum of 12 months; completed on a B-3 entry form; the importer pays duty and taxes on a monthly basis, calculated on the basis of $1/60$ of total value in the case of lower-priced goods (a formula car, for example) and $1/120$ for ships and vessels.

PRIMA FACIE

Latin for "at first sight."

PRO FORMA INVOICE

Issued to a potential purchaser as a quotation, an "invitation to buy"; is clearly stamped "pro forma"; becomes a formal order once it's signed by the purchaser. Importers may provide a pro forma invoice or a Canada Customs' invoice instead of a commercial invoice when entering goods into Canada.

QUOTA

A precise limit on the number or volume of goods imported annually, as determined by the federal government to protect Canada's domestic industries. Canada's clothing industry, for example, is protected by quotas. Importers of goods under quota must apply for a permit (form Ext 1466) to Foreign Affairs in Ottawa.

REMISSION

An abatement of duties owing; that is, duties are not paid at all — as compared to a drawback where duties are paid and then refunded.

RMD

Release on Minimal Documentation; computerized system developed by Canada Customs to speed up the processing of shipments; permits the immediate release of goods after which the importer or his or her customs broker has five days to complete all related documentation; available to any individual or firm able to post the required bond with Canada Customs.

SIMA

Special Import Measures Act, formerly the Anti-Dumping Act; protects producers from unfair foreign competition in the form of "dumping" and "subsidizing."

SUBSIDIZING

The importing of goods produced in their country of origin with the aid of government grants or other assistance.

SWIFT

Society for Worldwide Interbank Financial Telecommunications; fax transfer of funds through the banking system; a fast, but expensive, means of reimbursing a foreign supplier.

TARIFF TREATMENT

Duty rate established under the terms of a trade agreement with another country; Schedule III of the HS Tariff lists tariff treatments administered by Canada Customs.

TRANSACTION VALUE SYSTEM

Method of determining value for duty of imported goods, widely used by GATT members and implemented by Canada in 1985; based on the price actually paid for an item; replaced the more protectionist fair market value system.

TRANSHIPMENT

Shipment of goods through another country without entering the commerce of that country.

VALUATION

Process of determining the value for duty of an imported item.

VFCC

Value for Currency Conversion.

VFD

Value for Duty.

VFT

Value for Tax.

SELECTED BIBLIOGRAPHY

Appel, Robert S. *The GST Handbook: A Practical Guide for Small Business.* Vancouver: Self-Counsel Press, 1990.

Canada: Customs, Excise and Taxation. *Explanatory Notes* (Catalogue RV51-20/1-1992E). Ottawa: Canada Communications Group — Publishing.

Canada. Customs, Excise and Taxation. *Harmonized Commodity Description and Coding System* (Catalogue RV55-2/1992E). Ottawa: Canada Communications Group — Publishing.

Canada. Department of External Affairs *The Canada-U.S. Free Trade Agreement* (Catalogue E74-16-1988-E). Ottawa: International Trade Communications Group, 1988.

Canada: Revenue Canada, Customs and Excise. *The Customs Drawback Road...To Success and Profit.* [Ottawa]: Government of Canada, 1987.

Canada. Revenue Canada, Customs and Excise. *Customs 2000: Blueprint for the Future.* [Ottawa]: Government of Canada, 1989.

Canada. Revenue Canada, Customs and Excise. *Excise Small Business Guide* [Ottawa]: Government of Canada.

Canada: Revenue Canada, Customs, Excise and Taxation. *Index to Revenue Canada Services.* [Ottawa]: Government of Canada, 1994.

Canada: Revenue Canada, Customs and Excise. *The New Customs Act in Brief (1986).* [Ottawa]: Government of Canada, 1986.

Canada. Special Trade Relations Bureau. *The Export and Import Permits Act Handbook.* [Ottawa]: Department of External Affairs, 1991.

Canada. Statistics Canada. *Canadian Export-Import Alphabetical Index* (Catalogue 12-579E). Ottawa: Canada Communications Group — Publishing, 1988.

Coopers & Lybrand. *An Introduction to Canadian Customs Procedures.* Toronto: Coopers & Lybrand, 1988.

Dattu, Riyaz. "Customs Seizures: The Legal and Administrative Framework." Paper presented at the County of York Law Association Nutshell Programme, Toronto, February 28, 1989.

Davies, G.J., and R. Gray. *Purchasing International Freight Services.* Vermont: Gower Publishing, 1985.

Dearden, Richard G. "*Customs Valuation,*" *Canadian Trade Law Reports*, CCH Canadian (1989).

Government of British Columbia. *So You Want to Import.* Vancouver: B.C. Business Information Centre (601 W. Cordova Street), 1992.

Gray, Douglas A., and Diana Lynn Gray. *The Complete Canadian Small Business Guide.* Montreal: McGraw-Hill Ryerson, 1988.

Ingram, David. *David Ingram's Border Book.* Surrey, British Columbia: Hancock House, 1992.

Lindsay, Thomas. *An Outline of Customs in Canada.* Calgary: Erin Publications, 1991.

McGuire, Denis P. "The Adjudications Process: An Overview." Paper presented to the Canadian Association of Customs Brokers Annual General Meeting, Winnipeg, September 12, 1991.

Popcorn, Faith. *The Popcorn Report.* New York: HarperCollins, 1992.

Salembier, G.E., Andrew R. Moroz, and Frank Stone. *The Canadian Import File: Trade, Protection, and Adjustment.* Montreal: The Institute for Research on Public Policy, 1987.

Watson, Alasdair. *Finance of International Trade.* London: Bankers Books, 1990.

Brochures from Revenue Canada, Customs, Excise and Taxation:

The Business Number and Your Revenue Canada Accounts: January 1995

Business Number Services: January 1995 Goods Detained? (on CITES, the Convention on International Trade in Endangered Species of Wild Fauna and Flora) produced by the Canadian Wildlife Service, Environment Canada

Importations by Mail

Importing a Motor Vehicle into Canada

Importing Commercial Goods into Canada

Moving Back to Canada

Seasonal Residents

Settling in Canada

Thinking About Importing? What You Should Know

Your Guide to Importing a Vehicle from the United States into Canada

Brochures from the Canadian International Trade Tribunal:

Appeals from Customs and Excise Decisions

Dumping and Subsidizing Injury Inquiries

General Inquiries into Economic, Trade and Tariff Matters

Import Safeguard Complaints by Domestic Producers

Introduction to the Canadian International Trade Tribunal

STARTING A SUCCESSFUL BUSINESS IN CANADA
by Jack D. James, M.B.A., LL.B.

Everything you need to know to turn your good idea into a profitable business is explored and explained in this informative guide. This Canadian bestseller is chock full of practical, usable information that will help you master the start-up procedure. The skills you learn will help you every day and in every aspect of your business. $15.95

You'll be able to lay a solid foundation for future success by learning how to:

- Develop and reach your money goal
- Find the right business for you
- Save money when setting up your business
- Get financing
- Take advantage of government incentive programs
- Use Canadian tax laws to your advantage
- Set up proper records and maintain them
- Develop a professional attitude
- Find and keep good employees
- Design an operating plan
- Avoid accounting pitfalls

Also available —

Starting a Successful Business in Canada **AUDIO PROGRAM** on two lively and informative cassettes $16.95

- Fifteen experts reveal the key elements to starting a business off right
- Listen and learn at home or in your car!

MARKETING YOUR PRODUCT
A planning guide for small business
by Donald Cyr, M.B.A. and
Douglas Gray, B.A., LL.B.

Learn the secrets of successful product marketing. Marketing is not just selling and advertising; its objectives are to help you decide if you are developing the right product for the right target market, and if you are using the promotion vehicles and distribution methods to maximize the return on your efforts.

The in-depth checklists included in this book will take you, step by step, toward a successful, profitable marketing strategy. $12.95

It helps you determine the answers to questions such as:

- What is marketing?
- How do you find out who your market is?
- Can you do your own market research?
- How do you develop your product to fit the market?
- Which media do you use to let your market know about your product?
- What makes people choose one product over another?
- Are promotions useful marketing tools?
- What is the best way to get your product to your customer?
- How do you price to sell?
- What advertising strategies are most effective for your product?
- What legal and insurance considerations must you be aware of?

EXPORTING
A practical guide to finding and developing export markets for your product or service
by Anne Curran and Gerhard Kautz

Is your company eyeing international markets to expand into? This book will help you test the waters before taking the plunge, whether overseas or south of the border. Exporting can provide unlimited potential, but you can lose big money if you don't know exactly what you are doing. A careful analysis of your target country, plus a clear understanding of all the regulations, theirs and ours, are vital if you are to become a successful exporter. $19.95

This book takes you step by step through the process of exporting. It answers questions such as:

- How do I know if my product or service will sell?
- How do I work out what my costs will be? What do I charge my customer?
- What is a letter of credit and how does it work?
- How do I move my goods and what will it cost?
- What about the paperwork? What forms have to be filled out and what do I need to know to do it all correctly?
- What is the best way to ship my gods?
- How does NAFTA affect exporting to the United States and Mexico?
- What is a carnet and when can I use one?
- Should I use an international agent to help me?

ORDER FORM
All prices are subject to change without notice. Books are available in book, department, and stationery stores. If you cannot buy the book through a store, please use this order form. (Please print)

Name _____

Address _____

Charge to: ❏ Visa   ❏ MasterCard

Account Number _____

Validation Date _____

Expiry Date _____

Signature _____

❏ **Check here for a free catalogue.**

Please send your order to the nearest location:
Self-Counsel Press
1481 Charlotte Road
North Vancouver, B.C.
V7J 1H1

Self-Counsel Press
4 Bram Court
Brampton, Ontario
L6W 3R6

YES, please send me:

_____ copies of **Starting a Successful Business in Canada**, $15.95

_____ copies of **Starting a Successful Business in Canada AUDIO**, $16.95

_____ copies of **Marketing Your Product**, $12.95

_____ copies of **Exporting**, $19.95

Please add $3.00 for postage & handling.
Please add 7% GST to your order.